Last Stand of the Louisiana Shrimpers

Last Stand of the
LOUISIANA SHRIMPERS

Emma Christopher Lirette

University Press of Mississippi / Jackson

The University Press of Mississippi is the scholarly publishing agency of
the Mississippi Institutions of Higher Learning: Alcorn State University,
Delta State University, Jackson State University, Mississippi State University,
Mississippi University for Women, Mississippi Valley State University,
University of Mississippi, and University of Southern Mississippi.

www.upress.state.ms.us

The University Press of Mississippi is a member
of the Association of University Presses.

Copyright © 2022 by University Press of Mississippi
All rights reserved

First printing 2022
∞

Library of Congress Cataloging Number 2022017525

Hardback ISBN 978-1-4968-4140-7
Trade paperback ISBN 978-1-4968-4145-2
Epub single ISBN 978-1-4968-4142-1
Epub institutional ISBN 978-1-4968-4141-4
PDF single ISBN 978-1-4968-4143-8
PDF institutional ISBN 978-1-4968-4144-5

British Library Cataloging-in-Publication Data available

for
Myrian "Blond" Lirette & Marie Eschete
my Granny and Mawmaw
who in life fashioned a world worth living in

Figure 1a. *Rand-McNally New Commercial Atlas Map of Louisiana.* From *Commercial Atlas of America* (Chicago: Rand-McNally, 1913). Courtesy of the US National Archives.

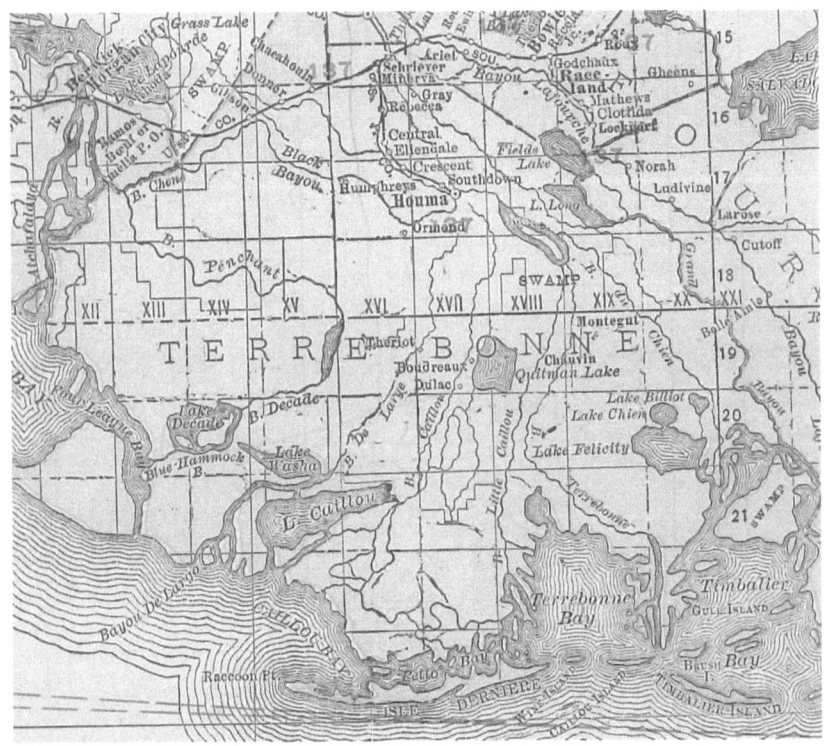

Figure 1b. Detail of Terrebonne Parish from *Rand-McNally New Commercial Atlas Map of Louisiana*. From *Commercial Atlas of America* (Chicago: Rand-McNally, 1913). Courtesy of the US National Archives.

Contents

xi	List of Figures
xiii	Acknowledgments

3	**UNMOORING FOR BEGINNERS**
11	Lesson One: Making Space
19	Lesson Two: Stories and Scholarship
24	Lesson Three: A Brief History of the Pre-Bust Louisiana Shrimp Fishery
29	Syllabus

33	**BLOOD**
39	Bloodlines
51	Blood Magic and Cruelty
64	Ecology and the Body

75	**WATER**
83	Bodies of Water
86	Names of Water, or the Idea of Order at Mare à Clay
98	Bodies on the Water
105	Land's End
113	Oil and Water
121	Gulf

127	**NETS**
133	Ghost Nets
151	Miraculous Draught of Fish

165	**FISH STORIES: A METHODOLOGICAL APPENDIX**
181	Notes
195	Bibliography
207	Index

List of Figures

vi	Figure 1a: *Rand-McNally New Commercial Atlas Map of Louisiana*
vii	Figure 1b: Detail of Terrebonne Parish from *Rand-McNally New Commercial Atlas Map of Louisiana*
13	Figure 2: Value of the Dulac-Chauvin Port, 2000–2019
32	Figure 3: Kim Guy
35	Figure 4: George and ChaCha Sevin
35	Figure 5: ChaCha Sevin
48	Figure 6: Glynn Trahan
60	Figure 7: ChaCha Sevin culling shrimp from pogy
65	Figure 8: The *Daddy Bucks* in the 2015 Boat Blessing
65	Figure 9: The Boat Blessing from the shore of Lake Boudreaux
88	Figure 10: Area around Robinson Canal, 1894
88	Figure 11: Area around Robinson Canal, 1941
89	Figure 12: Area around Robinson Canal, 1964
89	Figure 13: Area around Robinson Canal, 1994
90	Figure 14: Area around Robinson Canal, 2015
90	Figure 15: Lake Quitman, 1894
91	Figure 16: Lake Quitman and Lake Boudreaux, 1941
92	Figure 17: Lake Quitman and Lake Boudreaux, 2015
94	Figure 18: "Quitman's Lake and Impassable Swamp," 1856
95	Figure 19: Department of the Gulf Map No. 10, *Military Approaches to New Orleans*
102	Figure 20: Chad and Angela Portier
103	Figure 21: David Chauvin
106	Figure 22: Decercelier's *Carte du Missicipy ou Louissiane depuis la Baye de lascension jusqua la pointe de la Mobile*

108	Figure 23: John Ross's *Course of the River Mississippi, from the Balise to Fort Chartres; Taken on an Expedition to the Illinois, in the Latter End of the Year 1765*
115	Figure 24: Kurt and Claude Lirette
136	Figure 25: Steve Billiot as Cajun Elvis
137	Figure 26: Steve Billiot aboard his boat, the *Lady L*
152	Figure 27: Dawn on Lake Boudreaux
155	Figure 28: Chad Portier
169	Figure 29: Brett Lirette

Acknowledgments

The story goes that the scholar—solitary, lonely—lives a life devoid of human contact. Rather than taking refuge in people, the scholar seeks out the smell of old books, the reverb of tiny sounds (a pencil scratching, a page turning) in cavernous libraries and reading rooms, the cozy swaddle of a cluttered office. After a period of time—say, five years, the suggested duration of a doctoral program in the humanities—a work of original research springs forth, proof at last that the scholar has thought deeply and critically about a topic and is capable of documenting those thoughts in a book-length text. Instead of conversation and companionship, the scholar has interlocutors. If you are impatient to know who they are, you can flip to the end to read an alphabetized list of scholarly works that the scholar has read and engages with—at least in theory.

In my case, this story has some truth: after five years of graduate study, I emerged with a dissertation in hand. After another five years, I emerged with a book. You can see my scholarly interlocutors by flipping to the end. I spent hours reading old and new books, writing by hand and keyboard, curled over a desk in a cluttered but sunny office. But on the whole, this story is false and dangerous. This book would not have been possible without a vast network of people, opportunities, and support. This section is a small way to recognize that constellation.

Foremost, I want to acknowledge the heroes of *Last Stand of the Louisiana Shrimpers*: Steve Billiot, David Chauvin, Kim Guy, Claude Lirette, Angela Portier, Chad Portier, ChaCha Sevin, George Sevin, and Glynn Trahan. These men and women entrusted me with their stories, their hope, and their practices of labor. I hope I did right by them. I thank them for their openness and for trying to make a world more survivable. Also for the shrimp, crabs, crawfish, and squid.

Thanks also to others who let me interview them, allowed me to hang out on their boats and docks, and provided me with information crucial to this research: my pawpaws, Dudley Eschete and Clyde Lirette; Joseph Doan and the shrimpers moored in Intracoastal City; Carla Ghere; Mr. Harris; Mr. Houston; Trudy Luke; and Carolyn Tillman.

Thanks also to the following contributors to this project: Lindsey Feldman, who helped me shape my research when I was a fledgling ethnographer; Anne Dugas and Thu Bui of Louisiana Sea Grant, who helped me gain access to the community of Vietnamese shrimpers in Vermilion Parish; Jason Theriot, historian and fellow child of coastal Louisiana, who shared boudin and beer with me at his camp in Cocodrie; Shanondora Billiot, scholar of social work and fellow child of coastal Louisiana, who traded stories of scholarship and ethnography in southern Louisiana; Thurston Hahn III of Coastal Environments, who tracked down old, rare maps of the coast; Laura Ann Browning, who shared key historical ephemera and publications from Terrebonne Parish; and the special collections staff at LSU's Hill Memorial Library and at the Louisiana Research Collection of Tulane University's Howard-Tilton Memorial Library.

I thank the late Graduate Institute of the Liberal Arts, which counted me among its final cohort of doctoral students. The ILA, founded in 1952, was among the oldest interdisciplinary programs granting PhDs. For more than sixty years, it housed experimental scholars and artists whose imagination and curiosity crossed the boundaries of traditional disciplines. I was one of those lucky enough to be part of its community, which remained vibrant, creative, and rigorous even during the final days of the graduate program. I thank Martine Brownley, advocate for orphaned doctoral students; Katie Rawson and Jesse Karlsberg, who let me work with incredible freedom for my three years as an associate editor and creative technology strategist at *Southern Spaces*; David Morgen, David Fisher, and Joonna Trapp, who invited me to be a part of Domain of One's Own and the Writing Program; Abe Mohammadione and Vikas Shah, who gave me a chance to work on film sets and join the phenomenal creative and production team at Ideas United; and Peter Wakefield and Kim Loudermilk, who provided me with classes to teach and the mentorship to teach them well.

I have been lucky in this life to be a student to phenomenal teachers. Thinking that went into this book was first cultivated in courses taught by Tanine Allison, Jonathan Goldberg, Lynn Huffer, Sean Meighoo, Michael Moon, Bobbi Patterson, Bobby Paul, and Elizabeth Wilson. These teachers modeled both rigor and enthusiasm, and I am grateful that I could work out my preliminary theoretical agenda under their tutelage. A special callout to Anna Grimshaw and Allen Tullos. Anna provided the gift of an engaged practice of anthropology and a model of experimental scholarship that can nimbly navigate disciplinary convention without sacrificing artistic vision. Allen has been an emphatic supporter of my writing on Louisiana and has shown me how to balance empathy and critique when analyzing the often-frustrating places we are from.

My work would also have been impossible without my experience in Cornell University's creative writing MFA program. I am so grateful to my advisers and teachers there: Alice Fulton, Ken McClane, Ellis Hanson, Bob Morgan, Jane Juffer, and Jonathan Culler.

A first-generation college graduate, I am also greatly influenced by my earliest experience in higher education at Loyola University New Orleans, especially the mentorship of Katie Ford and Marcus Smith. Marcus opened the door to studying Louisiana, both in class and out, when he hired me as a personal assistant to recover his archive of New Orleans material flooded during Hurricane Katrina. Katie was my poetry teacher and thesis adviser. Chapter 3 of this book, "Water," begins with an extended close reading of "The Idea of Order at Key West," a poem I memorized and recited for her Introduction to Poetry course. Both during and since my undergraduate years, Katie has supported me with encouragement, advice, and friendship.

Angelika Bammer, a mentor, adviser, and friend, has had a tremendous impact on this work. It has been the greatest privilege of my life as a scholar and writer to work with her, and she has the rare talent to turn doubt into passion, fear into hope. I aspire to her generosity, curiosity, and sophistication. Angelika reminds me that I am a writer when I forget. And when I'm feeling adrift, she helps me find my moorings (and release them, one by one, if need be).

During the process of editing and transforming this book, I left academia to pursue a career in technology. It might be gauche to talk about my own work (in this, my book about work), but I would be remiss if I didn't acknowledge the stability and financial security that made creating this book possible and decoupled it from the urgency of the job market. Thank you especially to Abby Johnson, UX Research Manager at the Home Depot, for recognizing my value and giving me opportunity after opportunity.

Id also like to thank the amazing team at University Press of Mississippi: Vijay Shah, Joey Brown, Courtney McCreary, Todd Lape, Laura Strong, Ellen Goldlust, Kathy Burgess, and Carlton McGrone. I'd especially like to thank Jackson Watson for helping me navigate the publication process, Shane Gong Stewart for helping me finalize the manuscript, and Craig Gill for your support and editorial guidance over the last few years.

My friends have served as my first readers, critics, coconspirators, teachers, and cheerleaders. They have endured my improvised bits, complaints, jeremiads, baroque cooking, and shifting obsessions. Thanks to them, I have maintained something like optimism throughout this journey. Jay, Trish, Nasim, Sarah, Sasha, Rachel, Mael, Stu, Jesse, Laura, and Sally. Anne Marie, Danielle, Jameel, and Christian. Lindsey and the ethnographic adventure of 2013 taught me how to do anthropology—and made it fun. Fahamu Pecou, the shit. Clint Fluker, scholar, impresario, and confidant: I could not have made my way through writing this book without his friendship. To my podna, Brady.

My family has been unwavering in their love and support during the writing of this book. My dad, Kurt, makes an unnamed and heavily fictionalized appearance in the "Water" chapter. I thank him for being the "mayor" of Chauvin, for founding a cultural nonprofit with me, for teaching me the value of place and work and land and sea and kin and story. My mom, Sandra, makes only a cameo here but has nevertheless brought my world into being. She still teaches me to savor life, to appreciate the gift of others, and to love and serve with my whole being. My brother, Brett, played an integral role in my fieldwork. He accompanied me on interviews, kept me company between them, and served as my production assistant, key grip, gaffer, best boy, 1st AD, 2nd unit photographer, and sound engineer. Without him, my fieldwork would have been neither successful nor fun. Thanks also to my sister, Sydney, my sister-in-law, Annika, and my in-laws—Chris, Cindy, David, Christine, Daniel, and Joseph. Their support—whether manifested as childcare, food, conversation, drinks, jokes, mourning, or celebration—has been invaluable.

Since writing this book, I have come out as a trans woman, which has been my own practice of unmooring and of trying to make a world that is survivable. I guess it makes a little more sense why my book about Louisiana shrimpers returns again and again to queer theory to make sense of nonce worlds and the practice of self-elaboration. At a very practical level, coming out has forced me to reckon with my own ideas about naming, remembering and forgetting, and the fixity of identity. I have chosen, for better or worse, to have my birth name as my middle name for this book as a nod to the continuity of my publication history and as an homage to who the world thought I was for most of my life. My actual middle name, X, a variable, will take its place going forward.

My coming out has been fraught, especially here, in this age of stochastic terrorism directed at trans people, of the dissolution of rights to bodily autonomy, and of the machinery of governance mobilized to exclude people like me from public life. On a personal level, I have lost small portions of my network of care and belonging as some people, including some named above, have faded out of my life. But besides the loss and this dark age, this dark future coming to pass, I have found joy and love and hope and community. I have found life. Not the good life of the American Dream, but something better, something sustaining and experimental and, most of all, *livable*.

I would like to thank the people who have given me a supportive and affirming environment: my cis friends who have shown up, the moms of my eldest's Girl Scout Troop, my colleagues at Meta, my Chauvin family. I've reconnected with several people who are deeply important to me, whose love has been fun and comforting and has sustained me in the past year: Zee, Sydney (my sister), Louis, CeCe, Beth, Christian, Laura, and Catherine. But most of all, I've found my people, my community, my network of care and joy and queerness. To trans twitter and all my reply girls. To my comrades in activism. To my queer and trans community in Atlanta. Especially to the amazing, gorgeous women who have been with me in despair and celebration, who have helped me and allowed themselves to be helped by me: Jordan, Anna, Victoria, and my new bestie Lyra. And most of all, to Violet, who came into my life exactly at the right moment, rejuvenating me with love and creativity and brilliance and queer utopia.

For my wife, my partner, my friend (the second body for our single soul), Linda, I reserve the most profound gratitude. This was not easy, but you made it survivable, and it is a privilege and pleasure to share life with you, to author a world in which we can live together, to grow a family, to hope for a tomorrow better than today. You have gifted me with your hope, trust, and love, and I return the same with joy. You were there as I shattered, and your love has helped me rebuild myself, to become who I am. After I returned from fieldwork, Linda and I welcomed our firstborn, Phoenix Claire, into this world. Phoenix, like her namesake, has burned away an old world and created another one from its ashes. We welcomed our second child, Bernadette, in 2018. I am lucky to take part in the expansion of both of your universes. Over the past few years of plague and quarantine and transformations, we've built a little world together, something durable but flexible, a life worth living, a life full of love and closeness and absurdity and adventure.

Finally, thanks to Chauvin, Louisiana, a small hamlet on Bayou Petit Caillou, an hour southwest of New Orleans, a thirty-minute drive from the end of the road at the Gulf of Mexico. I am lucky to have been born there. I hope that Chauvin prevails so that others can be so lucky.

Last Stand of the Louisiana Shrimpers

UNMOORING FOR BEGINNERS

> This book deals with nothing other than hoping beyond the day which has become.
> —Ernst Bloch, *The Principle of Hope*

Over the course of the late nineteenth and twentieth centuries, shrimping played an important role shaping the south Louisiana imaginary. It moored people to a cultural past. It was a way to make a living. It offered freedom on the sea. Shrimping, the lifeblood of bayou and marsh communities along the coast of the Gulf of Mexico, fed generations of children who grew up to be shrimpers. Yet the twenty-first century has seen the decline of the shrimp fishery because of a rough slate of economic crises, a market flush with imported shrimp, the worst marine oil spill in history, and several calamitous hurricane seasons. As the shrimp fishery declines, so too do shrimp fishers. Why do they cling to this way of life?

◆ ◆ ◆

Say you have a ship. Say it is propelled by sails. Say you need it to be parked in a single spot for a while. You need to moor it: you drop several anchors into the water to keep the boat from drifting out to sea or tipping over. You anchor from bow and stern or perhaps use two anchors from the bow, one 180 degrees from the other. If you have a mooring, such as a pier or jetty or anchor buoy, you can tie up your boat from different locations along a side. In this case, we are talking about a ship, a sailboat, that is moored just off a coast in, let us say, the Gulf of Mexico. We use two bowers, anchors dropped from the bow, one heavier than the other. We position the ship in such a way that keeps it equidistant from the two anchors, one ahead of the bow, the other abaft the stern. This is what mooring is: to secure a boat by one or more anchors.

Say you want to sail away somewhere. The first thing you must do is unmoor. Today, *to unmoor* means a lot of things. It means to be adrift. It means to be cut loose from the things that anchor us. We use the word *unmoored* to describe a person or an idea that has slipped free from a kind of social, ideological, or imaginative bondage: it is a way of saying that a person disregards conventions of propriety or reason, that a person has gone off message or off script, or that an idea has taken on a life of its own and cannot be controlled by its fashioners. But for a sailor, *to unmoor* does not mean to loosen all anchors. It is a set of actions a crew takes before unfurling sails and sailing. To unmoor is to reduce the number of anchors to one so that after the sails are ready, the last anchor can quickly be hauled up and stowed for travel.[1]

It is easy to understand why we use *unmoor* to mean *unanchored*. For the nautically disinclined, it may be unclear why one would even want to reduce anchors to only one when the goal is to sail away. That final anchor does get hauled in before the voyage. Imagine, however, a sailboat, floating just offshore in the Gulf of Mexico. Waves rock the vessel, pitching it this way and that. Without an anchor (or a drogue, which does not reach the seabed but exerts drag on the boat), it would be nearly impossible to steer the boat to make the sails catch the wind. Unfurling the sails without regard for wind direction is extraordinarily dangerous. The last anchor gives the captain of the ship a chance to control the ship's orientation.

And what if this ship were moored at a wharf among other boats? A sudden tide or wake or wind on an unanchored boat might crash it into other boats, a mistake amplified into mayhem. The last anchor limits the reaches of human error or meteorological chance. The captain can control the unmoored boat through the anchor before canvas and wind and rudder can be used.

The kind of unmooring that was practiced when most large boats required sails to get anywhere lends itself to a much more limited, nuanced metaphorical application than the way we use *unmooring* to mean cut adrift. This kind of unmooring is not adrift at all: it is a stage of cutting ties to go on a journey. It is a controlled freeing, a shift from one type of control (anchored) to another (commanding sails). Instead of using *unmoored* to describe, say, a politician whose ramblings eschew political convention, accepted fact, and reason, we might use the word to describe the act of a politician whose utopian thinking never loses connection with the material and political conditions of a recognizable world, a politician whose unmooring is a thought exercise on the way to substantive policy change. Instead of using *unmoored* to characterize a population that feels ignored and unsupported by a dominant culture, we might use it to characterize a small group of people who live experimentally but in conversation with a mainstream culture. The metaphorical usage of *unmooring* implies something bad: being lost at sea, unable to find purchase on solid ground. But it can also mean a type of freedom: being unfettered by restrictions, able to move through the world without obstacles. In the United States, this unmooring is idealized. It is the life, liberty, and pursuit of happiness that we want to believe are not only unhindered by regulation but also entirely unshaped by government and tradition. We want our freedom to be original. We want to be born equal to pursue that freedom. But our freedom is neither unregulated nor original. We are not born equal, at least not in terms of ability to exercise freedom of self-determination. The nautical usage of *unmooring* explains this tension between competing forms of freedom and control. Instead of endless possibility, events are anchored in preparation to shift control from one agent to another. Instead of absolute control of these agents, all we have are a series of complexly engineered but imperfect safeguards against the threat of accident and chaos.

Say, now, that it is 2014 and you have a boat moored just inshore of the Gulf of Mexico in the state of Louisiana. Say you are a fifty-year-old white man dressed in a ratty t-shirt, torn jeans, and white shrimp boots. Your skin has taken on the permanent hue of skin just before a sunburn, but darker, with the texture of a leather welding glove. You need to finish attaching large nets tied to twin outriggers before you are ready to begin the May shrimp season. You tried working onshore at a machine shop and as a truck driver, and it didn't stick.

You've yoked your work to something you call freedom. Shrimping affords you something a job onshore does not. The trajectories of your life—the confluence of family and finances, of the hope to survive and the desire to be left alone, of the menace and comfort of a nautical disposition—have unmoored you. This unmooring is the unmooring of using the final anchor to reposition. It is an unmooring that does not drift too far from the networks of power relationships that have, you believe, left you high and dry. Being autonomous is the hallmark of your work ethic, but that autonomy does not prevent you from seeing yourself as part of a network of blood relationships, from feeling that an uncanny past is reemerging to steer you into a future that you hope will be somehow better or at least more or less the same as a present wherein you can provide for your household by dragging the waters near your home and divesting them of some of their sea life.

Say you cling to this work, the work of fishing, an industry that has been endorsed by no less a god than Christ himself. Say you cling to this work even when a handful of food inspectors let through a pink tide of foreign shrimp bred in fetid ponds on a diet of stiff antibiotics. You cling to this work even as your brothers quit it, finding fortune in oil and machines. When your children were small, they could not be pried from the gunwale on the secondhand skiff you got from your dad. But now, none of your progeny wants anything to do with a life of trembling marsh grass, brackish water, and crustaceans. But you cling nevertheless.

Why shrimp when there is no future in shrimping? Why persist in a job when you know, because you are not stupid, that there will come a time when there may be no more trawl boats moored in the bayous across coastal Louisiana?

I went to Louisiana, to my hometown, Chauvin, and asked shrimpers why they kept shrimping. I interviewed people who either made their livings on the water or used to do so, and I interviewed them at the beginning of a shrimp season that for many of them was shaping up to be the worst in recent memory. The dockside price of shrimp bottomed out to forty cents a pound for medium-sized shrimp during my fieldwork in spring 2015.

Even then, at the nadir of the shrimp price crisis that extended throughout that year and the next, the shrimpers I interviewed would not consider retiring their boats and getting a job in offshore oil, an industry that, unlike steel and coal and other iconic American blue-collar industries, still offered lucrative and mostly stable employment opportunities. They told me that shrimping was in their blood. They could not imagine doing anything else. Over the course of my conversations with shrimpers, I began to understand that their insistent dedication to a life on the water went beyond cultural inertia or a willful myopia about their own prospects. For these people, shrimping offered the possibility of imagining themselves as something other than bound to the relentless, totalizing control of social institutions and twenty-first-century global capitalism. Instead of surrendering to the market, to cultural prescriptions that cultivate a certain upwardly mobile, cosmopolitan selfhood, to tightening and expanding social networks wrought by new communication technologies, these shrimpers built a life based on the intense space of the boat, a place that collapses family and work and nostalgia and hope into a kernel of freedom.

This is not to say that shrimpers are beyond the influence of government or outside of capitalism. This is also not to say that shrimpers have a progressive agenda that rejects oppressive power dynamics or that they offer an unproblematic way of living. Although most of the shrimpers I spoke to were friendly, garrulous, charming, and generous, their stories revealed that they could also be competitive, vindictive, hypocritical (especially in their simultaneous rejection of government regulation and pleas for government aid), xenophobic, misogynistic, and ill-tempered. And while they imagine themselves living on the borders of institutional governance, they, like other Americans, find themselves subject to laws. They are consumers of regular American stuff, like television and fast food and brand-name clothing. And yet, through an embodied performance of an increasingly anachronistic form of work, these shrimpers carve out a new space of possibility: one that is both free and unfree, nostalgic and utopian, corporeal and immaterial. They long for a world that is organized differently than the one in which they find themselves and set about achieving it in the small ways of anchoring themselves in a cultural mythology, a network of belonging wherein they remain useful, and a negotiation with an environment that is often as deadly as it is nourishing. Most important, they build their worlds not through a series of political actions but in a subtle, everyday actions that reveal an orientation toward living a life worth living—even if it kills them. They do not wish to transform society to fit their poetics of the fishing life, but they do want to bring their family with them into a world of salt and sea and wriggling life hauled on deck. They want to eat from animals minutes separated from life. They want to be lit by the sun and the moon and halogen work lamps. They want to be free, for a time, from their phones and the constant obligation of visiting and attending appointments and paying debts and driving on routes predetermined. They want to be free to go back onshore when they feel like it. They want a mode of escape that also feeds their family, that ensures that their progeny continue a tradition of making a living that ties them to their parents and grandparents. They want the viscerality of a blood vocation. And so they play a game of freedom that I call *unmooring*: the strategy of releasing, as best they can, all anchors but one. The anchors they (attempt to) release are the ones that lock the landed firmly into recognizable networks of power: schooling, salaried or wage labor, upward mobility, the accumulation of cultural knowledge, the divorcing of the self from environment, the division of the self into qualities measured and collected as data, the surrender of the self to norms. The final mooring is the complex linkage that I term *blood*.

This is the blood of "It's in my blood." It's the blood of kinship. It's the blood that is the body's potencies, delivering oxygen as the body moves the muscles to perform labor. It's the blood, sweat, and tears shed by the father and grandfather doing the same actions, in the past, ghostly now but still buzzing with the vital force of a life in the making. It's the blood that courses through the next generation, most of whom will retain only a memory of their family on the water. And it's the blood that the shrimpers of coastal Louisiana use to orient themselves, to connect themselves to the land, and the final linkage before setting off to sea. It's the blood magic that transforms the boat from merely a tool into a transformational space, a machine of possibility.

This blood magic creates a space that anthropologist Kathleen Stewart defines as "a space on the side of the road": "the site of an opening or reopening into the story of America." She writes, "In other like 'occupied,' exploited, and minoritized spaces, [the space on the side of the road] stands as a kind of back talk to 'America's' mythic claims to realism, progress, and order. But more fundamentally, and more critically, it opens a gap in the order of myth itself—the order of grand summarizing traits that claim to capture the 'gist' of 'things.'"[2]

Stewart's project finds narrative rifts that challenge what we might call the American story, the one wherein individuals triumph in a wilderness through confederation, democracy, and capitalism. The story goes that driven by persecution, religious minorities braved the big Atlantic and set up a small world where they could get by on their own gumption and know-how. Taxed and oppressed, descendants of these settlers later fought, died, and lived for the right of self-sovereignty. Over the course of 250 years, America became the land of opportunity, where you can make it big if you have enough grit. It became the land of cul-de-sacs, plentiful groceries, and pensions. It became the global keeper of democracy, a place where everyone, no matter how much money they have, is middle class, middlebrow, and normal. Stewart looks for lived stories that punch holes in the American story, ones that create spaces wherein new stories, less granite, might emerge. In the game of mooring and unmooring, shrimpers open these rifts by living stories that counter the stultifying project of becoming good economic citizens who buys into what Lauren Berlant calls the fantasy of the good life: "upward mobility, job security, political and social equality, and lively, durable intimacy."[3] Although some shrimpers, particularly those born into successful shrimping fiefdoms, reach a sort of bourgeois class position, there does not seem to be a desire to actually jump classes. I spoke to shrimpers who owned and operated their own boats, and all they wanted to do was continue shrimping. The shrimpers who became the head of a fleet longed for the days when they were merely captains. Unlike other blue-collar workers, shrimpers have few illusions about job security. Even before the influx of foreign aquacultured shrimp in the 2000s and the 2010 oil spill, shrimpers understood that a single bad hurricane or a downturn in the oil industry could spell doom. The shrimp market boomed and busted. Shrimpers have always left the fishery for work in the oil fields, in shipyards and machine shops, and in service-sector jobs. Shrimpers also feel minoritized, left behind by what they see as political malfeasance, mainstream popular culture, and fetishization of technological capitalism.

This feeling of being minor extends throughout the small hamlets that cluster along the bayous of southern Louisiana, where shrimpers moor their boats. Self-identifying as Cajun, the people of Chauvin, Louisiana, like to tell stories of their difference. The story goes that, fleeing religious persecution and ethnic cleansing, Acadians—the French settlers who lived in what today is Nova Scotia and New Brunswick—sailed to Louisiana. It was a land of plenty.

It was a land where they could be left alone and develop their Cajun qualities. Cajuns don't read, but they're cagy. They subsist off the words old people say. They are different from any group of people in America. They have a knowledge that needs to be carried on, a knowledge that is a birthright, scrawled in blood and story. They speak. This is how the knowledge—which is not only knowledge but *wisdom*—transfers from generation to generation. Wisdom: how to do things, how to do them the right way for the right reasons. Doing, for Cajuns, is a type of pedagogy, a way to teach children how to be Cajuns. How to peel crawfish and shrimp. How to eviscerate a crab. How to cut thistle from an overgrown lot at just the right time to make a salad with the tender stalks. If you cut the plant too late, you might as well eat wood. Cajuns need to know how to harvest the knowledge from their families, which elders know how to tie knots useful for trawling, which ones know how to heal maladies, which ones know the particularities of the local language. Cajuns must be a lifelong learners, graduate students without the reward of certification. Cajuns must enjoy music made with accordions and fiddles and washboards. Cajuns must not only endure spicy food but *enjoy* it. Cajuns must eschew the insidious influence of the sitcom, the hip-hop joint, the animated GIF. Cajuns must live in the world (of mainstream culture) but be separate from it. Cajuns must be wrought of mud and floodwater and gumbo and muscadine wine and boats. Cajuns must have a nautical imagination. Cajuns must speak French. Cajuns must be tricksters.

The self-perception of people in coastal Louisiana as a minor people, Cajuns, who have a mythic predisposition to oppose the tenets of the American story, is not yet a rift in totalizing narratives. Instead, it is a counterstory, a story whose minor status does little to mitigate its totalizing force. The space torn open by the trawl boat, the blood mooring, and the embodied practice of unmooring is elusive, precarious, and flickers in and out of existence. It is a tiny world, a tiny living, where shrimpers can renegotiate the stories that govern their lives, whether those stories be the American story of the good life or the Cajun story of the autochthonic folk crafting a premodern life in places hidden from the colonizing force of American culture. These stories, including the Cajun one, anchor shrimpers to what has already been proven to be possible: the governance of people by both centralized institutions and distributed networks of control, the imagination of work as an entry into the good life, the impossibility of cross-cultural understanding, and the inevitability of globalized relationships. *Last Stand of the Louisiana Shrimpers* offers a course of study of how a group of people, clinging to a declining industry, carve out a space where they create survivable worlds through a simultaneously corporeal and discursive act of storytelling: the repetitions of labor, the sensory experience of working with animal life and machines on the water, the self-elaboration that seeks to imagine that the life they make is a beautiful one. They are suspended between the hardness of landed institutions, of prefigured modes of living, of totalizing stories, and the freedom of the deadly, mercurial, life-giving sea. Of course, they do not entirely escape the pull of the good life. They do not escape the blood-red politics of the white South. They will not survive if technology and global trade and climate change continue on their courses. But they also do not give in entirely. They carve holes in the good life where they can live. They carve holes where life and work are livable.

Lesson One

Making Space

I am drinking Miller High Life ponies and being sunned out and just saw everyone for Easter and Good Friday, and now it's the Octave of Easter and my grandpa cracks open another pony with his left hand, which is mostly intact—the ring finger ends at the second knuckle and sticks out from his fist like a loose piling. I am bayouside, sprawled on green-and-white folding chairs from the 1980s. The junky pier jutting into the bayou gets worse every year as the water eats away the pine planks, slowly prying the deck nails out of their holes. There are children who do not care about this or the splinters that catch their ankles or the gaps that yawn between planks, and they sit on the pier, play on the pier, perilously close to falling into the opaque bayou water. The priest floats by on a boat owned by Kimothy Guy, who everyone agrees is one of the best shrimp fishers in the parish. About ten days ago, the priest washed Kim's feet in church in the lead-up to Easter. Now the priest throws some holy water at me, and I bless myself at him.

It's the Boat Blessing, aka the Blessing of the Fleet, aka *la bénédiction des flots*. This is an old Catholic ritual wherein a priest smears God into the water so that fishers, like the apostles of biblical time, might catch a miraculous draught of fish. I'm in Chauvin, a "census designated place" in Louisiana, about an hour and fifteen minutes driving southwest from New Orleans, about thirty minutes driving from the place where the road ends at the Gulf of Mexico. Chauvin is a clustered place: dwellings organized into subdivisions along the main artery, Bayou Petit Caillou, where boats presently parade forth, trailing the priest ahead of the May shrimp season. If everything goes according to plan, this ritual magic will result in nets creaking under the weight of shrimp and the things that come with filtering the water through rope: squid, perch, sludge, hydrilla, aluminum cans, and plastic bottles. Everything will be thrown back, save maybe the squid, which are a secret delicacy here, prepared the same way you prepare any invertebrate from the sea: boiled with a seasoning mix called crab boil, served on newspapers, dipped in a dip made from mayonnaise and ketchup.

Here is a story people in Chauvin tell: the livelihood of Chauvin depends on the water to yield shrimp. Trawlers harvest and sell shrimp to dockside processors who sell to seafood distributors who sell to grocery stores and restaurants. In Chauvin, you have the luxury of buying directly from trawlers at dockside prices, say $1.50 per pound of raw head-on shrimp, size 21/25—the number of shrimp per pound—from a neighbor rather than $8.60 per pound at the Rouses Supermarket or $17.99 at Whole Foods.[1] But the story, as it stands, is wrong. The livelihood of Chauvin depends less on the shrimping industry—whose profit decrease each year—than on the willingness of people to imagine that the life of Chauvin depends on the water. Although the port of Dulac-Chauvin has averaged (without adjusting for inflation) about $50 million worth of seafood per year for the last twenty years, its rank among ports has dropped precipitously over the same amount of time (figure 2). Even accounting for cycles of boom and bust and inflation, the value of the port is going down. The people here work on offshore oil platforms, in machine shops or industrial shipyards, or at the Piggly Wiggly or Chase bank or local schools. And yet each year, the priest at St. Joseph Catholic Church leads a procession of trawl boats down Bayou Petit Caillou for the Boat Blessing. Shrimping is the only occupation to get a nod from the Lord. If we try to measure the success of the fishery by the value of its landings or the amount of new commercial licenses or the market share of the products, we will find that wild-caught shrimp is becoming a niche industry incapable of supporting the people who work in it. The people watching the slow parade of boats know that there is no future in shrimping in Chauvin.

But still, they pray for the industry. That this year might not be the last year to imagine oneself as one used to be. That this year be full of hot crustaceans leaking juices onto newsprint. That this year be the one when their children ask to hear a story about the good old days when everyone spoke French and got along, about a heritage that bleeds over into sacred nostalgia. A story about themselves as they imagine they should be: unique, humble, simple, hardworking, crafty, funny, pure, free. Voracious in appetite for food and God. Tenacious when it comes to weathering weather. This story is a highly masculinized version of events, centered on how a group of men see themselves. It's a story of a race of men with rustic intelligence, tellers of tales, men who have successfully escaped a life of tedium and wage labor, who have made

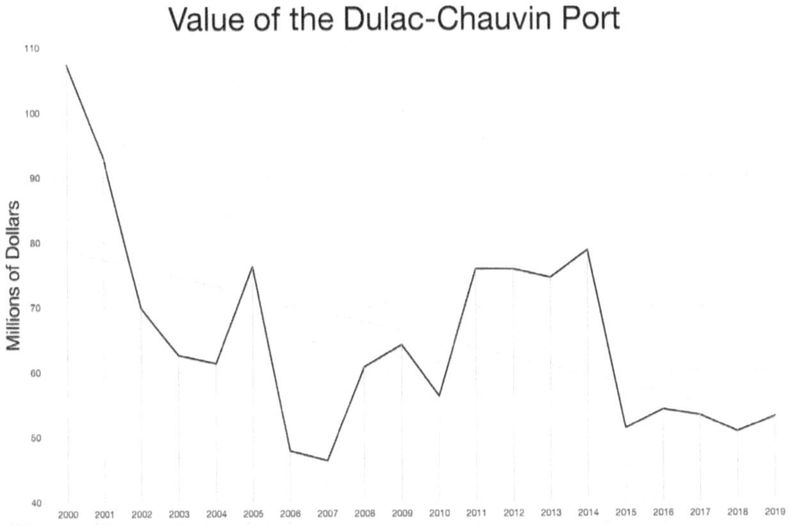

Value of the Dulac-Chauvin Port

Figure 2. Value of the Dulac-Chauvin Port, 2000–2019 (in 2021 US dollars). Source: National Marine Fisheries Service, Fisheries of the United States, 1995–2019. Adjusted value calculated with the Bureau of Labor Statistics Consumer Price Index Inflation Calculator: https://www.bls.gov/data/inflation_calculator.htm.

themselves in the images of their grandfathers, who have yoked their family and its domestic sphere to a boat, an insular place, both enclosed and mobile, serene, productive, real and unreal.

Needless to say, every year is a year of stories, whether or not one wants to hear them. This year, like other years, onlookers complain that there are fewer boats than the year before. They fear the day when their children finally rid themselves of the shrimp and ammonia stink of the Triple T processing factory on Highway 56. They fear the day when their children have left their stories behind for different ones, shared over cuisines that are utterly foreign, in cities and landscapes not scrawled in estuarial mud and sunset and seagull. This is a story of decline: people are abandoning traditional culture and labor, assimilating, selling out. But while we tell a story of romantic loss from shore, trawlers are creating worlds on their boats, worlds that may not prevent the ultimate end of the shrimp fishery but that nevertheless allow them to improvise a life worth living, a world that is bearable for a time, one that connects an uncanny past to a utopian future, flickering in and out of sight but burrowing deep into the physicality of environment: wind and marsh grass, the smell of peat, the viscosity of the estuary, the heat of sun and engine, the screech of winch and bird, the jerky slip of a sea creature in hand.

It is tempting to characterize the trawl boat, set in opposition to the imperatives of twenty-first-century American capitalism driven by instantaneous communication, commerce, and immaterial labor, as a utopian space. Utopia, literally "no place," offers a dream of a different future, one where the ills of today are reversed, where history has ended. In the idyllic imagination, the boat offers just this: an enclosed reality wherein shrimpers, acting as their own bosses, reconfigure the world to include only the things they love: the corporeal experience of the marsh, the taste of fresh food, the tight-knit family life of intimate coordination, the transmission of knowledge from old to young, the assurance of a type of ecological continuity. Imagined this way, the trawl boat is a nonplace, an optimistic direction for the future, the pure freedom of being entirely unanchored by material reality. Ernst Bloch, who attempted to recuperate the concept of utopia from its less-than-positive connotations among Marxists, might term this unfettered fantasy of the idealized boat an abstract utopia that has prevented the revolutionary potential of a future oriented politics.[2] Bloch writes, "Pure wishful thinking has discredited utopias for centuries, both in pragmatic political terms and in all other expressions of what is desirable; just as if every utopia were an abstract one. And undoubtedly the utopian function is only immaturely present in abstract utopianizing, i.e. still predominantly without solid subject behind it and without relation to the Real-Possible."[3] The abstract utopia is the idle hope we all have that things will get better. The hope for the good life.

To counter the impotency of the abstract utopia, Bloch introduces the concept of the concrete utopia, a possible future that lies just beyond the present moment and that can be anticipated through mediation with a specific, concrete history. This concrete utopian impulse will ideally spur action toward a better future rather than leaving hope stuck in an ahistorical wish for a world where wrongs are righted. Returning to my governing metaphor of unmooring, the concrete utopia allows for the drift of hope and speculation while one is still attached to solid ground. It is a way of positioning toward a future. According to Bloch, the concrete utopia "is concerned to deliver the forms and contents which have already developed in the womb of present society."[4] We might imagine what shrimpers are doing—continuing to fish despite the conventional wisdom that their industry is failing—as trying to reach toward a concrete utopia by bringing forth forms of living embedded in their understanding of history: an anachronistic return to the memory of their parents on a boat, of small families unfettered by mobile devices and extracurricular activities, of simplicity, of a form of self-governance that renders institutional regulation and even statehood irrelevant and moot.

To imagine a future involves attending to the invisible force of the past impinging on the present. José Esteban Muñoz, who resurrects the utopia in the spirit of Bloch, defines this as an act of world-making, of performing a future, defined "as functioning and coming into play through the performance of queer utopian memory, that is, a utopia that understands its time as reaching beyond some nostalgic past that perhaps never was or some future whose arrival is continuously belated—a utopia in the present."[5] For Muñoz, through imagining the past in concert with the future might enable us to construct some concrete utopia enacted in a troubled present. This practice is wrought with desire—specifically, the desire for a future of new and not-yet-conscious pleasures and relations: Eros, the combination of sexual pleasure and the will to live that, according to Marxist philosopher Herbert Marcuse, is a "unifying force that preserves all life."[6] Marcuse sets Eros in opposition to what he calls the "performance principle," the condition of labor alienation under capitalism. The performance principle—the normalcy of repressive civilization founded on exploitation—designates utopian practice as unrealizable fantasy.[7] Combining Marcuse's Eros-driven refusal of capitalist normalcy with Bloch's utopian thinking, Muñoz imagines a queer utopia that finds itself in the ghosts haunting shuttered spaces of counternormative sex practice and experimentations with new forms of connectivity. The desire, too, is hope—specifically, the affirmation of hope over fear as the primary anticipatory affect.

Hope is still of the potential, the magically possible. Fear is the imagination of a selfsame future: a future that is banally locked into the same systemic impressions of an eternal now. For shrimpers, however, the hope is both an orientation toward a freedom from the structures that configure and manage the forms of social and economic life *and* a mooring to a selfsame present that persists into the future. The shrimpers I spoke to would call Muñoz a dreamer, a communist, and much worse if I suggested to them that the future is queer stuff.[8] Rather than the Not-Yet-Here, shrimpers want to live in the On-the-Verge-of-Disappearing, the Just-Past, and for some, the Olden-Days. Although their attraction to the shrimping life is adjacent to Muñoz's formulation of an out-of-time queer utopianism, they desire a future still structured by heterosexual reproduction, organized around the family even as they desire to escape the logic of capitalism and expansive social networks.

Shrimpers negotiate memory and anticipation in service of creating another space where they can live differently. The no place of the utopia, even in its most concrete form, is simply not appealing to shrimpers, who delight in their embeddedness, their rootedness, even though they spend their lives on rootless water. For this reason, it might be best to describe the space that shrimpers inhabit on the trawl boat as a place between utopia (no place) and topia (a place). Philosopher Michel Foucault argues that "*utopias* afford consolation: although they have no real locality there is nevertheless a fantastic, untroubled region in which they are able to unfold."[9] Even the concrete utopia functions as a way to find a way to a better future, to console oneself with the hope that there is a way forward. The trawl boat does not offer consolation—or at least not consolation that is untroubled. Although there is a structure of escape, there is the necessity of return. Instead of utopia, the trawl boat is what Foucault calls a *heterotopia*: a space of disturbance formed by the alchemy of movement and story and improvisation and the game of mooring and unmooring from larger, totalizing cultural logics. He writes that heterotopias unsettle us "because they make it impossible to name this *and* that, because they shatter or tangle common names"; "they dissolve our myths and sterilize the lyricism of our sentences."[10] In other words, they can cut through the tightly woven nets that discipline the way we live: cultural narratives, institutions and their capacity to name, the quantification of human behavior by a statistical imagination. Although heterotopias collapse future and present, they do so in place, in a real place, in the materially rich space formed on the deck of a boat, on the rapidly encroaching littoral waters of the Gulf of Mexico. Heterotopias render us speechless or at least challenge the discourses that have structured the conditions for our possibility to act as self-identical subjects. They are ephemeral laboratories wherein those inside can experiment with the terms of living. Heterotopias are places (perhaps on the side of the road, perhaps on the water) that allow us to practice different ways of thinking, of surviving.

Although Foucault mentions heterotopias only once in his written oeuvre, he elaborates on this term in two speeches. In one delivered to a group of architects, posthumously published as "Of Other Spaces," he again contrasts utopia and heterotopia: the utopia is an unreal "placeless place," whereas a heterotopia is simultaneously real and unreal.[11] And in a 1966 radio address, Foucault describes heterotopias as "counterspaces," using several nautical metaphors that I find especially appealing when describing the world shrimpers are creating on their boats. He illustrates the counterspace of a potential heterotopia in an uncharacteristically cheery description of childhood make-believe:

> It's the Thursday afternoon in the parents' bed. On the great bed, they discover an ocean where one swims beneath the covers, and then the bed's a sky when one bounces with the bedsprings, and then it's a forest where one can hide, and then it's the night when one becomes a ghost in sheets. It's the pleasure, at last, when, upon the return of mom and dad, one gets punished.[12]

Here, Foucault figures a heterotopia as overlaying extant reality, a possible reconfiguration of experience, a modality of play. The bed, which is the boundary, can become something other than a bed. It can become the ocean, an image that not coincidentally suggests a type of freedom, of unknown danger, of adventure. The heterotopia, like the reconfigured life shrimpers lead on the boat, dissolves after a point. Here, the parents, who bookend the play of children with discipline, form the temporal boundary. In a heterotopia, as in Stewart's place on the side of the road, we can attune ourselves to the virtual, to the possible, to an opportunity to make for ourselves a world between and within the various preordained stories that structure our life. For shrimpers, voyages on boats have starting points and end points, are seasonal, and, like the bed the children play on, occur away from the disciplining gaze of some authority. The specter of regulation exists, but for a time, shrimpers can imagine themselves as free.

In both versions of the heterotopia speech, Foucault ends with an elegant simile about boats. In the radio address, he says,

> The ship—this is a heterotopia par excellence. Civilizations without boats are like children whose parents have no bed upon which they can play; their dreams dry up, espionage replaces adventure, and the ugliness of police effaces the bright beauty of pirates.[13]

Back on the shore of Bayou Petit Caillou during the Boat Blessing, I hear my grandpa complain, "They don't have the same amount of boats they used to." I want to say, "We are becoming a civilization without boats," but I don't because it seems rude: an apocalyptic complaint that is still out of place as a boat passes and blasts "Boogie Shoes," writhing with half-dressed twenty-somethings dancing around silent, smiling white-haired matriarchs and patriarchs on aluminum folding chairs. It's true, however: there are fewer boats this year. The boats themselves have fewer flags. Perhaps the music itself is just a little less loud. The boat, the lynchpin of the Chauvin imaginary, may end up a relic of the olden days, like the tools from when men gift-wrapped colonies of shrimp in purse seines, the trawl's predecessor. But now, for what could be a few more years or many more years, the shrimp boat is both a real part of economic life *and* the memory of itself as a real part of economic life. We mourn its passing from the banks, my grandpa and I, as we watch it pass in front of us, bobbing under the weight of its revelers. Emblematic of southern Louisiana "traditional" culture, the privileged site of male providers in small communities, a sacred spot, the trawl boat is a refuge of shrimpers made anachronistic by technological and economic development, a place for people out of sync with their era. It is impenetrable to outsiders yet permeable. As trawlers give up and the saltwater stretches further onshore, the trawl boat simultaneously fades away and moves further inland. It is a real place without a place, a threshold that collapses history and future, subjectivity and body, affect and myth.

It is this fragile space, the space of the boat and the possible modalities it offers of living and understanding, that this project tries to touch. The space of the trawl boat, though a counterspace to the kinds of official spaces of economic and cultural productivity, is something that came to be through a century of people negotiating technology, economics, survival, culture, locality, and ethics. Shrimpers have not designed the trawl boat to be an escape from mainstream life, nor do they talk about its revolutionary potential. The trawl boat is not particularly future-oriented except as a site where people imagine raising a family. Shrimping is a humble job that acquiesces grudgingly to more powerful economic interests, like energy corporations and government bodies. It does not even offer a place where wrongs are righted. Instead, it is an odd space born from dwelling in an environment, of subsuming narrative to ecology and ecology to narrative. The boat, the heterotopia par excellence, is the imaginative possibility that springs from the game of mooring and unmooring, a possibility that brings with it both hope and fear, the chance that the way we think things differently will be better than the ways we already think, the fear that we are fooling ourselves. There is danger: the boat, the fleeting utopia in the present, the utterly real and unreal place of reconfigured possible, might just become the fixed ur-myth of a new, stable, oppressive story that returns to a chauvinistic, sepia-stained past. Another cryptofascist holler. Another enclave that cannot live with others. And yet it could also demonstrate that there are alternatives to assent in the technocapitalist twenty-first century. Rethinking the boat, exploring the possible worlds made tactile by trawlers, we might be able to throw our dreams back into the bayou, the wet places, and see if we can grow back some adventure.

Lesson Two

Stories and Scholarship

Scholars have labored to create nuanced, complicated interpretations of place, history, behavior, social interaction, and art. As expertise passes into popular imagination, what began with precision and evidence takes on the arc of a story. Rigor falls away. Here are a few story lines about Louisiana that contribute to how people, including Louisiana residents, understand the place. These are rough, glib interpretations of scholarship, but they are the stories that have made it out of academia into the world.

This is a story History tells: the Acadians, gentle folk in concupiscent hills, loyal to God before the king, were uprooted and deranged by the British in the year of *dix-sept cinquante-cinq*. Some fled into New Brunswick, into the forests governed by the Mi'kmaq, learning to scalp redcoats in a brief guerrilla campaign and reemerging only later when the political situation in the region had stabilized. Some were packed into a miserable ship that sought to land at Williamsburg, but the governor of Virginia let them rot at sea, refusing them entry and then sending them across the Atlantic to a prison in England. Half or so died during the voyage. The bulk of the survivors went back to France, where they lived in sea ghettos in Nantes and La Rochelle, waiting for the next boat to arrive. Under Spanish rule, immigrants to Louisiana could cash in on attractive land grants, and a cluster of Acadians, many now intermarried with the continental French, returned to America. Prisoners in Canada, such as Beausoleil Broussard, the Che Guevara of Acadie and my great-times-seven grand-uncle, were eventually offered passage to Saint-Domingue, and from thence they headed for Louisiana. This is where Cajuns come from. They all became again a gentle folk in concupiscent alluvial plains, loyal to God before the state, until Uncle Sam forced them all to watch TV and speak English.[1]

This is a story Sociology tells: Cajuns, economically disadvantaged as a consequence of linguistic maladaptation and cultural insularity, remained a minority class in Louisiana until the oil industry made them all middle-class cowboys. Traditional work such as trapping, fishing, and farming gave way to industrial labor, exploited first by rich Creole plantation owners cum foremen who built the first refineries in Cancer Alley, the stretch of diked river between Baton Rouge and New Orleans. Louisiana's petroleum industrialization coincides with the rise of mass communications technology in the years after World War II, an event that exposed the Louisiana French to a broader world for the first time in a century and a half. Cajuns became dupes: of the culture machine, of the various industries that colonized their quiet Arcadia, of the US government, which demanded their acquiescence to humanistic democracy and laissez-faire capitalism. For the most part, Cajuns chose the wrong side during Reconstruction and later the civil rights movement and nearly elected Ku Klux Klan grand wizard David Duke into office as he ran *against* the first Cajun gubernatorial candidate in history, Edwin Edwards. They perceived themselves as dispossessed and underprivileged, especially as the oil industry evacuated Lafayette and New Orleans for Houston, but barely whimpered when community leaders bungled attempt after attempt to reintroduce French language and folk culture with public institutions and nonprofit organizations. Today, they are pawns in the claws of industry and state players, placated by a tourism economy and the spectacle of difference. But then again, who isn't? Cajuns are just like other middle-class groups in America, only perhaps more obvious in their nostalgia.

This is a story Politics tells: Louisiana is an odd state. It once had the largest free Black population in the country and its most terrifying slave auction. It springs forth from a contested geography: France, Spain, Britain, and the United States all staking claim at one time or another. It is a reduction of the largest land grab in American history, when Thomas Jefferson personally bought the Louisiana Territory from Napoleon without the blessing of the legislative branch of the government. It was unconstitutional, but it gave us the port of New Orleans, which, in the 1840s was the third-largest city in North America and the one with the most wealth. It is the only state in the United States to derive a body of law from the French Civil Code rather than British common law. Louisiana seceded from the United States in 1861, and New Orleans celebrated with a parade. A little over a year later, the Union took New Orleans and land along the Mississippi River and the coast, and support for the Union among the citizenry convinced the United States to welcome occupied Louisiana back as a state. In the 1930s, it was ruled by the Kingfish, Huey Long, who was more or less a communist autocrat. He modernized Louisiana with paved roads and free books and a university system and a public medical infrastructure. Sinclair Lewis thought Long might be the next Hitler, publishing a novel that imagined a Long-like US president who embraced concentration camps and a private army as a way of exercising political power. Lewis wrote his novel to damage the Kingfish's 1936 presidential campaign, when Long planned to primary FDR *from the left*. Instead, Long was assassinated by a doctor whom the senator might or might not have aggrieved through heavy-handed political machinations. Cajuns, mostly illiterate like other rural Louisianans, learned to read through Long's programs, entering the arena of American politics around this time. They tended toward the Democratic Party, voting in line with other groups of immigrant Catholics. Then they met the Bible Belt, liked what they saw, and became socially conservative. Louisiana is a red state where opinions on abortion matter during every election, where the continuity of big oil is the desired outcome of elections ("Drill baby, drill!") even after events like the 2010 explosion of the Deepwater Horizon platform, which put everyone connected with the fisheries in Chauvin out of noncleanup work. Populism, whether conservative or liberal, is always a good political strategy, appealing to a folkloric yearning for a precritical ethos where everyone performs heritage roles in a democratic economy.²

This is a story the Arts tell: Louisiana has a special connection to art and especially music. This probably has to do with the dusky bazaar that was the nineteenth-century French Quarter, embracing the expressions of transient people in a temporary city. It probably also has to do with the strength of fantastic history in the imaginations of its peoples: the memorialization of the Cajun deportation, the horror of slavery, the hope of the redemptory community of formerly enslaved people, the threat of extinction made each storm season, the culture of evacuation, the derelict aesthetics of Old South nobility meets urban density, the crazy reptiles that lurk and swim and bite, the tension between Catholic spookiness and voodoo spookierness, the cities of the dead where bodies rot in marble singles, duplexes, and mausoleums, the draw of the Gulf munching away at the coast, the enigmatic names of waterways (Bayou Go-to-Hell, Petit Mamou, etc.), the strange, Gambian-French-Chitimacha-Spanish-Choctaw-German-Cameroonian-Portuguese-Haitian-Italian-Mi'kmaquian-Isleño-Filipino-Irish-Houma-Dalmatian-Creole-Cajun mélange that constitutes local cuisine, the literature that reiterates the sublime properties of New Orleans, the relationship between nineteenth-century New Orleans and the Parisian salons whose members vacationed in the former colonial capital, the hybridity of its cultural and its artistic forms, and vampires (we must not forget vampires). Louisiana is the birthplace of jazz in the ghettos of Tremé. It is the home of bounce, whether Jazz Fest wants to admit it or not. It is home to the first opera house in the United States, the Old French Opera, built at the intersection of Toulouse and Bourbon in 1859. Or was it the Duchamp Opera House in St. Martinville, erected in 1830, the focal point of a place known as Petit Paris? It rested on the grounds of what was formerly Fort Attakapas, the place Acadian refugees were sent by the acting interregnum French *commissaire-ordonnateur*, Denis-Nicolas Foucault, who revolted alongside Acadians and French Creoles against the Spanish governor of Louisiana, was thrown in prison, and then ascended to the position of *intendant des* îles *de France et de Bourbon*, a position that saw him overseeing French colonial interests in Mauritius, Réunion, and Pondichéry. In other words, the Arts tell us, Louisiana culture was always already a global one.

These are the stories that undergird the stories we might tell next. Jesuit philosopher Michel de Certeau, when outlining his intellectual heritage in a chapter of *The Practice of Everyday Life*, writes, "In spite of persistent fiction, we never write on a blank page, but always on one that has already been written on."[3] Telling stories, especially repeating them, is a way to write something—a history—into a shared imaginative space. These stories flicker in and out of material spaces, encroach on them, shape them. In Louisiana, as elsewhere, a mythology of culture exists, and that mythology comes from different interpretations and reinterpretations. The page of Chauvin, the epicenter of my research, is well scribbled, slick with polished carbon and gum arabic and iron gall. For the most part, Chauvin's specific location has passed unnoticed by scholars, but the way people in Chauvin understand their cultural life and how they fit into broader cultural and political and spatial networks is shaped by the discourses that have sought to characterize, interpret, and define Louisiana in general. Both scholarly accounts and local histories, of course, are fictions in the way all fictions are: crafted by a certain education, a certain imagination, and ample perversity.[4] Bolstered by the enthusiastic scholarly arm of Louisiana culture, these stories threaten to become enclosures, cells, and walls. They threaten to weigh down the people who must live in constant negotiation with these stories and authorize outsiders to compartmentalize those people into fixed, restrictive categories.

Until recently, the main scholarship on the people of the Louisiana Gulf Coast concerned Cajun culture and history. This work includes histories of Cajun identification, explications of the particularities of Cajun ethnic heritage, and the collection of a vast archive of oral histories and local musical performances. The scholars responsible for building the foundations of contemporary Louisiana studies in the 1970s and 1980s—led by Glenn R. Conrad, Barry Jean

Ancelet, Carl Lindahl, and Carl Brasseaux—championed the study of Louisiana culture as legitimate scholarly pursuit. They legitimized a "Cajun revival" through scholarly discourse. Their work also set the primary academic idioms for future scholarship: history, folklore, and sociology. Conrad's *The Cajuns: Essays on their History and Culture* (1978), the Center for Louisiana Studies's first scholarly treatment of southern Louisiana culture, incited a proliferation of cultural histories, from sensationalist and nostalgic accounts of Cajun life to serious projects with social scientific aspirations.[5] Today's work on Louisiana has not strayed far from its intellectual heritage. Scholars are still concerned with issues such as cultural identity, representation, the articulation of "traditional" life, the collection of folklore and music, and the boundaries of the Cajun population.[6] This work generally follows several methodologies: historical analysis, ethnographic fieldwork consisting of qualitative interviews and participant observation, statistical accounting of demographic data, thematic analysis of a folk or ethnomusicological corpus, and/or cultural critique on the politics of identity and representation.

There is much value in the existing apparatus of Louisiana studies and in the methodological models within the field. However, I prefer to steer toward examining cultural identity where it is most nascent: the repetitions of work, the negotiations between current economic activity and extant cultural imaginaries, the role of memory and landscape in the will to survive. Instead of interrogating Cajun culture writ large, I focus on a small, disorganized set of workers who have been afforded cultural importance even as their economic livelihood is in question. Disciplinarily, my work pulls from history, anthropology, and critical theory—much in the model of Charles Stivale or Kathleen Stewart—and attempts to grasp small ways of being that are not quite incorporated into official stories. I fear that the aforementioned litany of stories, the popular understanding of scholarly work, overdetermine the trajectory of social and cultural activity. In other words, I seek to become unmoored from these stories in an attempt to find new lines of relation, new imaginaries, and new possibilities for the future.

The worlds summoned into being by coastal shrimpers are hard-won constellations of work and narrative, of a care of place and a care of environment. My efforts can be part of the great work of shifting the conversation from questions of authenticity, legacy, and folk practice into the realm of mapping intense and banal experiences embedded in environments, embodied labor, historical interpretation, and cultural play.

Lesson Three

A Brief History of the Pre-Bust Louisiana Shrimp Fishery

Before we can ask why shrimpers might refuse to quit shrimping—that is, how they might attempt to live differently in a fading industry on a disintegrating coast—we must understand how becoming a shrimper became possible and profitable. The industry rose quickly over about fifty years to become the top Louisiana fishery through specific technological innovations (canning, the otter trawl, the diesel engine). In addition to being profitable, shrimping has been paradigmatically different from other types of labor since its heyday in the 1930s–80s. Since the early twentieth century, most shrimpers have been owner-operators; unlike other blue-collar workers, they are their own bosses and have been as long as they can remember.

Before the rise and fall of the shrimp industry, the Louisiana fisheries were niche enterprises in a local world. The fishers of the New England coast landed the bulk of American seafood when fish scientists and fishery officials began quantifying landings. While Louisiana was sucked into the Confederate States of America's war to own people as chattel slaves, long-line fishermen in New England began accusing fishers using traps of overfishing. In 1871, this complaint, amplified by assistant secretary of the Smithsonian Institution and naturalist Spencer F. Baird, led President Ulysses S. Grant to establish the US Commission of Fish and Fisheries, the first institution to directly advocate for scientific research for the benefit of commercial fisheries. The commission compiled the first comprehensive study of the US fisheries, *The Fisheries and*

Fishery Industries of the United States, in 1887. According to special agent of the commission Silas Stearns, who studied the fisheries of the Gulf of Mexico, "It is to be hoped that the inhabitants of these shores will soon awaken to a realization of the store of wealth which beneficent nature brings to their very feet; if they do not, others will step in before them and bear away the first-fruits, for these well-nigh limitless sources of material prosperity cannot much longer remain unnoticed."[1]

In this version of the Gulf of Mexico, the waters are a vineyard and the fishers the absentee vignerons, cavalier with their stewardship. Stearns uses the language of ancient religions: the first fruits—the first harvests given over to God or clergy in tithe. Later, the *first fruits* will come to mean resurrection: "But now is Christ risen from the dead, *and* become the firstfruits of those who are asleep."[2] Here, at a point in history favorable for those who count and measure the facets of humans, the first fruits are the choicest commodities that will be exploited, sooner or later.

When the Commission of Fish and Fisheries compiled the 1887 study, the biggest fishery was New England finfish. Louisiana's finfish fishery was limited to the New Orleans market, to a small retail trade at the French Market, the bulk of which supplied restaurants and hotels.[3] In 1880, the oyster fishery was the most important, landing $200,000 of product versus $45,000 for red snapper and $41,000 for shrimp.[4] The oyster fishery, tended by Slovenians and Dalmatians who immigrated in the mid-nineteenth century and located chiefly in Plaquemines Parish, was the top fishery until 1925, when shrimping took over.[5] When the oyster fishery began to develop beyond the New Orleans market, it became more like farming: an oysterman harvests but also seeds the reefs.[6] Throughout the United States, shrimping has thus far remained a wild fishery.

Before shrimpers became trawlers and skimmers, they used seines—long, rectangular nets with a long edge of lead and a long edge of cork. A sailboat lugger would enter a shallow bay or lake, the men aboard dipping cast nets into the water to check for shrimp. When shrimp were found, the seiners would row out and encircle the water containing the shrimp, drawing the seine around it, with the lead line dragging the bottom and the cork line dragging the sky. The tallest shrimpers had to enter the water, holding the lead line down with their feet as their co-shrimpers unloaded the catch with dip nets.[7] Sometimes, there were no boats, and crews of six to twenty men set forth from a beach carrying a seine, trawling solely with their bodies.

Before the advent of ice and refrigeration, men built platforms in Louisiana's marshes to dry the shrimp in the sun after boiling and salting them. The founders of Louisiana's dried shrimp industry were Chinese and have nearly been forgotten.[8] Information about these early commercial shrimpers is fleeting and contradictory: there are scattered references to Lee Yim (or Lee Yeun or Chee Ken, among other names), who came to Louisiana either during the American Civil War or in the early 1870s and became the father of the shrimp-drying platform and potentially the namesake of Leeville in Lafourche Parish; late-nineteenth-century newspaper articles with passing references to Chinese or Filipino shrimpers; the establishment of the Quong Sun Company, which exported dried shrimp from New Orleans to China; and the names of ever-widening waterways such as China Bayou, Bayou Chine, and Chinamen Bayou.[9] Dried shrimp is still sold in small packages at the Piggly Wiggly in Chauvin. It is a rare delicacy, an exotic bar food, a snack, a supplement for cooking Louisiana food when the bounty of Louisiana is far away. Transporting shrimp at the birth of the Louisiana commercial shrimp fishery required removing all water so that the shrimp would not rot.

Unaccustomed to dried shrimp, Americans preferred their shrimp canned wet. Floating around the waters of Barataria Bay, George W. Dunbar and his sons George H. and Francis began canning shrimp in 1867, but the shrimp turned black as a result of a chemical reaction with the can.[10] In 1876, they patented a textile lining that kept canned shrimp pink and appetizing and moved their operation to New Orleans.[11] By 1880, the Dunbars had nearly doubled the value of the Louisiana shrimp fishery.[12] The canning operation in Louisiana initiated a minor feudal system wherein processing plants would employ seiners to operate factory boats.[13] The first fruits of the Gulf of Mexico were stuffed into tin cans bearing the Dunbar label.

The seine, requiring many bodies to operate, lent itself well to a factory model of labor: workers hauling in concert, earning uniform pay, with assignments to work a specific boat in a specific location. The waters with shrimp were far from the navigable waters that led to distribution channels and fresh markets. Vulnerable even in death, shrimp spoil quickly in their own liquids, their heads full of hungry enzymes.[14] In the late 1910s, processors began to fill holds in boats with ice and motored shrimp and oysters from beach and marsh and island to canneries using new gas-powered two-stroke outboard motors sold by Evinrude.[15] The shrimp fishery manufactured meat in an open air/open water assembly line: seiners pulled shrimpy life from the sea, icemen transported it via boat to the processing plant, pickers peeled off the carapace and discarded the enzymatic head, cooks boiled and brined the meat, canners filled and sealed the cans, and packers loaded the cans into boxes and crates to be shipped all over.[16]

In the 1920s, shrimpers became trawlers. The otter trawl, tested in 1915 and adopted by more than a thousand Louisiana fishermen in 1923, raked the seafloor of bayous and bays.[17] An otter trawl consists of a long, conical net held open by the shearing drag of two boards (called otter boards or otter doors).[18] The trawl could be operated by a boat with a small crew, and once motors winched the net in and out of the water, it could be crewed by one. The motorboats became a fleet of Lafitte skiffs, combing through the water, gathering up all its life. Other motorboats were iceboats buying shrimp from trawlers in the bays and ferrying the landings back to the processors, and the trawlers would stay at sea for days and then weeks at a time. For the next seventy-five years, the people of coastal Louisiana could rely on the water to grant them life they could exchange for money. When wildlife conservation committees partitioned shrimping into legal seasons to give the shrimp stock a break from being caught, shrimpers strung long lines of crab traps baited with chicken necks and catfish heads during the part of the year when they could not shrimp.[19] They strung gill nets and caught finfish. Oystermen collected oysters. Further inland, people farmed crawfish and hunted alligator. The store of nature washed life at their feet, and they noticed. The bounty of the water was limitless.

So too was the appetite for shrimp. With the rise of refrigeration, Americans farther from the coast of Louisiana began enjoying shrimp. By the 1950s, appetite for shrimp outpaced what domestic shrimpers could harvest. By the 1970s, this appetite outpaced what the world's shrimpers could catch wild. Funded by large-scale agribusiness corporations such as Ralston Purina and CP Group (Charoen Pokphand), shrimpers in Thailand began to turn to aquaculture to capitalize on the demand for shrimp, whose scarcity in the mid-twentieth century had made it a luxury food.[20] CP Group—which runs shrimp feed mills, processing companies, and other aquacultural and aquaculture-adjacent ventures—expanded shrimp farming to other Southeast and South Asian countries beginning in the 1980s.[21] Unlike Louisiana shrimpers, workers on Thai shrimp farms are wage laborers. Because shrimp are fragile little things, piling them into agroindustrial vats requires chemical cleansing of the water and antibiotics to halt disease.[22] With chloramphenicol, an antibiotic banned in the United States, Japan, the European Union, and Canada, shrimp farms in Southeast Asia began producing large quantities of viable but chemically tainted shrimp. Although other countries rejected chloramphenicol-contaminated shrimp in 2001, inspectors for the US Food and Drug Administration (FDA) allowed contaminated shrimp to enter the country, leading the price of domestic wild-caught shrimp to collapse.[23]

Since the crises caused by the 2005 hurricane season, the 2010 oil spill, and the 2015 shrimp pricing crisis, shrimpers in Louisiana have had increasing difficulties sustaining themselves and their families. A reprieve occurred between 2010 and 2014, when the price of shrimp recovered as a consequence of outbreaks of early mortality syndrome in aquacultured shrimp in China, Vietnam, Thailand,

and Malaysia.[24] Even large-scale agribusiness shrimp farms are subject to the precarious shrimp market, a global economy based on the fragile bodies of tiny marine creatures. In November 2013, the FDA issued a blanket rejection of Malaysian shrimp after repeated contamination with chemicals, disease, and decomposition.[25] These factors led to a comfortable 2014 season, followed by the collapse of the shrimp prices in 2015. As aquacultured shrimp returned to flood the US market, prices cratered, and people in the United States became aware of another sinister dimension of the global shrimp trade: some of the shrimp harvested on massive water farms were actually collected and processed by enslaved laborers.[26]

In the context of this staggering shrimp bust, I journeyed to my hometown in the spring of 2015 to ask shrimpers why they continued to shrimp. I might as well have asked them why they do anything at all.

Syllabus

What follows is an ethnography of down-on-their-luck shrimpers. While I describe more of my methodological concerns in "Fish Stories: A Methodological Appendix," the texture of this book derived from interviews, ride-alongs, participant observation, and archival research I conducted in Chauvin, Louisiana, in 2014 and 2015. I conducted in-depth interviews with shrimpers intent on persisting in the industry as well as some who have left it for adjacent fields. Their stories follow.

In conversation with these stories are theoretical diversions, critical analysis, quotations from a wide corpus of texts from different disciplines, and sections of fiction. Maybe some poetry. This book is not intended to be a traditional scholarly monograph; rather, it is an experiment that seeks to connect the lives this book is about with language and image and philosophical ideas. The book is organized into three sections, each of which explores the lives of shrimpers through metaphorical, scholarly, and literary riffing on a particular theme: blood, water, and nets.

The first section, "Blood," takes seriously shrimpers' claim that shrimping was "in their blood." While this phrase seems immediately comprehensible and a cliché, its meanings pull together the anxieties and corporeality of the Louisiana shrimper. The blood vocation champions work as a genetic trait, something that is embedded in the body of the worker. The repetition of this blood vocation as an explanatory device stands at odds with the end of inheriting shrimping as a vocation, as most children of the shrimpers I interviewed want nothing to do with their fathers' business. Beyond kinship, the blood vocation recenters shrimping as work done by a corporeal body, a style of work quickly becoming obsolete. In the corporeality of the shrimper, the physical rehearsal of labor, attuned to a rich environment that is an immediate, sensory present, creates a rhythmic space wherein shrimpers raise the specters of an imagined past in opposition to a future that grows darker. The creation of worlds through work combined with mournful and genealogical orientation is a type of blood magic: a sacrifice cut out so that one might live, transformed. The magic of the shrimping life, born in blood and from a sacrifice of livelihood and relevancy in twenty-first-century America, embeds—moors—shrimpers into their environment, their locality, and the matrix of blood that flows across family and cultural practice.

The second section, "Water," diverts from individual shrimping experience to explore the sea, a primal, asignifying function of unmooring. I begin with a reading of Wallace Stevens's "The Idea of Order at Key West," which wrestles with the ordering impulse applied to the inhuman chaos of the sea. Between the sea as unknowable freedom and the constriction of order and naming, we find the game of mooring and unmooring, of building levees and digging canals, keeping water at bay and bringing its effluvium into the solid parts of earth. Coastal Louisiana, which the Gulf of Mexico sips from, slaking its thirst for disordering stable things, is quite literally not on solid ground. I trace a local history of naming watery bodies and the erosion of the borders between formerly discrete places. In the water, there is a different play of memory and futurity: forgetting, letting some things drift back to a sea from which they slunk. I introduce the villain of the shrimping epic: the impersonal institutional agent, who unknowingly names local places, who enacts restrictions, and who let in the apocalyptic industry known as oil. I return to the shrimper, this time as a body on the water. Water is a deathly matter. Hurricanes periodically rob the coast of its life, scattering bodies across the littoral plane. I chart an alternative life on the sea, the one lived by an offshore oilman, which becomes part of machines of mainstream capitalism and normalcy but also destroys the land. Shrimpers' life on the water is a place of suspension, of self-erasure, of openness—and therefore, of possibility. Shrimpers described to me the sublime qualities of a life on the water, the majesty of birds and wind and spray, the menace of the dark cloud. But out there, in the ghost world of the sea, in the inevitability of a watery grave, also exists an opportunity to stand against both nature and institutional humanity, a model of survivability based on both agency and surrender.

In "Nets," I imagine how trapped the shrimper must feel. I wrote this section in the wake of the political disasters of 2016, when nationalism surged as a legitimate threat to both conservatism and liberalism, upsetting the regular and predictable conflicts between the Right and the Left. Britain decided to leave the European Union. The United States elected an autocrat billionaire reality-television star. Both campaigns employed xenophobic tropes, especially ones that characterized immigrants and globalization as major threats to blue-collar (white) voters. In the fallout from both elections, pundits declared that coastal elites, intellectuals, the political professional class, and other pundits had ignored the growing toxic discontent among rural and blue-collar whites who feel left behind by a swiftly deindustrializing world and a media coalition intent on pushing technologism and progressive identity politics.[1] So I explored the desire of the white, blue-collar men I interviewed to be free from governmental intervention. The shrimpers spoke passionately about how regulations hurt them, about how they could not stand to be part of a traditional workplace where they would be made to follow orders. They lamented the fact that governmental bodies ignore the knowledge the shrimpers have gained via birthright and experience. But even in the midst of a controlling society that targets increasingly subindividual parts of a person for modulation, shrimpers have, against odds, *made a life*. This, I say, is a miracle. Or at least a model for a miraculous refashioning of the world. Without an agenda, shrimpers engendered a world that they consider livable. They enact this world by gathering to themselves, as if with a net, the experiences and people that they care about. While they cannot escape the network of forces that seeks to control them, they can, for a time, form a local network where they can practice a world they imagine used to exist, a world which is yet to be.

Figure 3. Kim Guy, 2015. Photograph by Emma Christopher Lirette.

BLOOD

The inshore shrimp season had yet to start, so I hitched a predawn ride with Kimothy Guy to go crabbing in Lake Boudreaux (figure 3). His boat, a Carolina skiff, had crates of icy catfish heads stacked neatly on the port side of the wheel, next to empty plastic crates. Kim, a short but sturdy man in his mid-fifties, muscled out of the water wire traps yoked to foam buoys painted green and purple. He banged the traps on the side of the crates, loosening the locked grip of the crab claw. Then he baited the trap with a catfish head. As the sun warmed the April morning, the catfish heads seeped their blood onto the deck, slickening it.

My brother, who assisted me with sound recording during this crabbing trip, and I hung the bags we'd brought on our bodies to avoid dipping the equipment in fish blood. Eventually, we sat on folding chairs, our laps full of equipment and the soles of our shoes slippery.

That morning, Kim told me that shrimping was in his blood. The week before, Steve Billiot, a shrimper who moonlighted as an Elvis impersonator, told me shrimping was in his blood. The following week, shrimpers and people adjacent to the shrimp fishery in Terrebonne Parish told me that shrimping was in their blood. In each case, this claim was less information gifted by informant to anthropologist and more refrain: a rhythmic chant, an obvious truth, a prayer. Why else work the slow waters, this refrain asked. Why live there at all if not for the simple blood truth of vocation?

Something must have knocked shrimping out of my blood, my family's blood. Though my father learned French on trawl boats and his father met his mother over a trawl radio, no one in my dad's family works the nets today. On my mom's side, her father abandoned trawling for carpentry, which he passed on to his sons. For those with shrimping in their blood, the pull of blood must be strong. The shrimpers who have persisted have done so through oil and flood and imports. They have persisted even as their children have turned to more lucrative endeavors: working in machine shops, programming computers, nursing.

Here, we embark on a journey back to basic anthropological concerns: kinship, genealogy, social cohesion through imagining a sensical and sensible world of symbols like blood. Each Sunday, Chauvin Catholics, who are the moorings of Chauvin's spiritual sensibility, consume the Blood of Christ at Mass. One time, I went to a Mass at Saint Joseph with my mother. The homily was on the Eucharist. The priest said, "We eat blood all the time. When we fry up some meat, there's blood in the pan. We eat that. It's not gross." I like to tell people this anecdote to ridicule the simplistic faith of a rural people because I am a bad daughter. But it also shows that I am at least as bad an anthropologist: blood is more potent in Chauvin than in other places. The priest was explaining the mystery of transubstantiation in a way that makes sense to a congregation that wakes up before light to lure crabs with the scent of fish or pig or chicken blood, that hunts during hunting season, that spits out lead shot from braised ducks at an after-Mass dinner. Here, blood means nourishment and sacrifice, a connection to your family and the transubstantiation that occurs when the food you share moors you to them.

Fishing, of whatever sort, is a bloody affair.

Every few days, Kim buys catfish heads for crabbing. The blood in shrimping is of a different sort. You don't use bait to catch shrimp. You trawl. A boat lowers nets into the water, the nets catch everything, and then the shrimper culls the catch. In the local French, this is *trier*, which can also be used in English: the shrimper triés the catch; he was triéing when he cut his finger. Shrimp, like catfish, have things that will hurt you. For catfish, the dorsal and pectoral fins have venomous barbs that will puncture your skin. For shrimp, it's a rostrum, a serrated beak that juts out from between the eyes. Though it lacks venom, it can easily snag skin and tear it. It can make you bleed.

When triéing the catch, a novice shrimper will get picked. Even an unsuspecting shrimp peeler can get cut. Over time, shrimpers get better at triéing until either they avoid the cuts or they don't matter. O'neil "ChaCha" Sevin, a bait shrimper, has hands with hard skin, like saddle leather (figure 4). I doubt that he gets cut easily. ChaCha holds the distinction of being the only shrimper I know to outright deny, unprompted, that shrimping is a blood vocation.

ChaCha has been a shrimper his whole life. His father, George Sevin, was a shrimper (figure 5). His uncles shrimped and built boats. His brothers shrimped until the twenty-first century. The Sevins of Bayou Petit Caillou are locally famous for being shrimpers. George even tried to unionize shrimpers in the

Figure 4. George and ChaCha Sevin, 2015. Photograph by Emma Christopher Lirette.

Figure 5. ChaCha Sevin, 2015. Photograph by Emma Christopher Lirette.

1960 (to no avail). If anyone could claim that shrimping was in his blood in the sense of kinship, it would be ChaCha. But he denies that shrimping is in his or anyone else's blood. Instead, he theorizes that it's in the mind, a nonphysical addiction: "A lot of people go, 'It's in my blood, it's in my blood.' It's not in your blood. It's in your—I guess, your mind and your thoughts. It's always in your thoughts of knowing what I can go catch. Or not knowing what you're going to have until you pick up your nets. And when you're always thinking about that, then you can say, 'Yeah, I'm gonna always do it, because I'm not doing it for the money.'"

It's sustenance. It's a slow gamble. It's a cycle of anxiety and surprise. It's living in a state of unknowability, of fear and anticipation, and the rush of dopamine that accompanies success against the odds. Shrimping, for ChaCha, is a focal point of his dreams. What will the catch be like, how much shrimp can he catch, how much money can he bring in—these questions haunt ChaCha's mind like a nagging cut from a shrimp head.

In 2010, the BP-operated Deepwater Horizon platform in the Gulf of Mexico exploded and dumped 210 million gallons of oil into the water over eighty-seven days. Some of that oil bled into the Barataria-Terrebonne estuary. In addition to the ominous environmental impacts, which will slowly reveal themselves over the coming decades, the spill harmed consumer trust in Louisiana seafood. Because some waters were closed and the public was not interested in fish, shrimp, and oysters slicked with hydrocarbon oil, few people were fishing. Because ChaCha is a bait shrimper, meaning that he trawls year-round for shrimp intended to be sold live to fishermen, his business dried up. ChaCha would normally have supplemented that income by selling oysters, but that business dried up, too. He claims that he lost 90 percent of his income that year. The oil spill bled him dry.

In his rejection of the blood vocation—not just for him, but for other shrimpers—ChaCha strikes a Foucauldian posture: his argument traces the contours of the transition from a society of blood, wherein power speaks through blood, to a society of capital accumulation and biopolitical regulation. Michel Foucault makes this argument explicitly in *History of Sexuality I*: at the dawn of anthropological discourse, Europe moves from a "society of blood," in which "power spoke through blood," to one governed by sex, biopower, where "the mechanisms of power are addressed to the body, to life, to what causes it to proliferate, to what reinforces the species, its stamina, its ability to dominate."[1] But even in ChaCha's disavowal, his emphasis on the quantifiable aspects of industry, the pull of everyday normalcy in obsessing on the job and its rewards—the hungry curiosity of surviving by dipping nets into opaque waters—ChaCha still finds something *more* than mere sustenance or accumulation in trawling. Something ineffable. Something that, despite his protests, is in his blood.

To be clear, the seemingly abstract regime of biopower does not supplant the power of blood. Foucault's focus was not explicitly about labor. But to understand the potency of a blood-borne vocation, we must take into account how modern forms of capitalism reimagine selfhood through work. There's a tragic puzzle in attaching to an industry that's bleeding out for reasons of genealogical loyalty. It's an instance of cruel optimism, a resurrection of an imagined time when work might have been self-sustaining, family oriented. Saying "It's in my blood"—like a prayer to St. Jude, patron saint of lost causes—is defiant but resigned, an incantation of sacrificial magic, a mooring in eroding silt. Yet we cannot discount the fact that things *have* changed in terms of blood. At least on the Louisiana Gulf Coast, the shrimpers who trawl those waters are not subject to a power that spills blood, and the constraints of kinship no longer have the same influence over labor in a world of wires and capital. After all, look at me. A nonshrimper, the first in her family to theorize for an academic audience. Even as the shrimpers hold onto their blood, they too are concerned with futurity, the hope that they will have enough stamina to provide, that their children might grow up in health and live a prosperous life among others. They want to proliferate.

I propose rethinking blood as both a symbolic *and* material force—an imaginative force—that anchors these fishers to their work, to their families, and to their world. Blood becomes a biopolitical metaphor for all sorts of things: genetics, vitality, economy. But it is also something felt, something nonmetaphorically real: the hydraulics of the body in labor. The use of blood as a justification for labor speaks to something that both encompasses and goes beyond kinship and a figure of speech. Blood speaks to the experience of labor, the experience of longing and belonging, and the experience of loss. It is the goal and its inception. It's what proliferates. And it circulates, even to those for whom shrimping is not in their blood, who must content themselves listening for the whispers of blood. Blood goes beyond individual vocation: it is the basis for magic, memory, and an ecological model of care. It is the first and last mooring that anchors shrimpers to their work.

Bloodlines

Tharsalio: In this eie I fee
That fire that fhall in me inflame the Mother
And that in this fhall set on fire the Daughter
It goes Sir in a bloud; beleeue me brother,
Thefe deftinies goe euer in a bloud.
—George Chapman, The Widdowes Teares: A Comedie

Let's get something straight: blood has meaning in ways that other things do not. The mere sight of blood can cause someone to faint. When certain people see blood, their hearts slow, their blood pressures drop. They feel hot—or cold. They throw up. Perhaps there is some animal reason for this, related to a primordial hunt. Perhaps it is a fear of what is inside of our bodies. Whatever the case, blood has power, and its meanings are legion. The specific way the shrimpers I spoke to used it was informed by that legion, even though they might seem merely to be talking about kinship.

Introducing a special issue of the *Journal of the Royal Anthropological Institute* that focuses on blood, Janet Carsten writes, "The meanings attributed to blood are neither self-evident nor stable across (or even within) different cultural and historical locations."[1] Blood, unsurprisingly, is fluid. It flows across the surface of history and bleeds through the boundaries that might clot it. As a physical thing, blood is odd: a liquid that clumps together into a scab; a vital bodily fluid whose visibility outside the body can mean trauma; the medium through which our bodies maintain oxygen, nutrition, and warmth. Blood means life. Blood means death. Blood means passion when hot, the lack of passion when cold. When we are embarrassed, blood rushes to the surface of our skin and we blush. When we are horrified, the blood rushes from our face to give us an appearance of death.

We all know blood when we see it, but we might have a harder time understanding what it means in conversation. When Glynn Trahan, a former commercial fisher from Chauvin, tells me that shrimpers "have it in their blood. They love to do it. It's their way of life, and it's the way of life they love," what exactly does he means by "in their blood"? At face value, Glynn claims that blood reveals the truth of love. What is in the blood is what one loves, and if one can identify the concept (figured as a substance) embedded in blood, one can discover the object of a person's love, the vital essence of their subjectivity. Blood, after all, is the fuel of passion. When Glynn elaborates on the shrimping way of life, he offers a parallel interpretation of what it means for something, a labor, to be in someone's blood: the near-biological imperative of habit that shrimpers have *grown* to love because it is what they have always done. Blood: a rehearsal of industry that becomes increasingly comfortable, the relief of following a well-etched path back home. The rhetorical structure of Glynn's riff underscores this interpretation, emphasizing not only the definition by homology of being in the blood to being a way of life but the love that sustains the imaginative force of remaining in the shrimp fishery, which, at heart, is a familial love, one that is intergenerational. Perhaps shrimping becomes a way of life through a muscle memory, a blood memory, that stays with a body and accumulates there, that flows into successive generations of shrimpers.

The connection to kinship is more obvious in Kim Guy's statement that "my daddy [trawled] all his life. That's where I learned that from. And his daddy. So third or fourth generation. I guess it's stuck in our blood. We gonna have to do it." Here, *blood* means bloodline: the passage of traits from generation to generation. In Kim's genealogy, the process of inheritance includes the cultural and industrial knowledge that he learned at the feet of his father. Like genetics, the subfield of biology that studies heredity, the way that Kim talks about his bloodline feels simultaneously fatalistic and probabilistic: the inevitability of passed-on traits, predispositions that are not quite certain but that feel inescapable, not just likely but probable. The way Kim makes the blood vocation claim implies that the continuity of commercial fishing over four generations was happenstance. A chance, but one that becomes increasingly deterministic. He *guesses* shrimping stuck in their blood. This is the kind of repetition that happens intergenerationally: the body of shrimpers rehearsing the work of shrimping echoed by the bodies of their children rehearsing the same moves. The first daddy trawls, and the accretion of shrimping in his blood begins. If it sticks, he teaches his heir. Who teaches his heir. The bloodline flows into each instance of the Guy clan.

Jill Ann Harrison, fellow researcher of down-and-out Louisiana shrimpers, likewise heard the call of blood justifications:

There was no phrase I heard more often throughout my conversations with both current and former shrimpers than "it's in my blood." They used this phrase to explain why, despite all of the hardships and struggles, they continued to try to make it as fishers, and with this simple expression they demonstrated that trawling was not merely a job or a way to earn a living. Rather it represented the foundation upon which family history had been forged. In that sense, shrimp fishing constituted what they considered to be their genealogical destiny.[2]

I imagine that this explanation of labor in blood would resonate with the shrimpers I spoke with in Chauvin, none of whom were the first in their families to go out on the water and drag nets. Their experience of labor, of shrimping, is caught up in their experience of being raised on and off of water, of being taught by fathers and uncles and mothers and grandfathers. Kim still calls his daddy "Daddy" and visits him daily, learning new things about how to be a trawler. The genealogical determinism of Harrison's observation is evident in Kim's words. It is Kim's destiny to trawl, since his daddy and his daddy's daddy before him trawled the waters. He *has* to shrimp. The propensity to live the fishing lifestyle is a biological fact here, a gene. It's the origin myth for generations of Guy men, a shared and sacred story that informs the relationships Kim has with his father, with his son, and with his grandchildren. Bloodline: the physical mirroring that happens between parents and their issue. Blood: the liquid that flows in the veins of family members. An identity. But blood is also stock, a genre: a metonym for the kind of creature who can withstand the maritime life, with its boom and busts, its prickly full nets and the empty ones. The trawlers understand their work as requiring work—not just the physicality expected by blue-collar muscle labor, but the labor of surrendering to the fickle, abrasive forces that will inevitably leave shrimpers wanting.

Kim has three sons, only one of whom may enter the fishery:

My wife always says that our older boy [...] that's why he didn't want to come back [to Chauvin]: he didn't want to be a commercial fisherman. When he was young, he was only three months old, and he was on [the] shrimp boat, and he stayed with us the whole time. He would never stay home, babysitting with nobody. He would stay on the boat. That's what my wife said, "We kept him too long on the boat. That's why he don't wanna have nothing to do with it." He comes in the summertime when he has to, but as far as being one, he'll never be one. That's not in his blood.

Kim continued, "The way that things is: kids these days get on the computer or the internet or play video games, and the next thing you know, they never come out the house. They'll never know if the sun's shining or if it's raining. They stay in the house, and everything that they do is on the—on TV or computers and stuff. They don't have nothing to do with outside. It's different from us."

The quality of being in one's blood is both a marker of kinship and a marker of essential truth, even when those two things are at odds. Blood can do that: bleed through. For Kim, his bloodline, his genealogical destiny, involves shrimping. For his heir and namesake, T-Kim, it does not.[3] Shrimping is not in his blood, and he does not want to follow in his father's and grandfather's and great-grandfather's path. Kim and his wife, Melissa, believe they spoiled T-Kim for trawling by forcing it on him from childhood, but this explanation does not cohere with the innumerable stories of boys who grew up on boats and later became shrimpers. James Blanchard, one of the most successful shrimpers I talked to, started going out trawling with his dad when he was ten. He and two of his brothers still shrimp. As a boy, Steve Billiot would tie himself to his daddy so that when he would get up to trawl, the string would jerk Steve awake. Steve would then nag his daddy until he was permitted to come. ChaCha started trawling when he was still in elementary school and got his first job as a deckhand at fifteen. If exposure to shrimping in formative early years could knock the industry out of blood, Terrebonne Parish would have significantly fewer shrimpers. Kim's oldest son disrupts the genetic narrative of a vocation passed on through bloodline.

For most of the twentieth century, Chauvin's young boys saw shrimping as symbolizing the entryway to adulthood, to providing nourishment caught by hands roughened by salt and rope. On boats, boys became something like men. They learned how to give their bodies to the sea in exchange for commodities. They learned the ideologies of the self-made fisher, the owner-operator, beholden to no one, to nothing save blood. Commercial fishing became a way to make a living and accumulate wealth while still living at home, a place peopled by family stories and feasts, forging a tiny, insular, and immensely satisfying world. A world one would eventually be responsible for maintaining. A world that shared a common blood, a destiny, a practical continuity. Imagining life cycles this way—the human body a vessel that pours its world into another human ewer molded by hand—ties a loop in the linear rope of history, a knot. Instead of an uncertain, dreadful future, we reset each generation in a never-receding past. There is no origin to blood, just the pumping repetitions that circulate it in the family body.

Until recently, that world of enmeshed bloodlines must have felt so stable, fixed, and bounded, especially in opposition to the world of typical blue-collar industrial labor in the United States. The history of shrimping, of using trawls on motor-propelled boats, begins in Louisiana before the 1929 stock market crash set off a chain of events that includes the Great Depression, the formation of a government-funded social safety net, and the transformation from industrial capitalism to informational capitalism that characterizes the second half of the twentieth century. Anthropologist Paul Connerton argues that precapitalist social formations created a mode of living in which collective memory accretes slowly over a long duration through localized, small social networks such as families and interdependent systems of craftspeople and shopkeepers. These worlds are built through sustained, continuous relationships: master/apprentice, buyer/seller, father/son. Connerton writes, "There is an evocation of a whole lost world of more intimate social interaction here," the nostalgia for which creates "a *remembered village* and a *remembered economy* that serve as an ideological backdrop against which to deplore the present."[4] This lost world, held in place by blood vocations and a cyclical temporality, stood in defiance of the labor idioms of the twentieth century, the rationalization of time and career, and the imperative for each new generation to do better than the previous. What is ironic about this lost world is that it was founded only just beyond living memory: an ephemeral world of stability, offering a refuge under its veneer of timelessness and permanence, in the strange return of a precapitalist labor model during the peak years of industrial capitalism.

The return of kinship symbology through the blood vocation represents more than a retreat into the determinacy of filiation. The blood labor of shrimping, ironically, is almost entirely imagined as masculine, ignoring the most prominent labor of blood, childbirth. Though each of these men was born through a labor in blood, and though the tides by which they fish are connected to the cycles of the moon, which have been always linked to femininity and the menstrual cycles of their mothers and daughters and sisters, the blood labor the men speak of is not of childbirth.[5] Though procreative, the matrilineal is not the main focus; this blood is mainly passed from father to son. Passing shrimping along to the next generation is less the creation of something new than a cloning of particular genetic stock. Carsten writes, "Blood in Euro-American ideas of ancestry and descent is also generally understood to stand for permanence and fixity."[6] A bloodline continues from one generation to the next: the traits one inherits, fixed in genetic fatalism. Nature trumping nurture. Blood being, as it were, thicker than water. But Kim argues that the call of the water fixed his blood in place: "All we ever did was water."[7] He is incredulous that the water might not be enough for a boy; he does not understand and mourns for his sons who do not have shrimping in their blood despite nature and nurture. Kim resigns himself to a world where his sons reject the lost, placental world of their parents. In a world of instant global communications and mass multimedia, no one need be bound by heritage labor, at least not in their aspirations. T-Kim is a computer science major, not a fifth- or sixth-generation trawler.

Blood, however, moves in unusual ways. It can seep or it can spray. It pumps. It bleeds through. Tim Ingold challenges us to look at ancestry not as the point-to-point genealogies that envision a lifetime as a discrete unit that can be connected to another, but as, after Henri Bergson, "a meshwork of intertwined thoroughfares along which organisms follow their respective ways of life."[8] The dominant mode of genealogical charting, he argues, implies connections between stable, finished units: Kim's father, Kim, T-Kim. In this line, each person is a node, their name a metonym for a person as their status in a family tree. Instead, Ingold envisions bloodlines flowing like a braid, wherein the paths of a person's lifetime intersect with others between and across generations, where knowledge and traits are shared in an ecological process of becoming. Kim has two grandchildren who slept at his house the night before I went crabbing with him; they intended to go crabbing too, but were too *honte* (shy), when I showed up. Kim told me later that unlike T-Kim, these boys loved the fishing life, could not wait for summer to start so that they could go fishing with their grandpa. Sometimes blood leaps over a generation. Sometimes it flows into someone else.

Blood here is also tied to sex and procreation. We call someone a blood relation when they have come from the same bodies we came from or when they come from our own bodies. According to David Schneider, Americans distinguish between blood relations and legal relations, such as those between people bound by marriage: "The fundamental element which defines a relative by blood is, of course, blood, a substance, a material thing. Its constitution is whatever it is that really is in nature. It is a natural entity. It endures; it cannot be terminated."[9] Blood is permanent and fixed. You can disavow it, but you cannot divorce it. Kinship that stakes its authority through sex becomes naturalized as relations of the highest natural authority—as relations of, to borrow the language of Mary Douglas, the foremost anthropologist of natural symbology, purity.[10] The trawler's calling to fish is purified in the blood of his ancestors, is vindicated in the blood of his children. Talking about T-Kim's apostasy to a world of computers and immaterial labor, Kim sinks with disappointment and perhaps shame. The blood in his veins may not be the same as that flowing through his son's. T-Kim has in some ways disavowed his father, the work of his hands, the knowledge passed from generation to generation, a shared love of physicality, estuaries, and the quiet of working among grass, water, and crustacean. Perhaps we can say that the shrimping blood is a recessive trait, but the genetic metaphor obscures the affective, visceral component of blood, abstracting the blood vocation to a trait, absorbing its slippery meanings, scrubbing its persistent stains, and reducing blood to a fully comprehensible symbol of social reproduction.

The tendency to clean blood, to have it mean the biological linkages between people on a family tree, is widespread, even among the shrimpers who deploy blood in complicated ways. The process by which biology and quantification surpass the richness of blood metaphors in governance is what marks the beginning of what Michel Foucault terms biopower: "what brought life and its mechanisms into the realm of explicit calculations and made knowledge-power an agent of transformation of human life."[11] Biopower—the collusions among state actors, biological scientific disciplines such as genetics and epidemiology, capitalist and often transnational corporations, and statisticians—metaphorically exsanguinates the human. Biopower, unlike earlier examples of sovereign power, need not shed blood to ensure existing hierarchies. It merely needs to encourage and cultivate certain lives at the expense of others. It softly weaponizes knowledge. Foucault argues that our society went "from a *symbolics* of blood to an analytics of *sexuality*."[12] In the exercise of sovereign power, the king signs a writ that results in an execution of a criminal. The body, in asylums and hospitals and dungeons, becomes subject to so many bloody invasions. Foucault's symbolics of blood includes the blood taboos of kinship, which forbid incest, parricide, infanticide, fratricide. Blood formed a similitude between people. It could transform into the godhead in ritual. Blood sacrifice captured the dreams of ritualists everywhere. The analytics of sexuality, conversely, is more accounting than mystery, more interpretation and schematization than slippery symbol. Sexuality, a strategic deployment of biopower, seeks to define acceptable limits on human behavior, to valorize reproductive futurity. Most of all, it spreads a desire to know—specifically to know thyself, to become subjects of knowledge. According to Foucault, the exercise of power to end life had been eclipsed by the exercise of power to proliferate life, to shape it through both discourse and regulation, to allow its presence within reason.

The transition between blood and sexuality cannot be understood as a discrete genealogical line connecting two bounded and finished orders. Instead, the relationship between these two concepts of power looks more like a braid: blood continues to haunt the regime of sexuality. It recurs in nearly every aspect of life. Foucault writes,

> Beginning in the second half of the nineteenth century, the thematics of blood was sometimes called on to lend its entire historical weight toward revitalizing the type of political power that was exercised through the devices of sexuality. Racism took shape at this point (racism in its modern, "biologizing," statist form): it was then that a whole politics of settlement (*peuplement*), family, marriage,

education, social hierarchization, and property, accompanied by a long series of permanent interventions at the level of the body, conduct, health, and everyday life, received their color and their justification from the mythical concern with protecting the purity of the blood and ensuring the triumph of the race.[13]

Shrimpers deployed the thematics of blood in exactly this way. Blood comes to stand in for family, inheritance, and the familial project of settling somewhere and making a life. It also stands for education, especially intergenerational education, wherein parents teach their children how to be part of their family, how to carry on the family's blood through labor. The commingling of blood through marriage and procreation becomes a central concern, especially in marrying the right person. Melissa, for instance, accompanies him on every trawl even though she gets seasick. This behavior is considered hearty and hale. It means she has good blood. When the vocation gets knocked out of the blood, it is a source of grief, disappointment, and shame. It dilutes the thickness of blood.

Blood, at heart, is who you are. The most consistent way shrimpers spoke of blood was that blood is their truest essence, and in that essence is fishing. Blood is not just a way of life or a connection with kin: it is identity. Carsten argues that the most surprising quality of blood might be that "it is the stuff of truth": "But here the 'symbolic overload' of blood, its capacity to be read in so many ways, suggests that any one truth already implies all the other truths that may be embodied in blood. And this may connect to the way in which blood seems in many contexts to be perceived as a kind of essence—of the person, and of his or her bodily and spiritual health, disease, or corruption."[14]

At heart, blood is the secret self you can confess to others in private or wear in public as a badge of pride. Invoking blood is the naturalized way of justifying proclivities, of staking ownership over behavior, of making it a deep, immutable, pure, biological truth. Blood partakes in familial mythos: kinship breeds identity. A family becomes a genre of persons, all of whom behave in similar ways—or so the story goes. And the truth of that story becomes compounded by all the other ways blood can be true: it is the water of life, pumped through a body to make it something other than a corpse. That blood is associated here with labor is telling: only through fulfilling work might a person live. Only through a way of life one loves. In this repetition, however, blood implies less the network of temporal and familial connections that make shrimping a possible genealogical destiny than the stuff of the self.

Shrimpers—both large-scale fleet captains and small-time operators—informed me of their love of the commercial fishing life. They loved everything about it: the water and plucking food from it and the sounds of the diesel engine rumbling through the estuary and marsh. But most of all, they loved not being beholden to anyone, imagining themselves as part of a precapitalist fantasy where they worked solely because they wanted to. They loved being their own bosses. When Kim worked as a tugboat captain, his skin crawled. He felt anxious and trapped: "I just couldn't take the pressure of somebody telling me what to do." Karl Marx compared this feeling to an encounter with a vampire: "Capital is dead labour which, vampire-like, lives only by sucking living labour, and lives the more, the more labour it sucks."[15] Kim's work on a tugboat was about as rewarding as exsanguination because blood is life, and shrimping is in his blood. This, according to Kim, is the purest form of his identity, the best life he can imagine—the only life he can imagine. This dedication to shrimping extends beyond the bounds of genealogical destiny or duty: it is a story of love and commitment that is marrow-deep.

This is what Glynn Trahan told me about love:

A job is not a job if you like what you do: it's an adventure. If you look at work because you have to go to work, and you don't like it, you despise what you do, but you're only doing it because you have to survive and feed your family, and it's your responsibility to do so, then that's a job. But if you go out shrimping and you love to do it, you do it because you're out there. The scenery is beautiful, you know? The ocean's pretty. The water, the land, the different animals you see, the dolphins, the seagulls flying. There is just so much beauty out there. Imagine sitting down in an office inside of the building, and all you see is a computer and a telephone and people just running back and forth and listening to their problems—whatever the company's problems are—and you're just locked inside that building. You don't see the outside, you know, for twelve hours. *Or* you're out on a boat. When you get up, you have the beautiful sunrise. You work all day, catching shrimp or crab or whatever you're doing, and you have all of this beauty. You're outside enjoying the fresh air, the wind blowing, the beauty of the waves washing against your boat, or whatever it is that you enjoy. And then you have in the evening, you have the sunset, which is so beautiful out there. You just look at it like that, and you'll understand why people love to do it.

This explanation comes directly after he tells me that fishermen have fishing in their blood. Being true to your blood self, your truest self, is to go on an adventure, to live with love and vigor. Glynn finds intolerable the idea of being enclosed in a cubicle, disciplined by a boss, seeing the generic gray of the same inside day after day (figure 6). His body yearns for the touch of sun and salt and water, the oneness of an adventuring, maritime life. He invokes a picturesque world where a body can be part of an environment, where he is grounded in a location but free to move through it, to explore it, to let his

Figure 6. Glynn Trahan, 2015. Photograph by Emma Christopher Lirette.

identity likewise enmesh with the place. His aesthetics of trawling are contagious: blood-borne. It is difficult not to want to live in the sublime world he describes, communing with dolphins and wind and harvesting raw life from the seas. This is the inverse of Marx's capital: it is labor as a progenitor of life. Shrimping, despite the hardships, is capable of sustaining people, of making them buoyant and able to thrive.

Glynn recognizes the hardships that shrimpers face: "Even though a lot of people . . . they can't make ends meet, they still love doing it. Of course, you can't keep going in a hole, not making any profit, but . . ." For shrimpers to keep shrimping, they would have to have it in their blood, because there is little hope of financial success. Commercial fishers have to remain dedicated and loyal to their love, their blood; otherwise, they will not survive. Kim told me,

> If you want to [shrimp], you stay in the business. You gotta love your job. If you don't love your job, you never gonna succeed. Everybody say, "Boy I hate to leave." No. You gotta like your job if you want to keep your job. You can be making millions of dollars and you can hate the job and don't want to wake up in the morning to go. Us, we know we like to do this, so we love to get up and come do it. Ask some of my friends: "Aw, I hate to go. I hate to go." No, not me. If I'd hate to go, I wouldn't do it. I love to come do this.

While there is obvious enthusiasm in Kim's words, there is also the ghost of hardship. Shrimping involves an element of hardening one's heart against the elements and fickle economics of commercial fishing: one must weather the bad times. One must stay in business and drag nets. One must love the labor. It must be in one's blood. But Kim also mixes metaphors here: for most shrimpers, there is no keeping the job because no one is hiring them. They go out and catch shrimp and then sell it. It is not the kind of work that warrants a performance review. But it does require that the body work hard and consistently.

A typical shrimper, fishing state waters on a smaller boat, wakes before dawn. He leaves his family behind for up to two weeks at a time. He works in an environment that may contain another human body or two. He may hold conversations with buddies over the radio, but his socializing options are limited. He eats potted meat and crackers and fresh shrimp and crabs and speckled trout caught by hand. He slowly drags nets. He pulls rope and fixes machinery and deals with bycatch. He operates a winch. He operates an engine. He steers a boat and hides among fading barrier islands when the weather is bad. He releases nets into bushel baskets, lifts the baskets onto a table, and culls. He ices the catch. He swabs the deck. He repeats these actions day and night. He tries not to drown.

Although some boats are equipped with televisions and DVD players, most still feature only a staticky radio and today's country hits. The work is lonely and hard and wet. Between drags, the shrimper's body is in constant, muscular movement: lifting and carrying and picking and throwing and jerking and flexing. The body comes into contact with animal life, grabbing live shrimp and sorting their herky-jerky bodies. Removing live eels and catfish and turtles and sharks by hand, often ungloved. Fingers bear the marks of stingers and claws and jaws. The bodies of shrimpers are often wounded. The perils of bloodborne illness are rampant in the tepid Gulf of Mexico. Kim spoke of a friend dying of *Vibrio vulnificus*, a flesh-eating bacteria found in warm saltwater that enters the human body through a cut. But the most dramatic (physical) danger for trawlers is the threat of stormy seas, which can dash a trawl boat against sandbars and mangroves and rocky beaches or just capsize the boat, sending all bodies aboard into the drink. The least dramatic but most widely effective threat is the physical toll of working on a boat for forty years.

In other words, the work of trawling is the work of the human body, and that work, in turn, transforms the body. All the men I spoke to in Chauvin had skin baked thick and red by the sun. ChaCha stands about five feet, eight inches tall, all wiry sinew and muscle. His forearms are thickly roped from years of triéing and pulling nets and hauling bushels of shrimp. When he speaks, it is the sound of wood cracking, his vocal cords leathered from years of talking over a diesel engine and smoking Marlboro Lights. When he speaks, it's as if a statue has come to life, and the fissures in his deep skin make way for his muscles to realign his face. You can instantly recognize the places that ache him: the carpal bones and the elbow, the little bones of the ankle and the arch of his foot, the lumbar, the neck bones. For hours each day, ChaCha balances himself on water. He rocks when the boat rocks, and his fluidity of movement on the boat is aggressive and graceful. You can tell that it takes his blood some time to flow comfortably to his limbs each morning. His body is stiffening.

And whether he hates to go or hurts or is depressed, he wakes each morning to trawl. He knows the danger of stagnation, of not trawling when you must, even if the weather is bad and the catch is bad. He knows that he has to love trawling even if it hurts him in the short term. He knows that to survive as a trawler, he has to love it even if it kills him. In the spring of 2015, the price of shrimp reached historic as a consequence of a renewed flood of imported shrimp that undercut domestic prices.[16] For a shrimper to justify remaining in the industry under these circumstances, after already weathering a cataclysmic oil spill and forty years' worth of hurricanes and coastal erosion, however, requires more than mere love. It requires blood and the truths it brings. Harrison argues that the rewards of shrimping transcend the obvious economic benefits, that trawling is caught up in the familial and cultural identity. I do not dispute this. Trawling, a blood vocation, is indeed caught up in kinship and genealogical destiny and cultural identity. The magic of it comprises these blood meanings and surpasses them. The blood truth of shrimping is that it is an entry point to a counternarrative, opposed to dominant narratives that compel people to participate in the global logic of capitalism and that privilege the rationalization of kinship and time. And this truth is produced through an ecology and poetics of bodily practice and presence in place, one that has an audacious and anachronistic imagination. Seeing work through the call of a blood vocation requires shrimpers to envision work as something other than a means to survive. This magic is, of course, blood magic. The blood vocation of shrimpers speaks to the truth of the body and its place in an ever-proliferating world of work and water and blood kin and food and animal life and competing regimes of power and signs. More importantly, this blood magic is the last-ditch bulwark against a world that will not prevent these shrimpers from being crushed beneath the heel of the increasingly corpulent boot of global capitalism. Blood magic, as we all know, requires a sacrifice.

Blood Magic and Cruelty

I fhoulde loath the keeping of my blood, with the loffe of my faith
—Philip Sidney, *The Countess of Pembroke's Arcadia*

In 2007, I left Louisiana to live among distant and unknown blood kin in Acadie, the region in New Brunswick and Nova Scotia that still maintains an Acadian population. The idea was to enmesh with modern Acadian culture as a Louisiana Cajun. I was on a Fulbright grant to write poems there. I had just finished an undergraduate degree; while in school, I had evacuated New Orleans during Hurricane Katrina and preemptively evacuated the next year to Paris. The experience of forced and voluntary expatriation from southern Louisiana left me yearning for the comforts of an essential identity that I could trace through my bloodline. And so I traced my way to the root.

Moncton, the urban center of Acadie, is a town about twice the size of Houma, the biggest town in Terrebonne Parish at a little over thirty thousand people. A small, French-speaking Acadian elite ran the cultural institutions, including the Université de Moncton, my host institution. The names of the Acadians I met were all names I grew up with: Boudreau, Thibodeau, LeBlanc.[1] I stayed with Charles LeBlanc *dit* Chuck Emmrys, a psychiatrist and impresario of the local arts scene.[2]

When he met me, he embraced me as a *cousine*—my dad's mom's maiden name was LeBlanc. While the name opened the door, his perceived identification of a blood trait confirmed our relationship. He looked me over and said, "You look like you must have some Mi'kmaq blood in you." The Mi'kmaq are First Nations people who lived in the Canadian maritime provinces and who were allied with Acadian rebels during le Grand Dérangement, when the British forcibly expelled the Acadian population from the region in 1755. Some

Acadians took asylum with the Mi'kmaq and launched a rebellion.[3] Members of the two groups bled for each other until Joseph Broussard *dit* Beausoleil chartered a boat to transport six hundred Acadians to the French colony of Saint-Domingue, known today as Haiti. Beausoleil later ended up in Louisiana, and his people dropped the *a* from *Acadiens*, becoming Cajun. So the story goes.

In the construction of Native American or First Nations identity, blood reckoning plays an intense, bureaucratic role. Anthropologists Pauline Turner Strong and Barrik van Winkle write, "Indian identity is fixed, quantified, and delimited through an elaborate calculus operating upon 'blood': pure, full, or mixed blood; Indian, white, or black blood; Blackfoot, Luiseño, or Cherokee blood; blood in fractions, blood in degrees, blood in drops."[4] The quantification of blood matters for governmental control of who counts as being part of a particular tribe or nation. The United States has its legacy of one-drop rules, most notably in early twentieth-century legislation that defined people as Black if they had any Black ancestry as a way of drawing boundaries around those subject to Jim Crow laws. Blood, the eugenic ideal goes, must be pure. Today, the distant blood of my own Mi'kmaq ancestors would not and should not qualify me for membership in a formal band. My family, in its move to Louisiana in the late eighteenth century, lost its connection to its First Nation. For indigenous blood, one drop will not include you in a tribal roll, but, according to Strong and van Winkle, it can "enhance, ennoble, naturalize, and legitimate" as long as your blood contains "no more than a drop."[5] For Chuck, some ghost of the Mi'kmaq he saw in my face legitimated me as a cousin in ways that our shared name did not.

The conventional wisdom for the boundaries of Cajun identity is that ancestry matters less than a surrender to a particular way of life in a particular place.[6] In other words, blood is not so important. There are Cajuns named LeBlanc and Boudreaux as well as Schexneider and McGee, courtesy of German and Irish immigrants who married Cajun women.[7] My surname, Lirette, was never Acadian, even if the bulk of my family tree is. In addition to French populations, my family tree has historical branches named in the Canary Islands, in Italy, in Alsace, and in the United Houma Nation, a Native American tribe that currently resides in Terrebonne Parish. The genealogical emphasis on the Acadian origin story belies how people live their Cajun identity. In the most recognized form, this expression takes the form of a particular music played on fiddles and diatonic accordions (from our Irish and German cousins), of rural cuisine featuring rice, meat, onions, and seafood. For this version of Cajun identity, you can read Cajun scholars, such as folklorist Barry Jean Ancelet and historian Shane Bernard, who have documented the Acadiana region extensively. Less attention has been paid to the bayou regions of southeastern Louisiana.

Using spectacular displays of cultural expression to identify what constitutes a Cajun can obscure everyday practices moored in specific locations. These practices open rifts in the established narratives—from the big governing stories of America that compel us to work for a better life to the smaller, more local narratives that establish folk identities. For the bayou communities in southern Terrebonne Parish, the trawl boat, a vehicle of work, one tied to bodily practice and intergenerational connection, is also a vehicle of cultural identity. To be a trawler holds a certain prestige: the continuation of a lost world into the uncertain future. However, the connection of shrimping with blood complicates a purely material understanding of how a culture that persists in valorizing an industry with a bleak outlook comes to be. Imagining shrimping as something in the blood imagines an ancestral connection. At its fascistic worst, it suggests a longing for blood purity, where the magic elision between law and blood gives rise to a family of people all alike and to which one can belong. In Chauvin, you see "Registered Coonass" stickers.[8] People identify as Cajun. And though the stability of an ethnic label such as *Cajun* is undermined by its exclusionary mythology and inclusionary practice, the label allows the people who claim it to be proud, comforted, and knowable.

Strong and van Winkle take on this type of essentializing, which they portray as the inverse of the quantifying, bureaucratic essentialism of blood reckoning. They write about Kiowa writer N. Scott Momaday's use of the trope that "memory is in the blood."[9] Although the phrase first appears in a novel in figurative language, Momaday later uses it when discussing writing about the Kiowa: "The imagination that informs these stories is really not mine, though it exists, I think, in my blood. It's an ancestral imagination."[10] Though one critic has pointed to this language as being "absurdly racist," Strong and van Winkle argue that while it may be essentializing, it functions as a way of subverting the official reckoning of blood that creates the conditions for racial exclusion and fragmentation:

> To locate memory in the blood as Momaday does may be as essentializing as to locate identity in blood quanta, but Momaday's use of blood imagery aims not to differentiate but to relate; not to administer but to imagine; not to impose quantified identities upon others but to make sense of the intersubjective quality of his own experience; not to appropriate the land of others but to appropriate the experiences of his own ancestors[....] Momaday's "memory in the blood" becomes a refiguring of "Indian blood" that makes it a vehicle of connection and integration—literally, a re-membering—rather than one of calculation and differentiation.[11]

The image of memory residing in the blood, then, mobilizes an ecological attachment to place and people and stands in direct defiance of the relentless quantification that seeks to make people knowable and therefore able to be governed. The enemy, as always, is subjectivation: the process by which a person becomes a subject of knowledge and subject to power. One way to critique the "in my blood" trope is that it places identity back *inside* the person, into subjectivity, into the essential core of the human, whose whispered truth becomes vulnerable to normalization. But that is not exactly what is going in Strong and van Winkle's argument: the blood imagery aims not to administer but to *imagine*. Imagination here is the activity of thinking things differently, of projecting into a past that is utterly unknowable and owning that mystery, of placing it in the body. Certainly, the use of blood in this way still retains a tenor of genealogical facticity, but when Momaday disavows his imagination as "really not mine," he connects it to a shifting network of people, stories, and intensities that comprise his experience of belonging. His body and blood are also really not his but are ancestral traces, the products of people interacting with and through their environment, together.

This is a type of magic: bringing the dead back to life. Bringing the self to the seat of ancestry, tracing connections to people who are no longer people but stories. Necromancy is the art of communicating with the dead to get advice about how to live now: a type of fortune-telling. When I went to Acadie, I attempted to listen to the murmur of my dead ancestors in a foreign land. By the time I began my fieldwork in Louisiana, I was disenchanted. It is hard to power the engines of magic for long in a world where the bordering and fragmenting of people into categories and identities is institutionalized, where work never stops and few can get ahead. It is hard to believe in magic when the culture is algorithmic, where constituent parts of one's life are measured and collected as data to be sold, used to market products and retarget ads. In Acadie, there is an often-used term used for the type of nostalgic cultural celebrations that occur in Louisiana and New Brunswick, that imagine a life capable of being simpler, kinder, and more cohesive: *passéisme*. An obsession with the past. We can also call it *nostalgia* and mean a melancholic yearning for the past. The Greek roots of the word tells us that this dull ache is the pain of coming home, of being not quite there, of being just out of reach except in fleeting but vivid dreams.

So when shrimpers tell me that commercial shrimping is in their blood, I know that they are also talking about a kind of magic. In some cases, it is a particularly painful type of magic, one that requires sacrifice. Shrimpers sacrifice the security of a good, consistently profitable line of work. They sacrifice their bodies to the sun and salt. They increasingly sacrifice the ability to relate to their children, who embrace distributed networks of information and capital and the dream of one day jumping to a higher class. Shrimpers invoke their ancestral memory and in doing so—in imagining their ancestors toiling in the marshes and bays, raising children barefoot on cypress boats, surviving off land and sea—they are attempting to raise the dead and live among them. They reject a world in which family and history do not matter, where each of us is encouraged to live a normal life and to yearn for a good life. Lauren Berlant defines this good life as a sort of humble American Dream: a validation of the belief that work will allow us to get ahead, that we will be valued in the political sphere, that we can find committed partners and love them into old age.[12] How shrimpers might define the good life differs. Instead of upward mobility, there is the sublime experience of an estuarial life. Instead of job security, there is the repetition of hard, fulfilling labor whose fruits are delicious meals. Instead of political and social equality, there is the tiny family, floating on a boat, connected to an extended fleet by radio and custom. Instead of durable intimacy, there is the strange return of ancestors lighting the way through a foggy now. Instead of disenchantment, magic. Instead of statistics, blood.

I first trawled with ChaCha the summer of 2013, when I began researching commercial shrimpers. I had moved out of state in 2007 but visited ChaCha every time I visited my family. He was my main oyster connection and sold oysters by the sixty-pound sack for thirty dollars or so. That summer I met Lindsey Feldman, a doctoral student working on an applied anthropology project on the effects of the 2010 oil spill. We chanced to meet in the Chauvin library when we both brandished consent forms to a group of elderly women playing dominoes. I became one of her fixers, helping her gain access to my network of connections of possible participants, find housing, and pass the time. She mentored me in ethnographic methods.[13] My dad arranged for Lindsey and me—as well as my wife, Linda, and a female intern for our nonprofit, T-Possibility—to trawl with ChaCha during his morning bait run.

We woke at 3:30 a.m. Despite the darkness, it was muggy and hot. We drowsed and burned our lips on coffee in travel mugs on the way to Bait House Seafood, ChaCha's establishment next to the Toussaint-Foret Bridge in Chauvin. It was still dark when we arrived, the light hours away, but the boat was awash in floodlights, bleaching out the white deck. We stowed our gear in a tiny cabin belowdecks at the fore of the boat. ChaCha's boat, which was unnamed, had few of the trappings of home that bigger boats have. The tophouse was recessed into the deck, furnished with bunks that stored life jackets. The deck was all work: the engine controls near the stern, the nets and rigging directly abaft the shallow tophouse, with the culling table at center. ChaCha's deckhand, Joey, was browsing Facebook on his phone; despite his hip hop/country music swagger, he eyed us with caution. This boat was clearly a masculine space, and our entry was at odds with the way the morning arrays itself on most days: damp, lukewarm air drawing the sweat out of bodies in silent work, straining muscles against the nets ChaCha's daddy had sewn, tangled with the sharp and slick edges of sea life. There was to be mud and foam, menthol Marlboros perched on lips. As far as we could tell, ChaCha and Joey rarely spoke except to bark commands over the diesel engine and grunt assent while the radio blared top forty country singles. Maybe they did talk, worrying over the way business had literally been decimated the year of the oil spill, sharing the knowledge that ChaCha would not be able to pass on to his son, another twenty-something with no interest in trawling, especially now. We wouldn't know because we changed the space by being in it.

Deleuzian scholar Charles Stivale fell in love with Cajun dance while at Tulane University and subsequently wrote a book that developed the concept of "spaces of affect," proposing to "reflect on [the] affective in-between through the rhythmic constitution of bodies within the simultaneously sensory and territorial field of the dance and music event."[14] He argues that the space of affect, a space that contains the haecceity, or *thisness*, of a moment, is a confluence of bodies in motion, stimulated by sensual cues (smell, sight, proprioceptive movement, touch, sound) caught in a network of physical things and histories and possibilities. Although his analysis focuses on dance, an event that is commonly understood to be in the realm of the aesthetic, it is useful too for understanding the way blood and body figure in attaching trawlers to their labor. My gesture of aestheticizing trawling complicates the figuration of trawling as labor but does not seek to destroy its structuration as labor. Rather, as a space of affect, the event of trawling not only manifests as a moment charged with affect and physical connection but uses its affective dimension to carve out a fleeting moment where the terrible physics of power are momentarily suspended, where the body is freed of its language and overdetermination in improbable ways (always snapping back to determination). And it complicates the genealogical destiny component of this chapter's refrain, "it's in my blood." For if shrimping is in a person's blood, one place it enters is here in the moment of trawling, the physical rhythms that direct the course of blood to the task at hand. And this transmutation of labor into blood, of blood into family and memory and ancestry, into hope, is magic.

And by magic, I mean blood magic: the instrumentalization of the sacred or ancestral memory or imagination for a purpose and requiring some type of sacrifice. In this case, it is the sacrifice of the body to the caprice of the sea, of waking hours into a job that does not promise a good life of upward mobility or even financial maintenance. It is the sacrifice of the self in service of a lost cause, of tragic hope. Blood magic is a cruel magic, and not everyone believes in it. For the fisher who has fishing in his blood, he must surrender to a particular and precarious life. He must recognize, at least on some level, that what he is doing will no longer be sustainable as the twenty-first century erodes the small-time, family-based industrial model and replaces it with vast machines of industry and information. He must recognize and cope with the fact that what is in his blood may not flow in the blood of his children or their children and that what was once a given way of life will inevitably die out, leaving his family of tomorrow only able to imagine what it must have been like to wake up before dawn and rumble through a marshy bay, capturing thousands of shrimp in butterfly nets. And for the short term, the fisher who must fish because it is in his blood, who needs to transport himself to a world in the making where families worked on boats together, must reckon with his own dwindling economic prospects, especially in years of flood, especially in years of environmental cataclysm. Aligning the body to this doomed industry in an effort to appropriate and claim a connection to an imagined past, to make sense of the work of people to thrive outside of a world desperate to teach us to survive its own impossible systems, and to escape the tyranny of rational decisions is a hopeful and defiant act that is necessary to these fishers' survival.

Envisioning trawling this way, as both cruel and magical, enables us to understand persistent heritage labor in a deindustrializing society in a new way: as an embodied practice that feeds the senses, the imagination, and a sense of belonging not only to a community or culture but to a constantly changing and ever-haunted environment. This labor is still tied to the death march of neoliberal futurity, but it speaks to the transformative possibilities of acting in concert with the myths of genealogical and cultural inheritance, creating a livable world based on memories that reside in the blood. It is optimistic in a world that does not warrant much optimism. Trawling is an act that gives the trawlers hope. We can find evidence of hope in more prevalent everyday items: vitamins (hope for an eternal body) and food (hope for comfort and nourishment) and television shows (hope for a meaningful life). We desire things that give us hope. Berlant calls this optimism: "All attachments are optimistic. When we talk about an object of desire, we are really talking about a cluster of promises we want someone or something to make to us and make possible for us."[15] Promises reside in the regime of hope: they anticipate, expect, imagine something coming in the future. Desire, then, is a particularly future-oriented feeling, predicated on some incompleteness or inadequacy of the present. Or, according to Berlant, the things we desire and attach ourselves to are the things that make living livable. Except when they do not: cruel optimism. Berlant defines a relation as cruelly optimistic "when something you desire is actually an obstacle to your flourishing."[16] She identifies a relationship of cruel optimism in the yearning for the good life: the American Dream, self-sovereignty, health, romance, and economic success.

Even though shrimping counters the myths of the good life, it clearly inspires a relation of cruel optimism. The shrimpers shrimp to survive, to be a part of a family mythology, to align their experience with an aesthetics of living on and through the water. But continuing to shrimp in an era when farmed shrimp from Vietnam, Thailand, and Ecuador undercut prices, when giant oil rigs explode and taint the water, when the sea encroaches on its boundaries—to continue shrimping when shrimping will soon be an utterly lost cause will eventually hurt the shrimpers irreparably. And by hurt, I mean they will go out of business, and they will suffer because they have no income. For shrimpers who saw theirs as a blood vocation, incurring debt to do what they love is a puny hurdle. They told me, almost in chorus, "You have some good days. You have some bad." Shrimping offers something other than financial stability, something that has the capacity to escape into a ghostly past, to understand the world as organized by blood and bodies and myths even as we must bend to the free flow of markets and structural obstacles to flourishing. To not shrimp would be bloodless and unmagical.

ChaCha clearly recognized the cruelty of his attachment to shrimping. You could hear it in his voice, his gravelly voice cured on the boat, cutting through the thick noise of the engine. He spoke plaintively, resigned:

> When you go out to shrimp like this, some [shrimpers] shrimp in the morning hours, but a lot of them leave more at night. Some do a night and day, nonstop. I had a big boat where I worked night and day, but I got rid of it. My son showed no interest in it. I'd say about out of ten families, probably only two families stayed—in the last ten, fifteen years—the rest got out of the shrimping industry. They saw the amount of work and hours and they just got out. In my family, my dad and brothers [...] pretty much I'm the only one, the last still doing this thing. They all got out of it. My family was raised on a shrimp dock.

He couched the narrative of his work in family, reiterating the loss of a family business. For him, as for all the shrimpers I spoke to in Terrebonne Parish, the trawl boat, the shrimp dock—these are places charged with family ties, places that stood in for the site of family making. You could imagine the world ChaCha imagined as he talked: families staying close through sharing the physical burden of work, making a private world populated by diesel and water and marsh grass, surviving off of the bounty of a hard world that needed tending to. A blood family replenishing its bloodline through work and food and floating along in a private world of life and sensation.

This kind of narrative, the kind that romanticizes the labor that bends and breaks the bodies of shrimpers, was a common theme in my interviews. There was something *legitimate* about working on water, something different from the obvious realities that were equally liable to crush the shrimpers: the fast-globalizing world, the changing ecosystem, toxic chemicals. It pained ChaCha that his son "showed no interest" in shrimp, instead working in oil, an industry that has eaten away the coast with its channels and pollutants. There is a cruel irony at play, the person of ChaCha's son turning into a metaphor for the cruel optimism that characterizes his relation to trawling. The very things he hopes for in trawling—family, shared labor, connection to place and kin—keep him from connecting to a son who has industrialized as ChaCha struggles in a deindustrialized world.

ChaCha comes alive with movement and competency on his boat, managing a present with deft hands, creating a brief world that is something separate from his struggling life on land, something joyful. Trawling is not a frenzied activity. It involves riding a boat very slowly in water with nets down, lifting them at a certain point, and culling what is in the nets. Starting again. Restarting. Repetition. Giving up when you've caught enough or when you decide to give up. But ChaCha's movements had a rhythmic muscularity to them, a knowledge that flowed from bone to fish to water. He was caught in a network of intensities and stimulations. I was caught too, bringing with me identities and agendas that dissolved and resurfaced over the course of the trips I took with him.

On my first trip with ChaCha, the one where I brought another researcher and two people who just wanted to catch a ride, the presence of outsiders elicited a performance from the two men whose livelihood depended on executing successful morning and evening trawls daily. ChaCha's voice grated against the sound of the engine, telling stories of a family that made its life on the water, of feeling like the torchbearer for a punch-drunk industry trying to reclaim its legs. He humored general and leading anthropological questions. He led us through his day, its early waking, its many showers. All the while, his fingers sorted shrimp from crab from fish, the silver of tiny pogy fish tumbling across his hands the way a gambler in an old Western might walk a coin down his knuckles (figure 7). Though I had been trawling as a child and had fished for red fish and speckled trout in Lake Boudreaux with my dad and brother in a small outboard, the enthusiasm of my companions, ChaCha, and eventually his deckhand made the trip feel more exotic than it should have, as if we all had stepped out of a sleeping world for a three-hour trip. We returned with the rise of the sun. When I embarked for the trawl, my identities as researcher, Chauvin native, and activist rose to the surface to structure the relationship I would now have with ChaCha, a shrimper and lifelong inhabitant of Chauvin

Figure 7. ChaCha Sevin culling shrimp from pogy, 2015. Photograph by Emma Christopher Lirette.

and the water. I had no blood connection to trawling, and ChaCha did, even if he later denied the possibility of the blood vocation. In this play, ChaCha played the role of key informant and played it well, teaching us about the *vents de Carême* (winds of Lent) that brought the shrimp into position, the uncertainty of tracking crustacean migration, the ways of determining which shrimp are viable for bait and which are not. He told us what it was like to recover from the oil spill, the immediate cataclysm of it passing into a nagging memory.

Right after the 2010 spill, ChaCha was interviewed for a *New York Times* video feature about the human impact of the disaster.[17] In that video, he's torn apart. His voice strains under the thick weight of tears. His then-wife, Samantha, says that the stress has put a wedge between them. The accompanying article quotes ChaCha: "My wife cried and cried over this. Just the other night she told me, 'Thank God there isn't a loaded gun in this house.'"[18] Business was dead. The world closed in on him, and instead of embodying his work, he cleans fish with a nervous intensity, hoping that time would pass more quickly. He is mournful, especially next to his son, Stanley, who talks about seeking employment elsewhere, seeing no future in shrimp. In the article, Stanley encourages his family to sell their house and leave. In 2013, however, ChaCha was no longer on the edge of a breakdown. He recognized the downward slide of the fishery and with it his prospects in Chauvin, but he was avuncular, proud to pass on his knowledge. The trip had lulls where one could recede into the physicality of the moment, the feeling of the boat dragging across the surface of the water, the traction of thousands of marine bodies piling in the nets, the hypnotic process of culling, ChaCha's fingers dipping in water, stacking conclaves of foaming crabs, flicking fish and shrimp into bushels and tanks. It is impossible to say whether ChaCha was consumed with worry or whether he sank into the rhythms of work, unmooring from the dread of the shore, where he would face the prospect of selling his catch and staying whole.

I glimpsed a world that could be made on a boat. The sound of the engine roared around us, a force field of noise. I smelled the muddy water, its salts, the rot of *paille fine* grass in the clumps of land that floated around Lake Boudreaux, the sweet smell of live shrimp before they die and smell like fish. My shoes slipped across the deck in the slurry of grease and silt and water. I grabbed the shrimp, the slimy bodies twitching in my fist. I felt the thin mesh of nets caked with alluvial mud, the rough ropes that pulled them aboard. I was with my partner and a new friend and three people I barely knew, but even here, I could imagine how a family could form its bloodline on a boat: shared rhythms of bodies flexing and bending over for a common purpose, the shorthand instructions shouted over the engines, the enclosure of a small, bounded place floating along freely in an unrationalized landscape. It was a world of early morning skies, prismatic with new suns bleeding over the black night, of work and dexterity, of exchanging stories and acting in concert with others and the environment and industrial machinery. The utter *thisness* of the trawl is staggering: the scents and imbalanced proprioception, the pinpricks of pain when gored by the head of a shrimp or the lateral spine of a skittering crab, the Doppler slap of another boat's wake against the bow. But even in this sensorium, trawling is an action of long duration, something that can easily lose its magic when the novelty of anthropology disembarks, when the rhythms of hand and shrimp become constant; it requires some spell to keep up the enchantment. Throughout this chapter, I have called this spell the blood vocation, the fantastic scenario that a job can become so precious and potent that it becomes part of the body of a person, that an industry can dissolve into our most indispensable fluid. My peek into the trawling life in the highly artificial scene of research and industrial tourism suggested how this magic builds the foundations of an alternative, ephemeral, and potentially livable world, even if the cost of living there requires committing to an anachronizing way of life.

Our little party became part of an ecology that included bodies and watery ecosystems and animal life and temperamental weather and above all else stories. For that brief time, I could imagine a life that I had not previously imagined. Not an alien life: I grew up on and off different types of boats. I worked at sea, on an offshore oil platform in the Gulf of Mexico. I have slept in cabins in the swamp after a day of trawling, feasting on shrimp just pulled from the water. My dad taught me to hook worms and unhook fish. I grew up with guns—

shotguns and rifles—even though my dad was always more fisher than hunter. I was raised to love the great outdoors, to ignore the sips of blood stolen by mosquitos, to harvest wild thistle and blackberries, to wade through shallow water. In another life, this could have been my blood vocation. In another time, it might have been the only option I considered. The experience of trawling, on the 2013 trip and on others I have taken since then, offered a suspension of an identity I had worked hard to cultivate. It was a moment when a body gets tangled in networks of story and blood, of other bodies still and in motion, floating along in shallow water, extracting smaller, even more precarious life. In that moment, which constantly threatened to flicker away, disappearing back into the structure of my own everyday life, I had the capacity to get something stuck in my blood. I witnessed a rebel magic that let me touch a world that existed against the one we were all tired of knowing, the one where we would get back to worrying and disconnection and cynicism and fear about sustaining ourselves in a broken economy.

The sensation did flicker away, and I had to don the ethnographer's hat. I tried my damnedest to bring back the sorry world. I began with a wounding question to ChaCha: How did the oil spill affect you? He answered, "It's hard to explain to, you know, get back to it. It just feels dead. I guess they [would] have stopped it eventually, or it would have wiped everything out of the Gulf, or you'd have to find another way to survive. It's about having to go through change, not knowing what it's going to do to you. Until you experience stuff, you really don't know firsthand what usually happens. It makes you always have a question mark, always have doubts." ChaCha did not answer with statistics about profit loss, the future of shrimping, or the social reordering that occurred after the spill. Instead, he offered an answer based in feeling and anticipation. The difficulty explaining is the difficulty in re-creating the lure of sustaining fantasy. The fantasy that the oil spill shattered was not the importance of blood but the ability of industry to sustain a person. Too much has happened to get back to that fantasy; the seascape has changed. And now the industry feels dead: suspended, inanimate, a return to formlessness, to incorporeality. Like Berlant, ChaCha points to the sites of fantasy as a mode of survival. The oil spill, if left unchecked, would mean that he finally would have to abandon trawling. ChaCha's model of doubt also demonstrates the paradox of knowing in the space of affect: before something happens, no one knows what will happen; after something happens, doubts always arise. This movement is not a clear trajectory from innocence to experience; rather, it is a moment that colors both the prehistory of and fallout from an event with anticipation, doubt, dread, discovery, possibility. The trawl boat, a bounded territory, is a place where things do not quite need to make sense, a place where trauma and hope bleed into one another, taking a person on a journey from hope to corporeality to suspension. The trip, however, is limited, offering nothing but the chance to be a body in motion, connected to a flood of sensation and story for a few hours, holding life on shore at bay if possible.

In 2015 I again went trawling with ChaCha. This time, there was no deckhand, and I did not ask why not because I knew. ChaCha could no longer afford a deckhand. There were no extra tagalongs except for my brother, who I again convinced to swing grip as I filmed the trawl. We rode out later in the morning, in the golden hour, with the sun haloing ChaCha and Bayou Petit Caillou all green-and-brown bokeh. ChaCha spoke either in long monologues or in grunts of affirmation. He had made it through another few years, but it was obvious that the time had cost him. Diversifying to stay afloat, he had made enemies among other locals. He had been harassed by people jealous of his year-round license. And worst of all, the catch was about 80 percent pogy, a stinky fish also called menhaden that is used as fertilizer and in cosmetics but has little value for ChaCha, who cannot compete in the commercial pogy fishery. Crabs were overfished. Oysters had not rebounded since the oil spill. And the price of shrimp was dipping to historic lows.

ChaCha obliged me. He is a good sport. He answered my questions. And in doing so, he enlivened. He passed on knowledge, some of which I had heard before, some of which I had not. But the spell from the previous trip was broken. Perhaps it was just me all along: the excitement of breaking the grasp of the ordinary and jumping on a boat before dawn en masse. Perhaps it was the direness of the price crisis. Almost everyone I spoke to was afraid of not making it that summer. And I was bringing that fear to them in their last refuge. Late in the interview, ChaCha astounded me by rejecting the claim that shrimping could be in a person's blood. This rejection has tremendous meaning for someone like ChaCha: a man who is the last of his lineage to trawl, whose son had already rejected his father's industrial heritage before the 2010 and 2015 crises, whose whole life had been spent dragging nets and skimming and culling and icing and fileting and shucking and winding down after a long day trawling with a rod and reel in hand, pulling *sac-à-lait* and perch out of the bayou. For ChaCha, some of the magic of trawling had bled out.

Ecology and the Body

On the day of the 2015 Boat Blessing, my gear was soaked because I had been riding around on my motorcycle in a downpour the day before. I was running late. I missed the priest processing into the boat, but I did catch the first boats leaving. I drove my brother's Mustang with my camera and field recorder past the slow parade down Bayou Little Caillou. The Toussaint-Foret Bridge was open to let the boats pass, and I parked next door at ChaCha's place of business, Bait House Seafood. ChaCha was nowhere to be found.

I sat in the middle of the road where the swing bridge would connect Highway 56 to Bayouside Drive if it were closed. My feet dangled over the water. After a while, the boats began floating past me (figure 8). A curious thing happens when you are trying to document the Chauvin Boat Blessing: when people on the boats see you, they wave. A couple of people recognized me from the beginning of the parade route at St. Joseph's. Fewer recognized me as a family member. But everyone waved. Some hollered.

After the fifteen or so boats had passed me, I drove the Mustang to Boudreaux Canal. I parked just as the first boats approached the canal, which connects Bayou Petit Caillou to Lake Boudreaux, the terminus of the parade. Instead of filming the boats from there, I turned the camera on and began walking along the levee. I followed the boats, crossing Highway 56, climbing the crest of the levee that comprises the seawall at Boudreaux Canal. Then the land became less civilized.

Rain had turned the earth to slurry covered by dead palmetto branches and marsh grass and trash. The grasses grew so tall that I could see only the masts of the biggest trawlers. I could hear the loudest boats, too: not the roar of their engines, but KC and the Sunshine Band singing about the way they like it. The grasses parted in front of me. It was a trail. I had never been here before.

Figure 8. The *Daddy Bucks*, owned by the brother of the author's Aunt Nadine, as the lead boat in the 2015 Boat Blessing, with a priest at the bow. Photograph by Emma Christopher Lirette.

Figure 9. The Boat Blessing from the shore of Lake Boudreaux, 2015. Photograph by Emma Christopher Lirette.

The grasses were thick, their bases clumped with aluminum cans and cracked Styrofoam containers and cigarette butts. Small trees vined out of them, raking me. There were unripened blackberries, growing on bushes that scratched me. There was a cactus. I was able to avoid that one. The mosquitos feasted, biting through my socks and my shirt and my jeans. The earth slipped beneath me, and my shoes plunged in and out of the mud. I was caked and bloodied. There were fine scratches along my forearms.

I could see Lake Boudreaux lapping toward my trail and then dipping away as I climbed a small hill. Eventually, there was a clearing. The lead boat, captained by my Aunt Nadine's brother, Jerome, was dead ahead, but those onboard were too busy munching boiled shrimp and crawfish to pay me mind. I could see them, though, hosting the priest, waiting until he finished the ritual blessing to drink alcohol, and I filmed them (figure 9). The beach I was filming from was really just mud and dead grass, and I sunk into it. The water patrol that chaperoned the Boat Blessing ran their outboard up onto the bank and two police officers stared at me incredulously. I said, "I'm just filming the Boat Blessing." They said, "You should have worn long sleeves."

I had not planned on getting so close to the marsh that morning. I had almost justified missing the Boat Blessing entirely. I had attended to my own blood the night before: my wife was in town visiting for our baby shower. I had ridden my motorcycle the morning of the blessing from Kenner, where her family lives, back to Chauvin. Instead of documenting the Boat Blessing outright, I wound up documenting an impromptu journey into an unknown marsh ecology, with my body catching and tearing on the foliage. When you enter into an ecology, things connect to you, touch you, change you. You affect it, stomping through it. You are affected.

Beyond the slipstream magic of blood and its attendant symbolism, the truth of blood arises ecologically. Or at least, the truth of what commercial shrimpers told me was in their blood arises ecologically, and we might as well name it a culture of labor. Tim Ingold does not agree that culture should be defined as a system of inherited knowledge that makes the world comprehensible.[1] Instead, he imagines culture through what he calls a "sentient ecology": "It is knowledge not of a formal, authorised kind, transmissible in contexts outside those of its practical application. On the contrary, it is based in feeling, consisting in the skills, sensitivities and orientations that have developed through long experience of conducting one's life in a particular environment."[2]

Instead of transmitting culture genealogically, from one generation to the next, Ingold argues that we are constantly becoming part of our environment and that our knowledge and relationships (including kinship) are created by moving through and touching the particular environment in which we live. In other words, the idea of a culture of labor being in one's blood belies an orderly, genealogical schema that is at odds with the way that culture, kinship, place, and memory are generated.[3] Instead of abstract instances in a family tree, we are embedded processes in a rhizomatic manifold. As we move through the world, we touch one another. We touch the land under us; if there is no land, we touch the water. We touch the animals we pull from the environment and eat. We touch the razored vines of berries and are cut by them.

And the environment touches us back. Instead of imagining place as a blank stage on which we live our lives, we constitute place as it constitutes us. The place itself becomes the substance of our bodies, and vice versa, and so we live in a world of blood forged fresh for every encounter. Instead of linear transmission, Ingold argues for a much more complex path for the passing on of cultural knowledge *and* substance:

> It is from their emplacement in the world that people draw not just their perceptual orientations but the very substance of their being. Conversely, through their actions, they contribute to the substantive make-up of others. Such contributions are given and received throughout life, in the context of a person's ongoing relationships with human and nonhuman components of the environment. Thus, far from having their constitution specified in advance, as the genealogical model implies, persons undergo histories of continuous change and development. In a word, they *grow*. Indeed more than that, they are *grown*. By this I mean that growth is to be understood not merely as the autonomous realisation of pre-specified developmental potentials, but as the generation of being within what could be called a sphere of nurture.[4]

The shrimpers I talked to, then, are not necessarily the tragic last generation of shrimpers with a well of cultural knowledge that will dry up when they die. Instead, they are constantly negotiating with an environment, both the brackish water of Barataria and Lake Boudreaux and Bayou Petit Caillou and Bayou Go-to-Hell *and* the lifeworlds of kin on land and on boats and across lines of telecommunications. They contribute to their environment, changing it. They feed people across the nation and especially those whom they live among. The environment undergoes a constant transformation from sun and sea to crustacean and fish to net and motor to people, and the people come back through, forging paths in the substance of the place, paths in which resides memory.

Ingold argues that memory, like ancestry or substance, should be considered an embedded, relational practice that cannot be separated from the act of remembering in a place: "It is through the activity of remembering that memories are forged. This activity, moreover, is tantamount to the movement of the person through the world. Memories, then, are generated along the paths of movement that each person lays down in the course of his or her life."[5] The physical act of trawling created the conditions for the fishers to remember: they were not just retrieving stored information from a database, they were reenacting the times they'd had on a boat, creating memories by a nexus of recognition: the work, my questions, the land and seascape, the weather. They recognized themselves in their memories and longed not necessarily for a return to the olden days but for the ability to continue finding their way through a world of boats and blood. Describing how hunters and gatherers remember their skills and survive, Ingold writes,

> The important thing ... is that the process should keep on going, not that it should yield precise replicas of past performance. Indeed "keeping it going" may involve a good measure of creative improvisation. A skill well remembered is one that is flexibly responsive to ever-variable environmental conditions. Thus there is no opposition, in the terms of the relational model, between continuity and change. [...] Just because people are doing things differently now, compared with the way they did them at some time in the past, does not mean that there has been a rupture of tradition or a failure of memory. What would really break the continuity, however, would be if people were forcibly constrained to replicate a pattern fixed by genealogical descent.[6]

In certain cases, then, the danger for shrimpers would not necessarily be the increasingly hostile world they find themselves in but would rather be their own *passéeisme*, their yearning to re-create the world of their fathers and grandfathers. A cruel attachment: yearning to re-create a past that would no longer serve you. Luckily, for the trawlers I spoke to, they are plenty adaptable. Even when they are at their most mournful, speaking of the lack of shrimping in their children's blood, they are still making their way into a complex ecology that transforms their individual blood into something more collective.

Blood is an extremely transmutable symbol, as illustrated by the transformation of wafer and wine to the body and blood of Christ and the vampire mythologies of Europe and America, wherein blood transforms to a font of life. Since the 1980s, the sharing of blood is death by AIDS. Since long before that, mosquitos have been commingling drops of blood between the people and animals they suck on, transmitting yellow fever, a blood-borne illness that has left a recognizable stain on southern Louisiana history.[7] Today, we fear West Nile, dengue, and Zika from mosquitos. We talk about blood money—money paid in service of murder—but money also appropriates the vocabulary of blood. For instance, in 2010, ChaCha hemorrhaged money to the tune of 90 percent of his yearly income. Money circulates, and the market is stagnant. You inherit money the same way you might inherit your blood, by it flowing from your forebears. Poor economic conditions might suck you dry.

The words *economy* and *ecology* share a root: οἶκος (oikos), meaning "household." One is the management of the household, the other is the study of it. The economy, though we abstract it with its definitive *the*, is actually an ecological system that also remains embedded in local, relational encounters. Though the shrimpers I spoke to suffered anxiety about the downturn in shrimp prices, some were better suited to weather a financial bust than others. Also, while the United States dipped into recession in 2008, Louisiana experienced stability until 2010.[8] Unlike other agricultural or extractive industries, shrimping largely consists of owner-operated boats that work seasonally, with very few employees.[9] Recalling Marx, the trawler does not feed capital the way a factory worker does. ChaCha was self-employed with his wife, doing mostly direct retail business.[10] And by 2015, it was clear that the dead-end labor was sucking him dry. He said that this was the first year he had considered quitting altogether. He was the last of his family to stay the course, and it was bleeding him. With a few exceptions, the rest of the fishers dealt with docks and processors, with whom they might feud over price, a situation that puts shrimpers at a disadvantage. It is hard to have negotiating leverage when you have two tons of shrimp on a boat in the Louisiana sun. If we understand household in the limited, blood-kin way of genealogy, then things are dire indeed. If the shrimpers I spoke to were fulfilling their genealogical destiny, the ever-pumping machine of genealogy would also be inscribing the destiny of their children.

Their children are less interested in destiny.

Very few shrimpers had any indication that shrimping might be in their children's blood, which they had coauthored. Fewer still even had a mind to encourage those children to follow the fishing life. And why would they? The fleet can hardly bear new greenhorns, as one shrimper told me. With the competition from foreign shrimp and other burdens of fishing, it is hard to see how the twenty-first-century child of a shrimper would even consider working a boat unless their father already commanded a fleet. The cost of entry is simply too high. In southern Louisiana, an eighteen-year-old without a college degree would find a much more lucrative and stable income working in offshore oil. They would be able to advance more quickly than in commercial fishing, and because of the typical two-week on, two-week off schedule, they would still have the freedom to spend days on the water fishing if they felt it was in their blood. The sons and daughters of successful shrimpers found themselves in college, pursuing immaterial labor and starting families far removed from the trawl boat. One shrimper told me his daughter graduated from Yale University's law school and lives with her husband in Luxembourg. Kim's children were still in college. So were ChaCha's. I guess shrimping came unstuck in their blood.

In a broader view of a household, an ecological view, the boundaries of family and blood are more permeable. Janet Carsten writes, "As well as being subject to transformation within the body, blood can of course also be thought to be a vector of connection between bodies or persons. This may be articulated as occurring through the transfer of semen or breast milk (both, as noted, perceived as transformed blood), through maternal feeding in the womb, or through habitual acts of commensality, which are perceived to produce blood of the same kind in the different bodies of those who share food."[11] The family that eats together, sticks together and shares one blood. Blood forms a homology among life-giving substances: food, water, milk, semen. Blood nourishes the unborn through the placenta. If we lose too much blood, we will die. Bleeding and hunger make us feel faint. In the act of sex, genitals become engorged with blood, concentrating the magical liquid to the possible locus of conception or at least connection. The need for blood to sustain life is perhaps its most obvious meaning. The sharing of blood likewise marks the deepest bonds of interpersonal connection. We call our family *blood relatives* if they are related through birth. We become blood brothers or sisters when we cut our hands and press them to a wound on the hands of our closest friends. In the Christian Eucharist, the congregation becomes one body as they share the mystical flesh and blood of Christ. The feast, wherein one meal is transformed into the blood of several people, is a profound and common ritual that binds people together. In southern Louisiana, there is a special emphasis on food as cultural expression, but the sharing of food may be a more profound ritual than that, one that mirrors the sharing of blood.[12]

The work of shrimpers enacts the transformation of shrimp to blood. Though the bulk of shrimp hauled onshore is sold to distributors and then to factories, grocers, and restaurants, locals of Terrebonne Parish are flush with retail shrimp bought directly from trawlers—some of whom are blood kin and some who are not. On a diet of shrimp okra gumbo, fried shrimp, shrimp spaghetti, shrimp boulettes, shrimp jambalaya, and so on, the shrimp caught by Gulf Coast trawlers becomes literally incorporated into the bodies of their families and friends and neighbors.[13] Here, the shrimpers' labor, the work of their bodies, nourishes the bodies of others. Though their children do not retain the genealogical evidence of commercial shrimping, they experience the sacrament of breaking shrimp together with their families. People who have never set foot on a boat experience this proliferation of life through commercial fishing, and the economics of shrimp in small-town Louisiana touch more than the men who seem to be victims of the global economy.

My mom, for instance, spent years peeling shrimp for the Triple T shrimp factory. I grew up across from the factory, which left a stink of shrimp in the air that was sometimes blotted out by a miasma of ammonia. Even when no one in my family worked in anything connected to commercial shrimping, I can remember my mom, my granny, and my aunts peeling ice chests full of shrimp at the kitchen table. They had a bowl of white vinegar to dip their hands in, thereby increasing their fingers' purchase on a shrimp shell but making their hands sting when shrimp beaks would lacerate the skin. Afterward, my brother or I would drag an ice chest full of raw shrimp peelings back to the bayou, dumping the husks of shrimp life back whence it came, now a part of the sludge, returning what nutrition was left to what life could take it. Then the women in the family would distribute the shrimp into bags and freeze them. They would boil some shrimp for supper. They would later run water over the frozen tiles of shrimp, breaking off a quart at a time, to make the meals of the future. The family would survive.

The truth of blood goes beyond genealogical determinism, even if, as Carsten argues, its truth contains that meaning. The truth of blood—how a job can be in a person's blood—is the truth of a body making its way through a well-populated life, touching the earth, touching the water, and touching an extended and permeable household in which people eat together, play together, and work together. People come and people go. Necromancy is practiced as a course of belonging to an environment of people and places that have affected you. In Ingold's words, "The past may be absent from the present but is not extinguished by it. Death punctuates, but does not terminate, life."[14] An ecology of the world of the shrimpers of southern Louisiana contains not only networks alive in the present but the ancestral imagination that fuels new connections. And this magic, this uncertain projection, adapts to the exigencies the fishers face today: how to envision a world that includes them, how to belong to an environment that has only a tenuous grasp on its own continuity.

Back to the question of ChaCha's refusal to share the mythology of blood with his fellow trawlers: his ambivalence seems to come as much from a theoretical understanding of his life as the fact that of the trawlers I spoke to, he had lost the most in the last fifteen years. The defiant anachronism and ability to weather anxiety and to suspend the totalizing either/or logic of success that characterizes most of the fishers I spoke to is not something that can withstand unlimited hardship. The hope that comes from the blood vocation cannot be sustained without imagining an impossible future that rejects the fatalism of capital and of the normalizing technologies of biopower, wherein we become knowable, docile, disciplined bodies. And even then, one can still be crushed under the heel of forces beyond one's control, whether those forces are hurricane-force winds, a slow sinking into a gulf, crude black oil tarring up an estuary, or the price of shrimp from distant seas.

To imagine a better future: Is hope deadly? Not necessarily. The way we fantasize about the future, the way we attach to things, according to Lauren Berlant, is based on misrecognition: "To misrecognize is not to err, but to project qualities onto something so that we can love, hate, and manipulate it for having those qualities."[15] We imagine (even as our imagination is accurate). We tap into the virtual aspect of felt reality. This imagination helps us get through the present. It is "what manages the ambivalence and itinerancy of attachment."[16] This fantasy life is the surprising continuity of things through the constant change, through the precarity of our lives. It is a flexible imagination born in blood. For the fishers, it is a way of understanding how their bodies form a nexus of belonging to a given place, to a given people, to a given haunted career. This constitutive misrecognition allows us to live; recognizing its importance in how people imagine their connection to their worlds better equips us to attend to address the systems that are slowly, sweetly killing people.

This fantastic world-building does not lead to durable worlds—at least not in the sense of worlds that will shelter us and endure in stability. The world made by people who shrimp is summoned through a combination of physical repetitions and immaterial possibilities, yearnings, and orientations. It is a world that exists only in the present, in the making. Blood, figured throughout this chapter as an imaginative force as opposed to either pure materiality or symbol, offers a way to understand why shrimpers might unmoor themselves from the norms of self-interest under capitalism and moor themselves to a fleeting, declining industry. This understanding must come from understanding the course of blood for shrimpers: from kinship and proximity in the material world to the realm of recurrent and mythic pasts reconstituted in the present, from the corporeal experience of work in a teeming sensorium to the hope that by working the nets, they might be able to forge new bloodlines in a world that still values them. Analyzing the oscillation between actual material conditions of shrimping and the imagination that allows a continuing belief in blood magic also warns of danger of a blood-borne imagination: shrimpers who persist in shrimping, despite their strong blood, may one day finding themselves sacrificing more than their full participation in the American paradigms of upward mobility and capital accrual and the forward march of industrial history. They might not survive their imagination.

For the nonce, however, there is the possibility to live. To build a small world that counters the stories of disenchantment and alienation and economic liberalism that characterize twenty-first-century America. The blood vocation is a way for Louisiana shrimpers to enact a covenant with their place and people and continue to find meaning in the labor of their bodies. It allows them to transform their memories of their families, all together on a boat bobbing along on the edge of a great gulf, into something that can feed the people with whom they share the earth. Kinship, when thinking through blood vocations and blood magic and bloodlines, must expand to include a vaster network of people, places, movements, embodied experiences, and lives. The shrimpers I spoke to coauthored their world in blood. In that blood, they placed an industry that their bodies had known their whole lives, an industry that is being bled out by forces bigger than themselves. Their choice to heed the call of the blood vocation is dangerous, life-affirming, haunting. Though their descendants might not know the toil and peace of a life on the water, they will be indelibly marked by it. The people with whom the fishers share their catch are marked, as are the towns in which they live, the gatherings they attend, and the conversations they join. As soon as I stepped onto ChaCha's boat, shrimping was in my blood. It was in my blood when I first ate shrimp, boiled, at my mother's table. It was in my blood the day I was born.

WATER

> She sang beyond the genius of the sea.
> The water never formed to mind or voice,
> Like a body wholly body, fluttering
> Its empty sleeves; and yet its mimic motion
> Made constant cry, caused constantly a cry,
> That was not ours although we understood,
> Inhuman, of the veritable ocean.
> —Wallace Stevens, "The Idea of Order at Key West"

Genius loci: the spirit of a place. A protector ghost. The character, beyond the physical manifestations of a place, that imbues the place with its color, its memory, its atmosphere, its hope. In an ancient world, the *genii locorum* were spirits bound to certain physical locations, presiding over them like statued and invisible warlords or seneschals. Their territories had strong border police: genii locorum were stuck in their microstates but guarded them well. The genius of the spirit: anchored in place, it could shore up its power, creating corporeal weight.

In the world of cartography, every feature has a name. We identify settlements, rivers, lakes, forests, mountains, and deserts. We name the water contained by mud embankments, trussed with steel seawalls meant to prevent the backflow of water into the hinterlands. We name the water when it flows or stagnates in deep and wide grooves in ground cut by older waters. We name overgrown sandbars that have become islands over six thousand years only to slip beneath gulf waves over the last hundred years. We name the water when, in the Atlantic Ocean off the coast of Mauritania and Senegal, it joins the sky and spins toward America, bringing with it wind and flood. This instance, a genre of water we call hurricane, is less a feature of the landscape than a fury barreling toward the land. The ghost over the sea.

Just before I turned one, water named Juan dumped itself over my house. It poured into Chauvin. It poured and poured. And then the water, which was now called flood, rose. In coastal Louisiana, houses do not rest on the ground—that would be an invitation for the water to come in and bring with it the other machines of rot. So the water first occupied the space between the ground and the floor of my house. Next, the water crept to the subflooring and flooring. It took the foam cushion beneath the cut-pile brown carpet and then the carpet. My dad was there, sleeping on a sofa, then waking and sitting up ankle-deep in flood.

In 1992, different water, this time named Andrew, paid a visit to Chauvin. After tearing the roofs off marinas and spraying everybody in sight, it too renamed itself flood. When it finally left, our yard was ankle-deep in fish: redfish flopping drunkenly on the grass, drums with their heads hollowed out by maggots. These waters extended beyond the genius of the sea, overflowing the borders of named places. The waters went where they could go, and nothing could keep them fixed in place.

Each time the waters came, they took flooring and roofs and cars and lives. They took water's opposite: land. As the story goes, Louisiana loses one football field of land every forty-eight minutes.[1] Here is a historical trajectory of that loss in three moments:

Cutting through Louisiana is North America's greatest river, the Mississippi, which bisects most of the continent, draining its heartland. As planet Earth warmed after the minor ice ages of the sixteenth through nineteenth centuries, melting ice and increased rain inundated the whole of the Mississippi watershed every three years or so, creating what environmental historian Mikko Saikku characterizes as an inland sea.[2] When the weather is less wet, the waters of the Mississippi contract back into its main artery and its lesser ones—the rivers Ohio, Arkansas, Illinois, Missouri, Red, Yazoo, Atchafalaya. On the coast of Louisiana, the mouth of the river is less a maw, like the opening of the Saint Lawrence River, than a cluster of capillaries bleeding out into the Gulf of Mexico. The European who located the mouth of the river, René-Robert Cavelier, Sieur de La Salle, dedicating it and the whole of the delta to France, misremembered where he left it when he returned two years later, mooring in Matagorda Bay in Texas. After two years of looking for the mouth, his crew executed him.[3] Seventeen years later, the brothers Le Moyne—Pierre, Sieur d'Iberville, and Jean-Baptiste, Sieur de Bienville—found the mouth with the help of members of the Bayagoula nation. In 1718, Bienville seized the land where New Orleans stands today and set up some huts, naming it Nouvelle-

Orléans. Just before New Orleans turned one year old, unnamed waters from the incontinent river drowned it.[4]

Bienville thus began what we have been doing with the Mississippi since then: erecting levees, carving drainage canals, engineering the course of water. From this point on, landowners along the 2,320 miles of the main stem of the Mississippi River had to make their own levees to keep the river in its track—if they could. This model did little to stop the waters from flooding. The United States slowly began to brace the Mississippi with a "levees only" policy beginning in 1879, when the Mississippi River Commission, a federal agency, was tasked with stopping seasonal floods. We come now to the second moment: the Great Flood of 1927, when a Good Friday storm felled the walls intended to contain the river water. It was a cataclysm that claimed lives by the hundreds and homes numbering 637,000. The waters in the river reached sixty feet above sea level and cut crevasses, or breaches, in the levee walls. Water gushed through the crevasses with all the violence of Niagara Falls, turning the Mississippi delta south of Illinois into an inland sea.[5] The City of New Orleans blew up the levee downriver, sacrificing Saint Bernard Parish and the muskrat fur trade to preserve the French Quarter.[6]

In the wake of the flood, Congress passed the Flood Control Act of 1928, which transferred responsibility for flood control and the building of levees to the Army Corps of Engineers—and protected the federal government from liability.[7] Instead of reimagining the control of water, the corps doubled down on a policy of building levees. The levees, stronger and taller than the ones chopped apart by the 1927 floods, walled off 3,410 miles of the Mississippi River and its tributaries, with another 2,786 miles waiting to be graded to design specifications by late 2005.[8] This bracing interrupts the regeneration of land through sediment deposits in the river's flood cycle in the floodplains and along the river mouth.[9] So we sink. This is called subsidence. At the same time that the Army Corps of Engineers was toiling through its flood-control projects, the oil industry began dredging canals in a lattice along the coast, introducing salt to the inland waters and making the land much more permeable.[10] These large-scale rationalizations of the land, ordering the spongy dirt and chaotic waterways, create the third moment, the greatest flood: the reintroduction of the sea, which eats away at the coast. Coming up through shipping canals and brackish bayous, the sea salt kills the plants that hold together the sandy dirt. The wetlands fall away, and hurricanes maintain their mid-Atlantic strength as they break against the land. The relentless struggle to engineer water, to fix water in place, to contain its genius has, with cruel irony, made people more vulnerable to watery disaster. In 2005, a hurricane of middling strength named Katrina killed 1,833 people in five states, with 1,577 coming from Louisiana.[11] In the immediate aftermath of Hurricanes Katrina and Rita (which fell on the Louisiana coast less than a month after Katrina), the sea also claimed 217 square miles of land.

While it is easy to blame disastrous attempts to order the water on the governments and corporations that orchestrated the twentieth-century canalization of southern Louisiana, they are not alone in reshaping the environment. My great-grandfather, Henry "Tchonque" Eschete, tore a shortcut canal through the marsh, Cut-off à Tchonque, to get to his shrimping camp more easily. Lower Terrebonne Parish has canals bearing the names of its most embedded families—Sevin, Boudreaux, Falgout—dug by hand and spade. These lines, once the width of a pirogue, widened to boulevard, bayou, and bay. Now they are open water.

You can still see the names of the old places on maps, places that have been washed out to sea: Pelican Bayou, Big Misalle Bayou, Bayou Ne Touche Pas, Oak Bayou, Austrian Bayou, Crooked Bayou, Oyster Bayou, Bayou Big Parasol, Bayou Lucien, Flat Bayou, Lake Saint Jean Baptiste, Pelican Lake, Dog Lake, Caillou Lake, Hackberry Lake, Lake Raccourci, Lake Pelto, Bayou Go to Hell. Some of the bayous—slow-moving anabranches and distributaries of larger rivers—have become lagoons—fragile lakes with sandbars, reefs, and mangrove clumps as barriers to the Gulf. Most of these waters have become bays: the toothmarks of the sea eating the coastline. The bays widen, concavity giving way to smoother arcs, and we call this the Gulf.

In other words, we tried, really tried, to outsmart the sea. But we could not. Instead, we invited the sea in, to live with us, to eat us alive. We talk about bodies of water, and indeed, they are wholly body: you can feel these waters press against you as they encroach on the land, as they press into the floorboards of your home, as they spill over all your stuff. They wrangle other bodies further upstream and inland: the changing estuary, the northern migration of seagulls and saltwater fish and crustaceans into bayous that once were muddy but saltless. But water is also not a body: it spills, it seeps, it floods, it drowns. Its sheer fluidity obeys a different logic. Instead of accumulation, dispersion; instead of organization, repetition and rhythm; instead of fixity, a constant, variable cry.

The water caused constantly a cry in the fishers I spoke to. Life on the water is the only life they could possibly want. It is the only life they know. The sea calls to them, inviting them back again and again into the limitless world of water. Life on the water is in their blood, their internal sea. Water is an unreliable and dangerous siren. Over the past hundred years, it has drowned leagues of land, land that was once settlement, farmland, and guardian estuaries. As the sea brings its salt inshore, it has changed the habitats of shrimp, crabs, and oysters and killed trees. At first, the introduction of saltwater was welcome: it expanded the shrimp fisheries inland, coinciding with the expansion of the shrimping industry from dockside seiners (wage laborers employed in casting nets by hand) to a fleet of entrepreneur-captains that persists today. The returns diminished because the saltwater also has a poisonous quality, killing the plants that hold together the land. Brown and white shrimp need the fast-eroding, brackish estuaries of the coast to grow large enough for humans to eat. If the sea's encroachment is not stopped, there will be saltwater until the levees and floodgates surround some but not all the human inhabitants of Terrebonne and Lafourche Parishes.[12] While shrimpers in Chauvin acknowledged that this kind of intervention reduces flooding (for people in the protection zone), they also see it radically changing their land and livelihood. If it is not stopped, the fisheries will be all gulf, the hometowns people have lived in for a couple hundred years will be gulf. And the fishers will have to move north, to where the land is sturdier and fishing jobs are scarcer.

Shrimpers can find jobs in oil, the industrialized and toxic return of life on the water. In Louisiana, men can make good livings working on offshore oil-production platforms, drilling rigs, crew boats, and tugboats. They can support the oil industry onshore, too, with welding, mechanical skills, and shipbuilding work. The security of the oil industry comes at a cost: the 2010 Deep Horizon blast blackened the Gulf of Mexico with its crude, viscous fuel. The oil coated fish and oysters and pelicans. It coagulated into tar balls, which had previously been an occasional nasty surprise in a trawl or on a beach, a trace of the industry that basically kept Louisiana financially solvent for the better part of a century. Oil is water's dreadful other in coastal Louisiana: a capricious, generous, and vicious genius loci of the Gulf of Mexico, its necessary mob boss. Though shrimpers cry constantly about the oil industry, they also claim that they couldn't do without it: if oil left Louisiana, their livelihoods would be over just as much as if their homes sank underwater. With government-subsidized channels and canals and pipelines and processing plants, however, the oil industry provided avenues for saltwater to drift inland. It drives Louisiana's changing geology, geography, ecology, and economics.[13] Oil has made life on the water complicated and the fishers ambivalent. It has introduced another dimension of fluidity *and* order.

In "The Idea of Order at Key West," Wallace Stevens writes of a great ordering a woman sings into being. She mimics the sea and so masters it in her singing. Her art is a rational world-making. But the water she mimics is inimitable: it is body and not body. It is a formless, unintelligent chaos, an inhuman. The singer entrains the sea to her world-making:

> ... And when she sang, the sea,
> Whatever self it had, became the self
> That was her song, for she was the maker.[14]

The sea becomes a reflection of the world the singer is making in the singing. You cannot listen to the crashing of the waves without hearing the singer's meanings. This world-making organizes the chaotic liquid world of the sea. But Stevens, the great rational transcendentalist, hedges: What self could the sea, a body and an empty shirt, have had? What is the self of the Gulf, the same one that long ago played muse to Stevens, the same one that is invading the Louisiana coast?

When we imagine the sea as a body, wholly body, we do not imagine it with the organization of a human body. There is no liver of the sea, no spleen. While we might term the terminus of a river a mouth, it is a mouth that can consume the whole of the river's body in a nightmare grin. The features and structures of bodies of water are in constant flux, shifting in flows of water that constantly rearrange, make and unmake sea beds and dead zones of hypoxia that prohibit marine life and currents and waves. The most salient parts of the sea—the borders and the water itself—flutter like the empty shirt in the Stevens poem ("Like a body wholly body, fluttering / Its empty sleeves.")[15] The empty body of the sea, a body filled with flattened intensities rather than discrete organs, recalls a concept from Gilles Deleuze and Félix Guattari: the Body without Organs. They write that the Body without Organs "is continually dismantling the organism, causing asignifying particles or pure intensities to pass or circulate, and attributing to itself subjects that it leaves with nothing more than a name as the trace of an intensity."[16] An organism is an organization of life into a specific arrangement of organs—tools to maintain that life. The constituent parts of an organism have meaning and order. Deleuze and Guattari have a blessed rage to disorder. Stevens attributes a rage to order to the singer/world-maker of his poem:

> The maker's rage to order words of the sea,
> Words of the fragrant portals, dimly-starred,
> And of ourselves and of our origins,
> In ghostlier demarcations, keener sounds.[17]

One way to read these final lines of "The Idea of Order at Key West" is that art's task is to order the chaotic world and our chaotic selves. Stevens champions artifice, the triumph of humans over nature, the mastery of the self. This interpretation makes sense for the tightly ordered poem, with its iambic pentameter and precise vocabulary. In the penultimate stanza, the order-making of the singer permeates the world even after she ceases to sing and the speaker turns back from the beach ("Why, when the singing ended and we turned / Toward the town, tell why the glassy lights, / [...] / Master the night and portioned out the sea.")[18] Here we can read the ordering impulse transferring from the singer to the speaker of the poem, who finds new order in the lights of fishing boats. The final lines support that reading, but we can also read the sea as a constant challenge to the will to order. The sea, a Body without Organs, introduces asignifying particles, pure intensities into the well-ordered world, disrupting our structures of meaning, our belief in the stability of identity or origin. And we rage.

With water, rage is futile. A rage for order imposed its levees on the Mississippi River. Hurricane Katrina drove up the river's mouth and found the best backdoors and canals and cracks and made New Orleans a lake. Coastal restoration projects dump sediment and Christmas trees and old ships to try to rebuild barrier islands that lost the siege of erosion. A rage for energy and products and transportation and capital caused us—and by us I mean the living things on planet Earth—to lose the battle against the sea, as glaciers melt and join the horde of water. From aqueducts to dams to levees to freshwater diversion, we have been in an arms race with water since we decided to impose our order on it. Water, however, is not in an arms race with us. It is motiveless, inhuman, a fluttering and empty shirt, elemental. Its old chaos is unaware of us.

For shrimpers of coastal Louisiana, life oscillates between an ordered world of land, where they face the tyranny of capital, culture, kinship, and identity, and the disordered world of water, where they face an inhuman force of shifting allegiances, asignification, freedom of movement if you can learn to ride the waves. Life on the water is at once dangerous and peaceful, flexible and relentless, experimental and selfless. While it is certain shrimpers bring with them the traces of themselves, their origins, their ghostly demarcations, they also face a vastness that diminishes those things, including the ties of blood vocation and family that provide them with moorings. One thing that distinguishes a shrimper from a person with a conventional job is that the shrimper must learn to be suspended, to float in uncertainty. To ride the currents wherever they may go. Life on the water is attractive to fishers not only because of its nautical beauty and the inertia of heritage but because it offers a method of coping with an ordered world that has left them and many other people behind. While imagining shrimping to be in their blood provides shrimpers with a counternarrative that reimagines a world of hope and magic different from the banality of everyday American life, the blood vocation is still a way to anchor themselves, to be grounded in the physicality of work and the intimacy and belonging of shared familial destiny. Life on the water, in opposition, is a world of pure unmooring: the release of all anchors except for the one that compels a person to return to land. Getting on a boat and spending a few weeks beyond the three-mile limit while trawling for cheap shrimp is not escape, it is a therapy. It is listening for an inhuman noise that we might understand and sing. Those who make their lives on the sea are like the singer in the Stevens poem: "there never was a world for her / Except the one she sang and, singing, made."[19] Their encounter with the water reveals the possibility of redirecting the rage for order away from ourselves and toward making an inhabitable, mutable, and doomed world livable.

Bodies of Water

And God said, "Let there be a firmament in the midst of the waters, and let it divide the waters from the waters."
—Genesis 1:6

The story goes that the day after God created the heavens and the earth and portioned off light from dark, he set to organizing water. God chose sky to ply water from water: a portion of the water would cover the earth, and a portion would be locked in the firmament, which he names Heaven. Ground did not come until the third day, when God raised dry land to collect the water into seas. This is the origin of the word *levee*, from the French *lever*, to raise. Sometime later, according to the story, he will break the sky and flood the earth along with its scummy life. And yet he chooses one small family to live on the waters that have drowned every breathing body. Once the waters go back to wherever they were before, Noah and the rest get to reapportion earth, to name the water between tracts of dry ground.

In lower Terrebonne Parish, the bayous and canals are separated by wet, marshy ground that is sinking into the Gulf of Mexico. At some point, the waters will tear down the dry land raised by God. Or at least, water will do what water has always done with land: carry it bit by bit out to sea. Coastlines, alluvial deltas, and islands have been shaped by millennia of rushing, trickling, rising, swelling, leaking, and relentless waters.

Joke's on us for believing in borders when it comes to water.

We imagine water as a body, something contained, the discrete fullness of an entity, whose depths are internal. Derived from Old English, *body* means a fleshy organization, the beginning and end of an individual self, that which holds our vitality or soul or epiphenomenal consciousness, the limit and structuring principle of our experience of life. We use body metaphors for collections of things and people: a writer's body of work, the body politic, a multinational corporation, the Corpus Hermeticum and Corpus Aristotelicum, the US Army Corps of Engineers, all of which take their name from the verbal form of *corpus*: "to make a body." We imagine these collections to be organized the way we are: into subcollections of organs, into structures that allow for individual differentiation working toward a common purpose, into hierarchy and demarcation and workflows. The body of work by a poet such as Wallace Stevens can be divided into categories such as juvenilia, major books or works that might signify an aesthetic shift or the introduction of additional concerns or exigencies, prose that promotes his ars poetica, and unrelated prose. We would imagine that the major poetical works serve as the organizing principle for the rest of the body. It is easy to see how we might mistake a corporate entity for a person: there is a central command whose goals are divided into manageable tasks given to highly differentiated members of the organization. We might consider a corporation like British Petroleum, whose executive faculty sets the agenda for the company, whose public relations department speaks with its lips, whose engineers and inspectors see with its eyes, whose legal team listens with its ears and manipulates other entities with its hands, whose oilfield operators and roughnecks and roustabouts bend its back on the continental shelves. But what is the organizing principle of water?

To consider a body of water a corporate entity is ludicrous. The Gulf of Mexico is not a collection of water and fish and oil. It cannot be, because the things in this body of water are in constant circulation. Unlike the God of the Bible, we cannot ply water from water, at least not on the global scale necessary for water to incorporate into something more discrete. And yet we try. We cling to the idea that the water can still be body, wholly body. And why not? The human body varies between about 48 and 65 percent water.[1] The rest is all lipids and bone and fiber. The human body pulses with the currents of blood. We contain oceans within. Herein lies the difference: blood and the other waters of the flesh are for the most part internal; water—the sea—is external. There is no internal to the sea, at least not the way we mean *internal* as a signifier of hidden constitution, organization, subjectivity, and truth. We might say that we can feel our truths in our bones, that our vocation is in our blood, or even that we act in primordial lunges toward survival, a program etched into the stuff of our genes. With the sea, we might say that it rises. It drowns. Its waves crash against shores, and sometimes the sky twists it into storms. The sea can contain anything, growing with each accumulation suspended in its waters but not incorporated into its body. It can expel its contents in unexpected places: bodies blistering on beaches hundreds of miles from where they were once quick with life, tires caught in nets far from any road. No matter what falls into the sea or what is spit from it, the sea is still ultimately the sea.

Names of Water, or the Idea of Order at Mare à Clay

The old people, as the oldest shrimpers I spoke to referred to their parents and grandparents, came up in the time of seines and cast nets, of canots (sailing luggers with hinged keels designed for navigating shallow waters) and pirogues (originally dugout cypress canoes; now flat-bottomed, sharp-hulled rowboats) and challons (like pirogues but with blunt, flat-nosed bows). In the old days, as the oldest shrimpers referred to that epoch, each particular flow of water, each water limned with land was named, committed to a navigational memory. ChaCha Sevin's father, George, a retired shrimper in his late seventies, described the way people inscribed their names on the waterways:

> I've seen some places, like the families, that's [no longer] still there, like some of them markers. Like the Mare à Clay [for] old man Clay Lecompte. Right there at Robinson [Canal], that point they got where Placid [Canal] is at, that would go all the way to the Mare Bleue back there. And they'd plow right there, make them a garden and all, and they'd hunt. We called the pond the Mare à Clay. Every one of them other ponds had a name. It's unbelievable what they had in them ponds. They had bass in there, neg—if that would be right there now, it would be unbelievable. And I think it's the oil industry that killed it.

In the old days of lower Terrebonne Parish, people ordered the small world by naming its small features. Ponds (*mares*) and ditches (canals, cuts, *coups*, cutoffs) were named for the men who were their stewards. Mr. George, remembering the slippery way names and families and ponds disappear from a world he could navigate by naming, does not believe that people today would believe the granular riches hiding in the watering holes. Back then, there was enough land to plow a garden and hold animals suitable for hunting. Back then, water had its edges, making it easier to name.

If you look at the comprehensive cartographies undertaken for more than a hundred years by the US Geological Survey (USGS), the mapping arm of the Department of the Interior, you will not find the Mare à Clay, the Mare Bleue, the Cutoff à Tchonque, or even Placid Canal (figures 10–14). The USGS nevertheless represents the best attempt at recording the names of the waters of the Louisiana Gulf Coast. These maps divide the land and sea into quadrants of knowable places, naming each place with institutional aloofness. The 15×15-minute maps of the area are named for Dulac, even though Chauvin is at its center. The four 7.5 × 7.5-minute maps that comprise the Dulac quadrant are named Dulac, Lake Quitman, Montegut, and Lake Tambour. Lake Boudreaux, the larger lake, more important to both Dulac and Chauvin, was actually labeled as Quitman Lake in the 1894 survey (figure 15), an error rectified in the more precise 1941 mapping (figure 16). Lake Barré fills the Lake Tambour quadrant, whose namesake does not even appear on the 1894 survey. In the 2015 survey, Lake Barré is labeled Gulf of Mexico, even though Lake Tambour, which is still labeled, likewise lost its southernmost shore to the Gulf. These maps, though lush and useful, impose an order that is possible only for those who must not daily navigate the marshes and ridges and waterways.

Would the USGS today believe the quality of bass in the *mares* right there at Robinson, where Placid is? Would they believe the bounty contained in those ponds, the biodiversity, and the wealth of life, which was so remarkable that it became a historical and spatial marker for Mr. George?

The answer, as we must know, is yes. Governmental surveyors and scientists believe what they can measure, and with enough time, funding, personnel, and political will, we could have measured the Mare à Clay, even in the old days. Today, if we could find the pond, we could plumb it, catalog it, and overwhelm it with our prowess at knowing. Our measurements, written on ledger or typed into a spreadsheet, would then become facts: markers—historical, spatial, and schematic—that we could use to navigate the broader corpus of knowledge about wetlands, biodiversity, hydrology, subsidence, erosion, industry, crustaceans and fish, marsh grass, mud, people willing to live on saturated earth that is falling into the sea, people who yoke their livelihoods to the life they find in water and estuary and forest and field, people who are getting older but still can remember when the littlest things had names and landmarks and seamarks were not just coordinates on the way to a destination but stories.

For example, let us return to Lake Boudreaux, erstwhile Quitman Lake. Although I had fished Lake Boudreaux and its marshy passes since childhood,

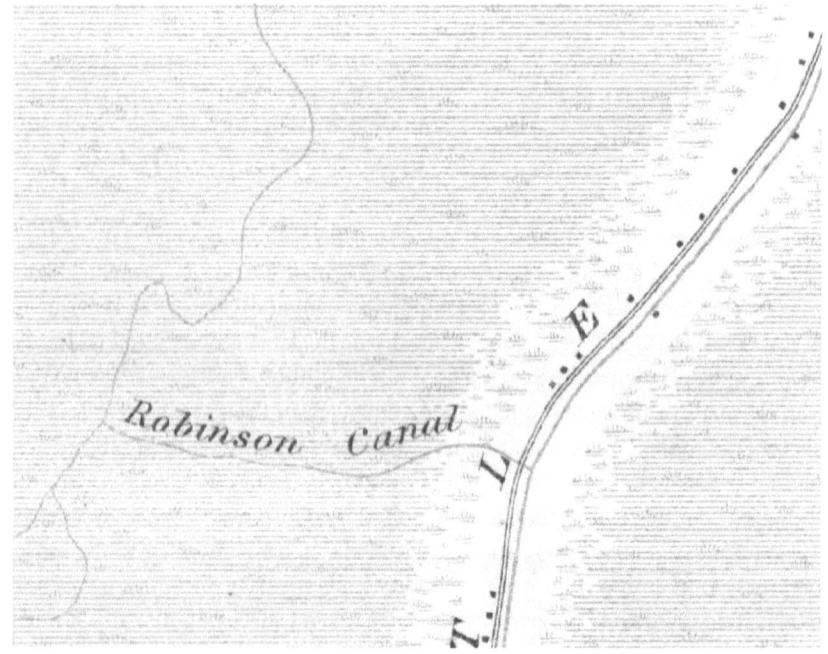

Figure 10. Area around Robinson Canal on the US Geological Survey map of Dulac, Louisiana, 1894. This is the approximate location where George Sevin placed the Mare à Clay, though the map does not chart the *mares* and cuts George describes. Courtesy of the US Geological Survey.

Figure 11. Area around Robinson Canal on the US Geological Survey map of Dulac, Louisiana, 1941. The Mare à Clay may be in one of the ponds surrounding the canal. Courtesy of the US Geological Survey.

Figure 12. Area around Robinson Canal on the US Geological Survey map of Dulac, Louisiana, 1964. What appeared as ponds on the 1941 map have now been combined into larger bodies of water. Courtesy of the US Geological Survey.

Figure 13. Area around Robinson Canal on the US Geological Survey map of Dulac, Louisiana, 1994. Again, what appeared as ponds on the 1964 map have now been combined into larger bodies of water. Courtesy of the US Geological Survey.

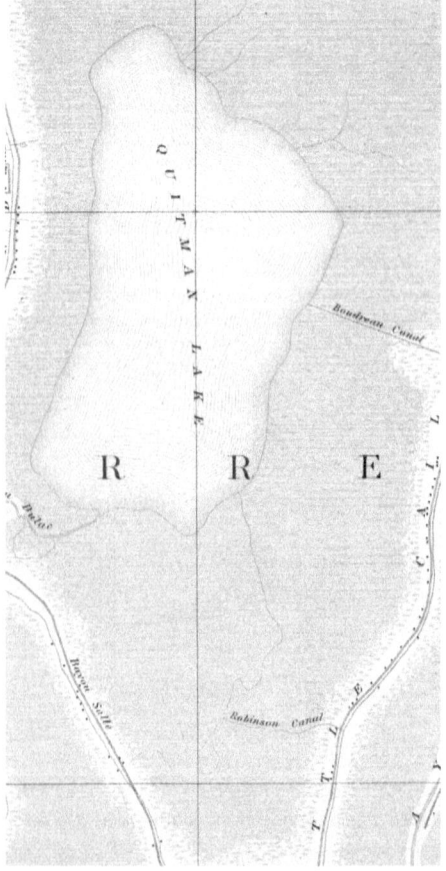

Figure 14. Area around Robinson Canal on the US Geological Survey map of Dulac, Louisiana, 2015. Unlike the earlier US Geological survey maps, this one includes satellite imagery as well as shaded relief (the deep green is shallow water, whereas the brighter greens and browns are dry land or trembling marsh). On the earliest map, the ponds either did not exist or were not surveyed by the cartographers. On this map, the ponds have been replaced by shallow open water flanking isthmuses created by the rising water and sinking land. Courtesy of the US Geological Survey.

Figure 15. Lake Quitman on the US Geological Survey map of Dulac, Louisiana, 1894. The map does not show Lake Boudreaux. Courtesy of the US Geological Survey.

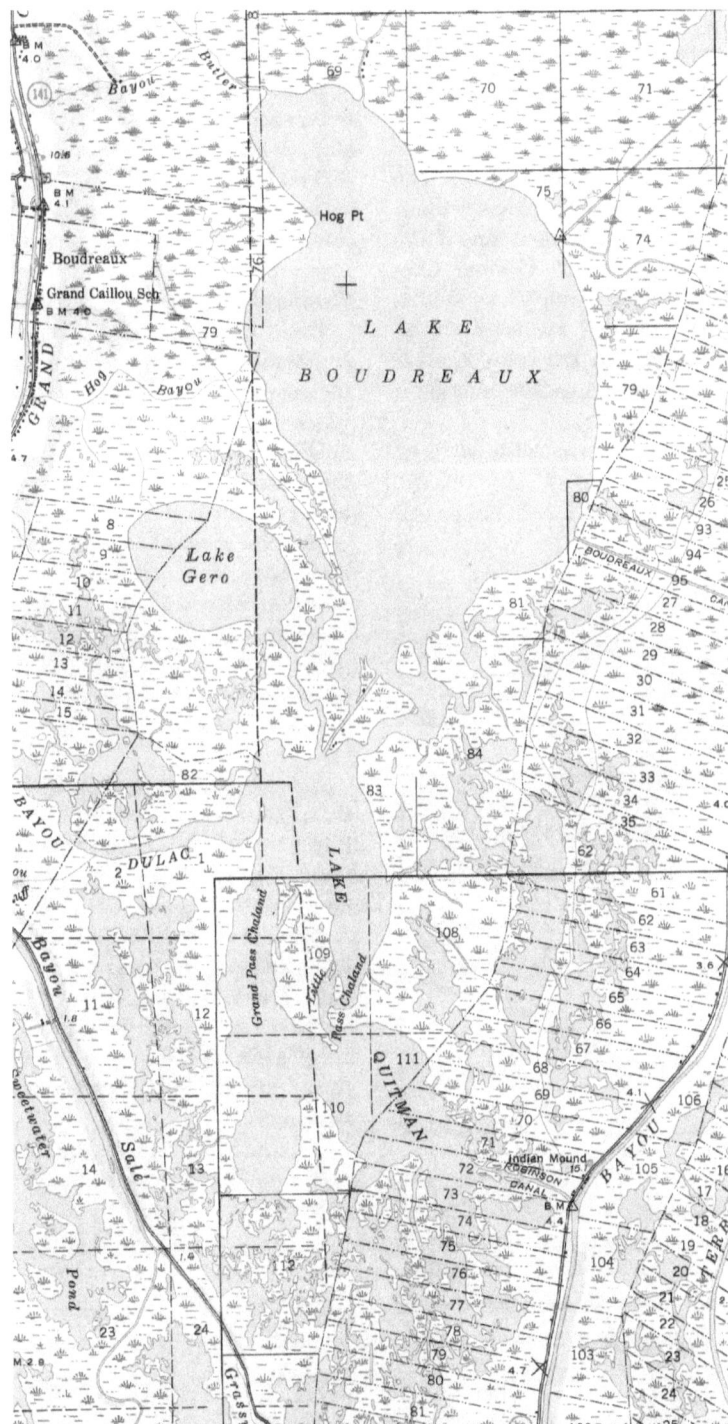

Figure 16. On the 1941 US Geological Survey map of Dulac, Louisiana, Lake Quitman has become Lake Boudreaux, while Lake Quitman now appears below. Courtesy of the US Geological Survey.

Figure 17. Lake Quitman and Lake Boudreaux on the 2015 US Geological Survey map of Dulac, Louisiana. Courtesy of the US Geological Survey.

I had never heard of Quitman Lake (or Lake Quitman) until I began scholarly research on the area (figure 17). My dad had heard of it because he's interested in local history and genealogy, but he only knew two things about it: that historian Alcée Fortier described Chauvin as "a post-hamlet in the central part of Terrebonne parish, [. . .] situated at the head of Quitman Lake," and that the name *Quitman* referred to a soldier, though he could not remember where he'd learned that information.[1] I asked my grandfather, whose daddy cut the Cutoff à Tchonque and who ran a shrimp-drying platform in the marsh below Lake Boudreaux, whether he had ever heard of Quitman Lake. He said no. In 1938–39, the US Board on Geographical Names, a body within the US federal government ordered into existence by President Benjamin Harrison in 1890 to oversee naming conventions, decided that Lake Boudreaux was the correct name for that body of water, "not Quitman Lake."[2] *Houma Courier* columnist Bill Ellzey flirted with this mystery in 2012 but seems to have stopped at acknowledging the discrepancy.[3] It is here that this story becomes a story of remembering and forgetting names.

The people of Chauvin, for instance, have forgotten that Quitman Lake is named for John A. Quitman, a general, congressman, pirate, plantation owner, and governor of Mississippi. He gave Narciso López soldiers and money to wrest Cuba from Spanish control and add it to the roster of US slave states. When this effort failed, he resigned his governorship. He owned Live Oaks, a plantation in Dulac (though not Dulac Plantation). He never quite lived there, but he sent overseers, including his brother and son, to force enslaved Black people to produce sugar and molasses.[4] Historian Robert E. May describes Live Oaks as "particularly fearsome": "Labor conditions were brutal, and transfer to the Louisiana place was sometimes used as a punishment for unruly slaves at Quitman's other holdings."[5] For Quitman to get to his lake, he would have had to go through John M. Pelton's Dulac Plantation. There is no compelling archival or ethnographic evidence that explains why the people of Chauvin have forgotten the radically pro-slavery Mississippi governor who owned and punished human beings the next bayou over. Contemporary maps show Quitman Lake surrounded by "Impassible Swamp," so perhaps those on Bayou Petit Caillou just did not know what was going on with Bayou Grand Caillou (figures 18 and 19).[6] Or perhaps the presence of large-scale institutional slavery was too distasteful a memory to cherish. The people of Chauvin have also forgotten Colonel James Baker Robinson, who owned a plantation and a crew of slaves near present-day Robinson Canal and about whom there is scant information. Yet the names of slavers and their plantations trace the waterways and lands of lower Terrebonne: Sarah Bridge after Sarah Plantation, Woodlawn Ranch Road after Woodlawn Plantation, Barrow Canal after plantation owner R. R. Barrow, Quitman Lake, Robinson Canal.

Figure 18. "Quitman's Lake and Impassable Swamp" on William McCulloh's 1856 plat map of the Chauvin area ("Township 19S, Range 18E, Southeastern District West of the Mississippi River," https://wwwslodms.doa.la.gov/WebForms/DocumentViewer.aspx?docId=522.00853&category=H#1). Plat maps often include the names of people granted land before the US Land Act of 1820, but this section included no grants. The land may nevertheless have been inhabited. This map also does not show Boudreaux Canal, perhaps indicating that it came later.

Instead, people in Chauvin have reordered its ghosts so that the only ones that remain are the stories of survival. So the story goes for Lake Boudreaux: when an unnamed storm washed Old Man Boudreaux's house out into the lake, he cut a *traînasse* (a small canal cut by hand for the use of a single person or family to reach a larger waterway; from the French word *traîner*, which means "to drag") in the trembling marsh to where it moored. The bank was solid enough that men and beasts could stand along Boudreaux's Canal, and they pulled by rope pirogues full of beams and flooring and other architectures. Old Man Boudreaux rebuilt his house where it stood—at a guess, the site of the future Boudreaux Canal Store and School. Instead of memorializing the breaking of Black bodies across an "impassable" swamp or the carving of the wetlands to make it easier to transport sugarcane, we instead celebrate the way we might tame a landscape with our shovels and boats and frontier ingenuity. But names, like the floodwater of Old Man Boudreaux's unnamed hurricane, have a hard time letting the dead stay buried.

Anthropologist Tim Ingold writes, "Places do not have locations but histories. Bound together by the itineraries of their inhabitants, places exist not in space but as nodes in a matrix of movement. I shall call this matrix a 'region.' It is the knowledge of the region, and with it the ability to situate one's current position within the historical context of journeys previously made—journeys to, from and around places—that distinguishes the countryman from the stranger. Ordinary wayfinding, then, more closely resembles storytelling than map-using."[7] Ingold's project of embedding spatial knowledge in a dynamic unfolding of

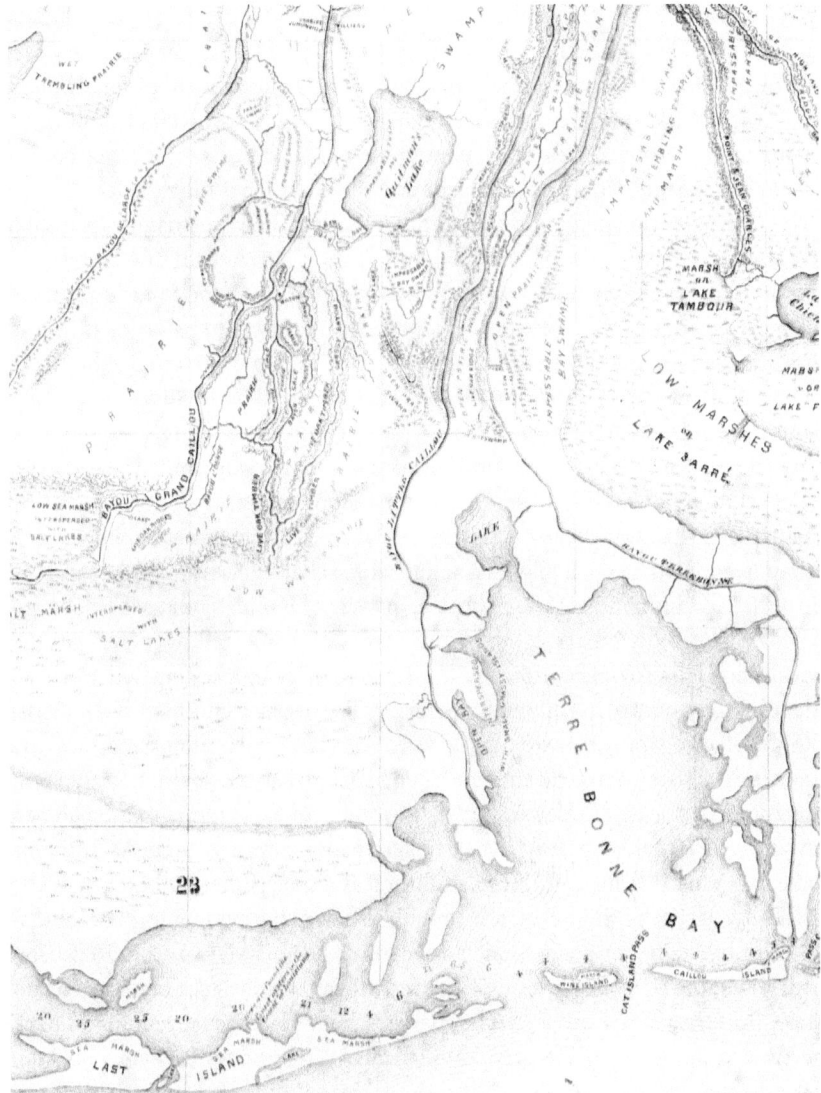

Figure 19. Portion of Department of the Gulf Map No. 10, *Military Approaches to New Orleans*, 1863. Note the imprecision of the mapping of Lake Barré, or is it low marshes? The figuration of the border between land and water reflects the uncertainty of the coastal land/seascape.

reality through movement and environment correctly returns our conversation to storytelling. For Ingold, movement in a place is a reenactment of local movement, and this wayfaring is both a way to get from place to place and a way to create a world knowable by the people who must live in it. His regional matrix with crisscrossing paths beaten by old feet and waterways traversed by old hulls is especially seductive when thinking of the isolated marshlands along coastal bayous in the nineteenth century. To the twenty-first-century eye, a world of *traînasses* and shrimp-drying platforms and lonely pirogues piled high with muskrat bodies looks rough in a cozy way: a world small enough to name its smallest features, small enough to not need to commit those names to paper. Like other lost places, lower Terrebonne Parish is full of lovely stories, and their repetition orders how we think of it today, how we imagine its future, how we mourn its return to the sea. And though I, as a child of Chauvin, do not wish to disbelieve those stories, I must speak up on behalf of the stranger.

Space, geographer Doreen Massey warns, is the suspension of multiple histories, "an inherently dynamic simultaneity": "Such a way of conceptualizing the spatial, moreover, inherently implies the existence in the lived world of a simultaneous multiplicity of spaces: cross-cutting, intersecting, aligning with one another, or existing in relations of paradox or antagonism."[8] The estuaries of coastal Louisiana, like all space, contain incongruous accidents of histories. It is a permeable waterscape. A palimpsest of stories, remembered and washed away, negotiated by the living interacting with a changing environment and the material and immaterial things the dead have left behind. Ingold, who does not cite Massey in his theory of place and region and storytelling, privileges the local knowledge of the country folk, who are happy to reorder their world in their image. Country folk, though, are forgetful. Governor Quitman and Colonel Robinson, two strangers who neither were born nor died in Louisiana, let alone in some impassable swampland at the edge of the country, demonstrated that they could shape that local knowledge from afar. They had money, slaves, and an incentive to remake the land in their image and to name it. Although Quitman's lake was renamed by both locals and no less a governmental body than the US Department of the Interior, his name still lives in the opening waters that once unofficially bore names such as Mare Bleue and Mare à Clay. Robinson lent his name not only to one of the most heavily trawled waterways off of Lake Boudreaux but also to the village of fishers whose legacy stretches back to the old days—my great-grandfather Henry "Tchonque" Eschete, Old Man Clay Lecompte, and Kim Guy. Beneath the names of Quitman and Robinson lie the sinister ghosts of a slave economy that tore through human bodies in the same cavalier way these planters tore through the marsh to transport their sugar and indigo.

The stranger, abstracted as an institutional force, becomes the charting of land rights and ownership in the township plats, the tactical mapping of the swamps for use in the US Civil War, the topographical surveying of the USGS, and my project of making my local knowledge strange enough to comprehend the contradictory yet comprehensive mapping of a land drowning in gulf. All of us strangers and all of us countrymen—we rage to order the external world. We name bodies of water as if they are people we know: whole, discrete, with discernable characteristics and identities. But in an ironic turn of events, the lake that strangers once knew as Quitman, which became Boudreaux at some unknowable point in time, has now subsumed the lesser bodies of water in its proximity. In other words, Lake Boudreaux has swallowed other lakes, lakes with names like Gero, Robinson, and Quitman. If not for a few ridges and *marais flotant* (floating marsh), knotted together with loose clumps of peat, Lake Boudreaux would have swallowed what the old people might have called the Mare à Clay, a place that, thick with unbelievable bass, people could tell stories about, recognize as a marker and find their way around a large, indiscrete world.

Bodies on the Water

Water makes many Beds
For those averse to sleep –
—Emily Dickinson

In the old days, when old shrimpers felt a storm was coming, they would drop anchor and sleep. Here is the story of the Picou Cemetery, a hundred-year-old graveyard built on a thousand-year-old mound erected by people in the Coles Creek culture. There was a hurricane from the era of naming storms after what they destroyed—the 1909 Grand Isle Hurricane. Old man Picou, out fishing, felt the atmospheric pressure dropping, saw the shadowing of the sky. He moored himself right in his oyster reef. He rode out the storm, rocked to sleep in a marsh. When the weather cleared, he rowed back home. He found his wife and children in the trees that used to grow on the banks of Lake Boudreaux. He buried them in the Indian mound.

Conventional wisdom today holds that land is safer than water when it comes to cataclysmic storms. In an era when we can watch weather forecasts and receive storm warnings by push notification, an era when there are roads and cars and GPS, conventional wisdom holds true when we evacuate to the hinterlands. But for those who live on the wettest edge of the land, who ply their trade on water, sometimes it is safer to just ride out the storm in a boat. This is not to say that the Gulf represents safety to the fishers of coastal Louisiana. How could it? As a serial hurricane survivor, I can vouchsafe that leaving a flood zone by land is preferable to dropping an anchor on a skiff. But the waters that saturate the marshes and swamps and make the border between land and sea diffuse have a rich and ironic relationship with its tenant bodies. Every fisher I know tells me of the pleasures of being "on the water"—never *in* the water, because that would be death or some other failure. A person drowns in water. A body floats on the water. The fishers I know *live* on the water, buoyant, floating on a sea whose inchoate and capricious ungovernability buffers them from a world of order, docility, and discipline. Speaking of the pull of the sea, fisher Kim Guy said, "[When] we grew up, us, it was water. All we ever did was water." His body could not wait to get back to the water. It could not bear to be moored.

I pressed fishers on what drew them to the watery life aside from the fact that shrimping was in their blood. They said that life on the water was peaceful. Quiet. Isolated from the quickening world on shore. Throughout their lives, it was water. All they ever did was water. Though several fishers said they took the still moments between catch and cull to pray or meditate or obsess over the size of the landing, the physical immediacy of dragging nets and floating through widening waterways enclosed by paille fine marshes, the steady intensity of the Gulf's pulses, rocking them, the alchemy of sun and storm and seagull cry and diesel engine—these bodily responses allowed them the shield against the banality of life and death among people. Former shrimper Glynn Trahan told me that the shrimping life is "probably one of the best lives I've ever lived." What other lives has Glynn lived? The life of a father raising children in a world that will not protect his favorite life. The life of a husband suddenly within arm's reach after a life at sea. The life of a son who struggles to maintain a legacy he traces through his father. The life of a man whose friends are dying. The life of an American citizen in an age of global military police actions, mass shootings, ethnic nationalism, hyperpartisanship, and hyperconnectivity. According to Glynn,

> Because you're out there, you don't have this everyday thing, where you're hearing about somebody got killed in an automobile accident or this plane went down or these bunch of soldiers got killed fighting in a war, or every day, you find out somebody near you or somebody you know has been diagnosed with this terrible disease, and they're not going to live for another two or three months or whatever. This person worked his whole life and getting ready to retire, and he's—you only hear these bad things. Out there, you don't hear all of that. Now, with the cell phone, now, you can kinda get all that news, thing is not as good as it was, let's say thirty years ago. Because thirty years ago, when you was out on a boat for a week or two weeks, you knew absolutely nothing that was going on unless, you know, somebody sent you a message by VHF radio or whatever. Everything was just so tranquil out there.

Out there, on the water, you can escape the quotidian world of information. You can take pleasure in not knowing. Blood ties, whereas water unties. On the water, you are incomunicado. You do not have to face the fragile bodies of loved ones, bodies that threaten to become merely bodies—and soon. Later in the interview, Glynn mentions the things most of us would first mention as components of the everyday: the business of errands, commerce, and obligations that sustain life. Life on the water, it is clear, offers an escape from these things. But Glynn's identification of life on shore with banal grief and communication touches on the capacity of water to wash away the very networks that give us significance, that make us selves.

The unmooring of the body on the water echoes my assertion that the sea, with its seething planes of intensity, functions as a Body without Organs, one that can free a person to consider the possibility of thinking and living differently. The life of the body on the water offers escape from both the banal everyday *and* the intense events whose interpretations tentpole a life's meaning. Deleuze and Guattari offer a therapeutic suggestion: "Where psychoanalysis says, 'Stop, find your self again,' we should say instead, 'Let's go further still, we haven't found our [Body without Organs] yet, we haven't sufficiently dismantled our self.' Substitute forgetting for anamnesis, experimentation for interpretation. Find your body without organs. Find out how to make it. It's a question of life and death, youth and old age, sadness and joy. It is where everything is played out."[1]

The body at sea, unlike the body on land and among people, is devoid of signification: there is only work and rest. The body pulls the nets and releases the marine bodies trapped therein. The body culls the product from the trash. The body waits. The body must become attuned to the wind and tide and sun, but it must also be willing to improvise, to try things that might not work. The body has to let go of a self and surrender to work. This is not to say that trawlers or fishers do not take with them articulate and inarticulate knowledges and skills or that they somehow achieve the eldritch Deleuzian ideal of the Body without Organs. The former would result in no productive fishing. The latter is either death or nirvana, each being the horizon of possibility but not an actual way to live and not one that Deleuze and Guattari actually recommend.[2] When Deleuze and Guattari write, "The BwO is what remains when you take everything away," they follow with, "What you take away is precisely the phantasy, and significances and subjectifications as a whole."[3] Life at sea offers a brief and bodily collapse of being an orderly subject expected to control one's own destiny. On the water, a body *can* bracket the dreams that make it a self onshore. The shrimper onshore faces the insurmountability of the global flow of seafood that has determined his profession to be anachronistic. He faces the pressure of living up to his blood, the internal waters that can pump strict and contradictory identities into being, a matrix of genealogy and inner truth. He faces the expectation we all face: to lead a good, orderly life, one where you provide for yourself and yours, one where you accumulate wealth and feed yourself at regular intervals and pay attention to your weight and cholesterol and try to avoid addictions and crutches and fantasies. Life at sea may require a certain acquiescence to a fantasy of control and competence, but it does not require you to be who you are.

This is also not to say that fishers intentionally use fishing as a way to escape identity or people or the crush of global capital or their modes of living. Several shrimpers described trawling as "a cruise," a vacation, full of the sublime encounters of beauty and a respite from the stressors of their onshore life. It is a respite, but it is not a pleasure that remains stable. Chad Portier, a commercial shrimper and boat builder, manages captains and crews and runs his fleet with his wife, Angela, and captains a boat with a crew (figure 20). In the middle of explaining how he succeeds in commercial fishing, he reveals his anxiety about staying in place, especially on land:

> We fish twenty-four hours a day when I fish. I don't care what it is, I fish. I can't sit on an anchor; it drives me f—crazy. I just can't stay in the house. I'm not that kind of guy. I'm inside like I'm in jail or something. I got to get out of there. But when I'm on a boat, I use it to—and [Angela] would try to—she would come fishing with me all the time when we first got married. She was one of the best deckhands I had, actually. She would cook. She would pick. She would just take one drag off. Some of the best times of my life, really.

Chad runs an insomniac, wandering operation: he needs the constant movement of the water, the constant productivity of seafood extraction. But more than that, he needs not to be moored, whether at sea or on land. The stability of solid ground is the worst kind of anchor: a chain sunk deep into the ground, something that thirsts for the relief of a hammer and chisel and a weak link. Though both Chad and Angela are born-again Christians—an identity that sets them apart from the sensual Catholicism of their neighbors—Chad's fear of being grounded nearly caused him to say "fucking crazy" in front of his wife before he disciplined his speech. He is not the kind of guy to be yoked to the domestic sphere. There is something he wants to say about what he uses a boat for, how it remedies the doldrums or cabin fever or whatever it is you call the state of wishing you were elsewhere, adrift, and subject to the vagaries of the elements and the harvest and the mystery of what bodies the water holds. His marriage was forged in that elsewhere, the flow of labor in and out of the flow of water. It is not hard to believe that those were indeed the best years of his life. The best life he ever lived.

The male body at sea is the ideal body on the water for the fishers I talked to.[4] When Chad and Angela honeymooned on their boat, Angela played deckhand

Figure 20. Chad and Angela Portier, 2015. Photograph by Emma Christopher Lirette.

to Chad's captain. The restless muscularity of the young shrimper is a signifier, on and off the water, of potency and ability to provide for self and community. Chad was not the only one to eliminate sleep from the commercial shrimping playbook. Shrimping czar, ex-trawler, and activist David Chauvin scheduled two two-and-a-half-hour naps each day when he captained boats in his midtwenties (figure 21). Dropping his sleep allowed him to manage both daytime and nighttime drags. I met David in his office at his fleet compound in Dulac. Though he has been in the shrimp fishery for about thirty years, putting him in his late forties, roughly the same age as Chad Portier and Kim Guy, David had less of the sun-hardened, ropy look. He wasn't stout or sunburned. His face did not have a hard-earned topography of cracks and craters. With his dark hair tapered into an Ivy League haircut and his pressed polo shirt, David looked like a senator from central casting on his day off. He and his wife, Kim, travel to seafood expos in Boston and fund-raisers in Washington, D.C. They advocate online for down-and-out shrimpers, and David knew more about the global seafood trade than any other person I talked to in Terrebonne Parish. And though his appearance might suggest that his was a life of white-collar comfort, his alert, aggressive movements—from the explosive way he stood to deal with some urgent shrimp business to the coiling anger in his posture when he described the conspiracy of loopholes and lobbyists that threaten his livelihood—support his tales of asserting his leadership as a young captain on the water. Chad noted, "The way [a fisherman] walks is the way he's gonna fish. You can see. If he's always going, always doing something, he's a good fisherman, because he's always gonna be thinking of the next place to go check or the next

Figure 21. David Chauvin, 2015. Photograph by Emma Christopher Lirette.

place to do this or do that." David was not one to drag around. The male body on the waters of coastal Louisiana, according to its shrimpers, should have a nervous competency, a nautical wanderlust, and a willingness to both throw itself onto the sea and persist there.

But the body, no matter its hardness, can break against the sea. The same anxious spirit of adventure and prospecting that propels successful fisherman onto the water chances to leave the bodies of fishers imperiled. Boats break down. Engines break down. And when the storms come, a body needs to prepare. Kim Guy tells a story of his body on and in water:

> We got stuck in a couple of storms at the dock at my house. We couldn't—we couldn't go anywheres. The engine in my boat was broken, and we was trying to get it repaired and we couldn't go up the road, and we stayed stuck, tied up at the dock. I had pieces of my engine in my truck on the road, and I knew it was going to start getting—water was gonna get high outside. So I took off walking on the levee to get to the road. And I went move my truck further up on the road over there, to where I wouldn't lose the parts on my engine. And when I came back the current was going pretty good and I'm—I slipped on the levee and I missed the rope and I didn't stop till I got to the road. I couldn't catch onto nothing. They had so much current, and I didn't stop till I got back to the road. And then they had to throw my life ring all the way from the boat with a long rope, so I can get back to the boat. That wasn't too fun. I didn't think I was going to make it back to the boat. And they didn't have nobody around because everybody had left for the storm. Everybody went up the road.

> And we was stuck down here. [...] My wife would remember because she was scared to death. She was trying to throw the rope to me and she don't know how to swim and—I didn't have no choice, I just—tried clinging onto the steps of the house, and I miss a step to the house, and—I didn't stop till I got back to the blacktop on the road in front of the house over there.

This is a story of a body caught in the current, washing it back again and again to a place of danger. Kim could not tell me exactly when this had occurred, but it had been in the last fifteen years, an age of cell phones and weather reports and paved roads.[5] As tranquil as the water seems when it is contained within its borders, it threatens to spill out and bring with it the full force of a murder-drunk god. A genius loci with incomprehensible motives.

When a body drowns, it first loses ability to panic.[6] Shouting and splashing precedes the event of drowning. In the final minute before losing buoyancy, the body uses its arms to push the water down and tilts its head to the heavens. This is not voluntary. If the drowning body bobs its nose or mouth above the surface of the water, it only breathes and continues pushing down. When a body drowns, it loses the ability to swim or grab a life ring. The body cannot kick its way to safety or give a constant cry. It cannot invite another body to save it. If another body—one that is not drowning—swims out to trawl the drowning body out of water, the drowning body will grab the live one. This is not a choice. The rescuing body, weighted with a drowning body, begins to drown. The method to save a body from drowning is to first let it drown. Once it sinks, it is safe to fish it out and perform revival methods. But savior beware: at this stage, it is also easy to let go.

Land's End

The body begs for a system that will not break—
—Katie Ford, "The Vessel Bends the Water"

Say you are in New Orleans and need to travel to lower Terrebonne, but you are in an age before water-control efforts killed the forks of the Mississippi River (figures 22 and 23). Say you want to visit the pre-ruin resort on Last Island. First, take an upriver steamboat to Donaldsonville, where the Mississippi forks into Bayou Lafourche.[1] Embark on a skiff and travel downstream to Lockport, to where the Barataria and Lafourche Canal Company cut a channel into Field's Lake, to where the B&L Canal Company cut a channel into Lake Long, to where the company cut a canal into Bayou Terrebonne, which B&L kept navigable by dredging its floor.[2] Follow Bayou Terrebonne until it widens into ocean. To the east are the Timbalier Islands, and if you follow them, you will eventually arrive at Chenière Caminãda and Grand Isle. Right ahead and stretching to the west is Caillou Island, which itself hosts a resort that includes a few hotels.[3] To the north is Terrebonne Bay. To the south is open gulf, broken by Wine Island and then Last Island, Isle Dernière. There, book a room at Eliza Pecot's Ocean House, wage your wealth at Captain Dave Muggah's Billiard House, forget your troubles at Mr. Martin's Fine Bar.[4] Say you want to drink to the end of the land.

In the 1850s, members of the landed gentry could escape the humdrum life of a slave-owning planter or a high-profile politician by repairing to an "island of tranquil delights."[5] The bourgeoisie—the teachers and merchants and doctors and tailors—also found themselves on the last islands. Being so close to the mouth of the ocean and away from land when railroads and steamships were only beginning to connect people to people may lead to a type of revelry that borders on madness. For example, John Thuer, a music teacher at the Thibodaux Female Institute, spent the summer of 1854 on Caillou

Figure 22. Portion of Decercelier's *Carte du Missicipy ou Louissiane depuis la Baye de lascension jusqua la pointe de la Mobille*, 1718–29. Courtesy of the Archive nationales d'outre-mer, Aix-en-Provence, France.

Island. He proclaimed himself Finn-Fon-Boo, the vice governor of Rogue's Harbor, Caillou Island, and sent the *Thibodaux Minerva*, a four-page Know-Nothing partisan newspaper, an allegorical satire of island fauna in the form of an advertisement for a "Sub."[6] In Vice Governor Finn-Fon-Boo's telling, the tribes he governs consist of Finns, Pokers, Scarlatinos, Shakers, Singing Filibusters, Sneaks, Pietists, and others that seem, based on the puns littered through the descriptions, to correspond roughly to sharks, rays, shrimp (or dogs), otters, mosquitos (or seagulls), roaches, and crabs. Or perhaps there is a deeper or double satire occurring: *poker*, slang for "penis" in the nineteenth century, according to the Oxford English Dictionary; *scarlatina*, a word used for scarlet fever, which can develop into rheumatic fever, a symptom of which is rheumatism, a condition for which Thuer sought relief on the island; *shakers*, a religious sect that featured ecstatic trembling, equality between men and women, and celibacy; *pietists*, the name of an anticlerical strain of Lutheranism.[7] Finn-Fon-Boo also repeatedly refers to the "lords of creation," a highly arch term that by the mid-1800s was used to mock male dominance over society.[8] Thuer's motives for writing and publishing this account are inscrutable. Though the text describes itself as a job advertisement, it includes no instructions for applying. Thuer has no other published output, and his Swiftian prose is either silliness or diffuse mockery of something lost to printed memory. Perhaps the islands were infected with mirth. Perhaps vacationers were energized by the impossibility of the fragile world of recreation, of sea breezes and fresh seafood, of dancing with strangers, and of shirking the landed life of responsibility and industry. Perhaps they were drunk on the dangers tucked into the delights of the water.

According to another missive from the barrier islands, this one from Last Island in 1855,

> Standing at sunset on its beautiful beach ... stretching along its semi-circumference of some twenty or thirty miles; tessillated, as it were, by the inimitably fine tracery of the surf, and your brow fanned by the cooled and invigorating expirations breathed from the lips of Æolus—the mind becomes largely excursive, not to say romantic, till its whole history seems at once comprehended by the magic of your intuition, or you find yourself almost unconsciously weaving the thread of your imaginings into the woof of reality. The intonations in the voice of the surge seem to laugh for a moment at the folly of reckless adventurers, then to chaunt songs of applause at their success, or sigh a sad requiem at their misfortunes. Regarding its crescent form, you think of its adaptedness to piracy, and are told that it was one of Lafitte's favorite haunts.[9]

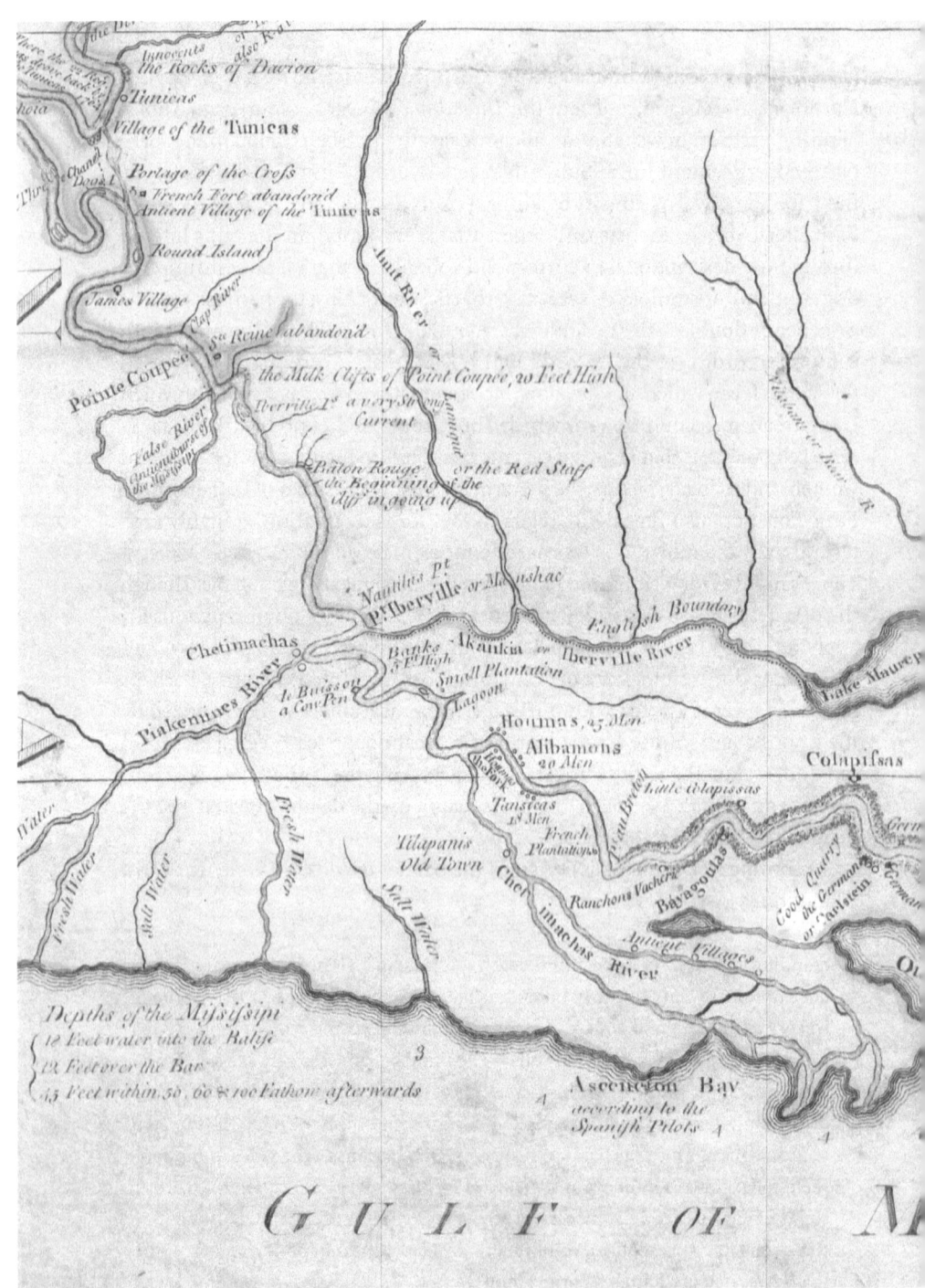

Figure 23. Portion of John Ross, *Course of the River Mississippi, from the Balise to Fort Chartres; Taken on an Expedition to the Illinois, in the Latter End of the Year 1765* (London: Sayer, 1765). Courtesy of the Louisiana Research Collection, Tulane University, New Orleans.

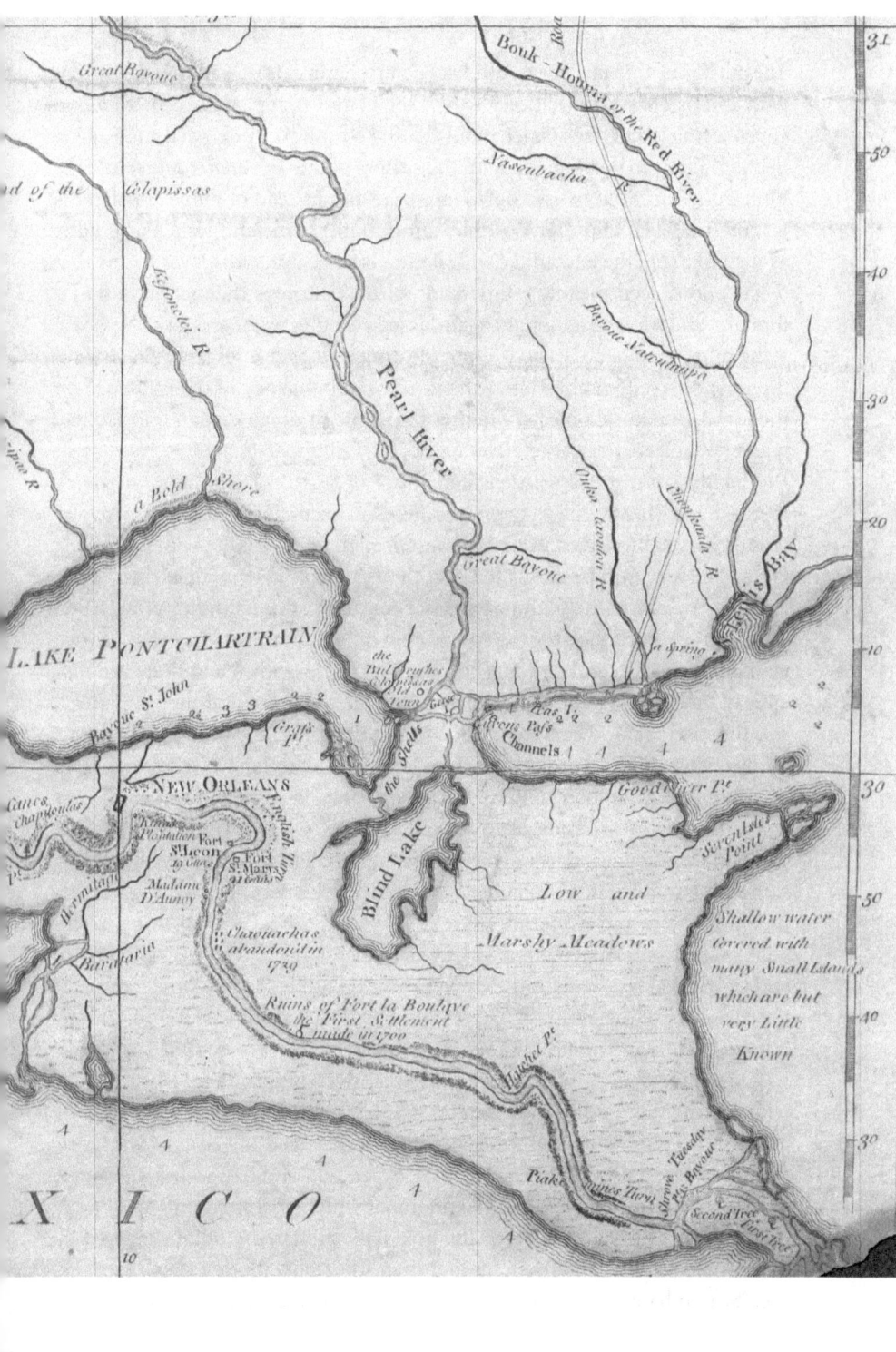

The author of this piece was "Studyx," a faux-Latin nom-de-plume consistent with the ostentatious diction of the sketch, and it appeared in the *Houma Ceres*, a four-page newspaper published by Know-Nothing partisan Eugene William Blake in partnership with the editors of the *Thibodaux Minerva*. Like Finn-Fon-Boo, Studyx uses florid language, but instead of aimless satire, his writing imitates Ralph Waldo Emerson in both theme and tone. For Studyx as for Emerson, the encounter with nature is occasion to discover truths that create and exceed meaning. Emerson writes, "Nature is the incarnation of a thought, and turns to a thought again, as ice becomes water and gas. The world is the mind precipitated, and the volatile essence is forever escaping again into the state of free thought. Hence the virtue and pungency of the influence on the mind, of natural objects, whether inorganic or organic. Man imprisoned, man crystallized, man vegetative, speaks to man impersonated."[10]

The mind is a storm whose waters form the world, which evaporates back to mind. For Studyx, the watery mind takes an excursion to the shark-shaped islands, carved by water and air and most of all thought. Studyx, witless prophet, flattens history into place, his magical thought creating a mythic truth of the last island heard in the inhuman cries of the ocean: this haunt for pirates, this watery grave. For Emerson, the co-creation of reality is a volatile event. Stories gain heft and flesh and pop into the world. They lose form and flesh and disappear. Emerson, a naturalist who disputed the existence of things unnatural, saw the mark of God carved into inchoate things, into the things we become. Studyx, who imposes order onto the island by way of fancy, writes that he is disappointed when confronted with reports that in some prehistory of Last Island, a wild horse, rising from the foaming sea, was not the devil and thus was tamed. Emerson writes, "There is throughout nature something mocking, something that leads us on and on, but arrives nowhere, keeps no faith with us," and "The beauty of nature must always seem unreal and mocking."[11] The Gulf exceeds our imagination. It speaks to people on vacation, mocks them, and sighs a sad requiem for their misfortunes. And the people, impersonating the surreality of the limitless waters troubling the beach of Last Island, trusted it to keep faith and not kill them.

August 10, 1856: the waters rose and silenced the party on Last Island. Those with summer homes saw those homes splintered and rushed out into the open gulf. A witness said people were "hemmed in between the rush of waters in front and rear."[12] Bodies were pinned between gulf and bay, water and water. Those with families sheltered in the hotel, which shattered and cast them into the sea. The bar splintered. The pool hall splintered. Bodies sheltered in overturned cisterns and tried not to drown. The tight embrace of parents and their scared babies: the water smashed it and took the babies. During the eye of the hurricane, when the storm became death-still before resuming, humans chained themselves, arm in arm, to a beached and broken ship, the *Star*, that was supposed to rescue them but crashed instead. These people survived. The waters rose in the night, swallowed more people. Then the flood followed the storm to crash against the mainland, bringing the dead with it. The living left behind by the waters made their way to the *Star*. They, the 250 spared, were half of the resort, and they stayed on the boat for three days.

Last Island went underwater. What emerged were two islands: Isles Dernières. There were no signs of human habitation left. In 1962, the Whiskey Pass Association, a group of well-to-do businessmen in Houma, erected a twelve-foot-tall cement pyramid on the shore at Whiskey Pass, a *traînasse* dug by the 1856 hurricane. On top of they pyramid, they erected a six-foot-tall, 1,376-pound statue of the Virgin Mary carved from Carrara marble. They named it *Our Lady of the Sea*. In 1967, the shore fell away beneath the statue, so it was moved inland on pilings by the grace of the Louisiana Land and Exploration Company. In 1982, the waters rose to overtake the statue, so the Whiskey Pass Association mounted *Our Lady* on a sixty-foot-tall piling jutting out of her sea. LL&E became Burlington Resources. Burlington Resources became ConocoPhillips. The company wanted *Our Lady* off its land in Houma. Roxanne Sevin, Cha-Cha's sister, offered her land in Cocodrie, and so the Whiskey Pass Association commissioned a forty-foot piling to be thrust into the mud, and *Our Lady* was bolted to a steel armature.[13]

The fall of Last Island, like the effects of the hurricanes in 2005 that sunk the fisheries, like the oil spill that doused the Gulf in tarry oil in 2010, was an accident. As philosopher Paul Virilio theorizes, "The word *accident*, derived from the Latin *accidens*, signals the unanticipated, *that which unexpectedly befalls* the mechanism, system, or product, *its surprise failure* or destruction. As if the 'failure' were not programmed into the product from the moment of its production or implementation."[14] The body begs for a system that will not break, but the point of systemic failure, according to Virilio, is built into the system. For the last vacationers on Last Island, the system that broke was a system that trusted the sea not to swallow it, that imagined a sandy oasis away from the rot and swelter of Louisiana in the age of yellow fever, that invited people to come and see the fun of aquatic revelry and reverie. An accident, according to Virilio, results from a failure of imagination: something takes us unawares, something we should have seen from the beginning. Or perhaps those erased by the sea on Last Island knew. Historian Alain Corbin, who documents the transformation of the sea from abyss to beach resort, writes, "The discovery of the dangerous beauty of the shores refreshed the pleasure that individuals could experience in simulating their own destruction."[15] Corbin cites the new delights of sinking feet into wet sand, of swimming out into the surf, practices that gained popularity as vacationing rose in the mid-nineteenth century. But he could also have described the feeling of perching in a cypress hotel, floating on the brief mound of sand, dancing above the swirl of tide and eddy. The land at Last Island, as we know, ended. Those who danced upon that doom danced in spite of its pressing failure. It was an accident, one that, in the final accounting, people did not prepare for, even if they could feel it coming. And so they disappeared.

Shrimpers of the Louisiana coast, like other residents, recognize a primary danger to their livelihood that has less to do with economic realities than it does with the existential threat of the water that is ending the land. When I was a child, my dad brought me to a beach cleanup event on Isles Dernières, which was, as far as I can remember, a series of large sandbars in open water with marsh grass and seagulls and empty plastic bottles and chip bags and cigarette butts and the crushed bodies of crabs and broken, salted branches. When Mr. George Sevin was a child, the old people drove their horses and buggies all the way to Caillou Island, fording the bay, which was shallow enough that it did not swallow man and beast. The shrimpers I talked to believe that the oil industry and the US Army Corps of Engineers are to blame for the erosion of their land. According to the conventional wisdom, the oil companies dug canals and allowed saltwater to enter the brackish and fresh estuaries inland. In addition, the levee system built by the Corps of Engineers prevents sediment from depositing, which would rebuild the coast as the Gulf reshapes it. The shrimpers see the commercial and governmental reshaping of their landscape as a profound and misguided reordering of a natural system. Their rage against this reordering is also a rage against their own precarity, hemmed in by the rush of water to the south and the relentless works of those would remake the sea into a colony of the land.

Oil and Water

The year is 1992 and the man wishes he were still a shrimper. It is four in the morning. The smell of the pogy plant lacquers the insides of his rusted-out Toyota pickup, gas-station coffee cooling in cups made from petrochemicals. The pogies in the factory rot on conveyor belts a hundred yards off, and their stink will settle into the vinyl and felt of the parked truck while the man sleeps on an oil production platform in the Gulf of Mexico. Each week when he returns, after driving three hours back to Chauvin with the windows down, the man's wife—who keeps her hands well-vinegared in the shrimp factory across from their small house—will not kiss him until he has rinsed the scent of pogy off of him. When he shrimped, his wife was with him, and they stunk together.

He goes to the heliport. There are men from nearby Eunice and New Iberia and Jeanerette and men—like him—from the bayou parishes of Terrebonne and Lafourche and Assumption. There are men from Dallas, Texas; and McDonough, Georgia; and Philadelphia, Mississippi. A sixty-year-old Black man who has never been and will never be hired as a company man, tries to lift his eyelids and fails. There are some white men by a freshly made canteen of coffee. They are large and boisterous. One—a redhead with glasses and clean overalls and clipboard—bellows a story about a certain type of industrial grease used on the platforms. The man remembers the story because he has told it himself: after a day spent cranking wrenches, a stupid, young coworker goes to take a leak, forgetting to wash his hands raw beforehand. He drives home, where he and his wife—well, you know. The next day, the woman complains of a funky discharge. Suspicious of her husband—who, it must be admitted, had a problem with infidelity—she seeks the counsel of a doctor. Everyone knows this bit, and they laugh the punchline into place. The sad hilarity of swapping fluids. The industrial slapstick.

It's the man's turn to tell a story. During his seven days off, he was putting up a fence around a backyard because his children were entering the age of walking too far. There comes—and this never happens, he swears in a way that implies that of course it always happens, we're in Louisiana for Christ's sake!—a gigantic alligator. Not being a man of the law, he had to act like a beast. He grabbed a barely used twelve-gauge shotgun and locked his tendons into a shooter's stance. His firstborn is with him. Strangely, people have gathered to watch as the man shoots at the alligator, and they clap when they see the geyser of blood spurt from the place where the buckshot tore a hole in its belly, flipping it over. It was a proud day of improbable ballistics, and the man might have ended it with a Southern and Seven had he not given up alcohol in 1988 after he killed a man he never knew while stoned on beer and Percocet. He brought his child inside and called Wildlife and Fisheries to dispose of the body. He hoped he wouldn't be fined for this, and he wasn't. You can kill an alligator if it threatens you. This is known as self-defense.

In the helicopter, the man floats over the coast, latticed with canals and pipelines. He floats over one hundred miles of water, to a scaffold of steel and oil that towers over the water. In another time, the man would have been on a boat burning cheaper fuel, collecting shrimp into a net to sell to families he had known his whole life. Instead of fulfilling what others in his hometown thought of as a blood vocation, he chose a world of metal islands that sucked the black blood of earth the way water is sucked through a straw. In his mind, this is still a world of water. The men on this platform in what is known as the Eugene Island field, check charts and valves and keep the pipeline clot-free. These are not the cowboy days of drills and the loss of limbs. The day starts at six in the morning and stretches to six in the evening, full of vigilance and boredom and answering alarms signaling that something is slightly off and the machines need tending. The man eats hearty meals cooked by a man who drives in to the heliport from the Westbank in New Orleans, the only African American on the platform. They watch hours of HBO and LSU football and cooking shows together. Onshore, the man will rent movies he watched offshore to share with his family. He leads a symmetrical life: one in the damp mud in which he and his family have planted themselves, living and dying in continuity with larger families and networks; the other in the Gulf of Mexico, where a new society is re-created week by week. He is a lead operator but not a foreman. When he's left in charge of his platform, his attitude shifts from deferential to commanding, and his favorite command is "Listen." He's a storyteller even though he is rarely a good listener, talking through his coworkers' stories, remembering details that were almost surely lost to time until the exact moment he recollected them.

Figure 24. Kurt (left) and Claude Lirette, 2015. Photograph by Emma Christopher Lirette.

Onshore, he's a storyteller (figure 24). He tells stories of the days when he was a drinking alcoholic. Of days when he trawled. Of days when his mother trapped furs during the winters when she was thirteen years old. Of days of labor and days of loss. Of days on a water teeming with life, not surrounded by a water from which he cannot harvest. These stories are the only way in which he connects to other people. He learned French not as a child (his parents kept the language to themselves, a private speech) but as an adult, working the trawls with older men who chose a life of water and fish over land and money. Still, he is embarrassed by his French, speaking only a few sentences that he's memorized well over the years, returning to the harbor of English once a conversation has moved into the realm of content. Over time, he has amassed hundreds of acquaintances whom he might readily ask for a favor. He rarely has use for favors owed.

His doctor, a man with whom he has a cousin-like relationship, looks forward to his visits except that it becomes clear over time that years of drinking have wrecked his body: he has cirrhosis, he has hepatitis C, he bleeds easily, and so forth. There's a tragic jocularity between them. The one man making light of his own frail body, almost (but not quite) desperate to please a man who has the kind of wealth and privilege the man sometimes (but not always) wishes he had. The doctor isn't sure what to make of the man, whether he and his sick body and his life of day-in, day-out toil are conspiring to tell the kind of joke a doctor would never understand or whether the man is like the doctor: precise and overflowing, in a state of constant repair, a person who by some grace became recognized by others as having the power to heal.

Back offshore, the barometric pressure is dropping. The horizon becomes as dark as the sea, and it is hard to see the jack crevalle skimming the surface of the Gulf. The waves are rough. They are sending helicopters to evacuate the platform because Hurricane Andrew is crossing Florida and coming to flood the man's home. He waits out the storm with his wife and two children about five miles north of their home, in the new house built at five feet above sea level in which his brother and his family reside. Though the land on which the eight-hundred-square-foot home stands is at four feet below sea level, it is raised up on stones. Flooding has more variables to factor than mere elevation: The strength of levee and pump. The slowing power of the barrier islands and the marsh and the cypress ridges. The height of the storm surge and tide. The precise location where the water tears a rift in the levee. The day after the storm, the man brings his family back to their house via pirogue—the road is flooded. Only a few houses lie between them and their first glimpse of what damage Andrew has wrought to their house when the flash of silver marks the passage of a fish from flood to boat. His wife screams with equal parts shock and delight. The children grab the fish and put it back in the water, and it swims away. Later, this memory will be the inverse of the day the floodwaters retreated: finding shovels so that his children could help him shovel rotten drums and redfish from the yard.

As soon as his household and hometown are in living condition, the man drives his truck to Intracoastal City to begin another hitch on an oil-production platform in the same waters that deposited fish in his yard.

This is the story of the shrimper's shadow, the offshore oilman, who decided at some point not to go down with the shrimp fishery, who found the possibility of making a living, a good living, on the water. Like the life of a shrimper, the life of an offshore oilman requires a dual living arrangement: life on land, life at sea. But unlike the shrimper, the oilman's time is precisely bisected, time here and time there demarcated, accounted for, adhered to with discipline. To work for the oil companies is to work for a vast and bureaucratic corporation, to be regulated vassals to a distant and potent political and economic machine that requires docile bodies to show up on time and not make a mess of the job. The job is, like the job of a shrimper, extractive. One pulls living bodies from the sea. One sucks the remains of bodies long dead from rocks. One extracts a commodity to sell on the open market. It would be easy to mistake the life of an offshore oilman for a seafaring life: it requires that people work, in this case, in the Gulf of Mexico. Like shrimping, working offshore is mostly a lonely world of men isolated from family and society. Like shrimping, the work of working offshore is simultaneously backbreaking and boring. It is unsurprising that shrimpers turn to oil when shrimp prices bottom out. According to Jill

Ann Harrison, who studied the industrial choices shrimpers made once it was clear that the industry was in decline, the oil field attracts shrimpers because they already have the necessary skill sets to be good workers.[1]

The year is 1956 and another man, an uncle of the man from 1992, wishes he had better equipment: an engine that didn't require so much wrenching, nets that didn't require so much mending, a bigger boat with better quarters, a taller draft, a more impermeable hull. He wishes his shovels didn't have pockets of rust brushing the tiny seabob shrimp with a faint red sludge. Seabobs are a species of small, unregulated shrimp mostly sold to shrimp-drying platforms and thence to Asian markets. They are called seabobs because their legs and antennae make them look as if they have six beards, *six barbes*. The man wishes the Chinese guy still owned that platform in Dulac. When he did, a man could make a living catching seabobs. But without the bigger engines and better nets and nicer boat and most of all a capable and willing crew, he can't compete with the slick skiffs crowding Lake Caillou and Oyster Bayou.

He heels his skiff against the wake from a ship. There is an oil well in Bay Sainte Elaine, and the way out to Caillou Island is perilous: the wash from the different industrial boats pushing schooners and skiffs onto banks and clumps of flotants, the sharp hulls of the ships cutting through skiffs darkly trawling the night waters, the sheen and rainbow of the oils they float on the water. The man's uncle, Nonc Natole, is a short man with ropy arms and a nut-brown face. One night he was out trawling out by Pass la Poule in Lake Pelto in a forty-foot skiff. He had a few deckhands with him, but maybe they were drunk or snoozing or playing a good game of Pedro while the night skimmers dragged the waters and collected the soft bodies of shrimp. A big ship with a sharp V-shaped hull cruised right through them, shattering Nonc Natole's boat. The guys on the ship, who were transporting something or other to a new oil rig beyond the islands, could barely see the half-drowned men, bobbing and splashing with the half-dead shrimp cut free of the nets, among the cypress splinters and diesel slick. The oil guys hauled them in, and the Coast Guard had to land them back home. You can't very well ask a big oil boat to turn back inland.

The next week, the man gets rid of his skiff and fills out an application in shaky ink. He isn't the first. Old man Tchonque had to sell his oyster leases to the Boudreaux Canal Store to get out of the debt accrued over years of not breaking even, keeping only the salt-cured camp and drying platform on a small, sandy island surrounded by a ditch he'd started calling the Cutoff à Tchonque. He was getting into carpentry with his son. This man has his eye on oil. Years of tuning his inboard skiff motor have turned his hands into an extension of a machine, fingers nimble enough to coax dead metal back to hot life. The next week, he's out on a rig with a roughneck's salary, overalls with his name embroidered on them, and a good hard hat. He's not even that far out, traveling by crew boat out of Morgan City, down to Vermilion Bay, near a peninsula called Cypremort Point. The man wonders why the hell somebody would name that spot Cypremort, which means "dead cypress" in French. But then again, he has buddies who come trapping almost as far west as Cypremort Point, and there are lots of strange names for the coves and cuts and bayous and lakes on the way, places that in English would mean Bayou Don't Touch Me and Mean Bayou and Bayou Carrion Crow. On the rig, the man lives in a world structured by tool and platform and hierarchy. Instead of himself or his daddy, he listens to the foreman. His main job is to change the oil on the engines, to keep the pistons lubed and pumping. The man would be happy with anything as long as it paid more than the $1,800 he made the previous year; he and his family had survived mostly on the shrimp he could barely sell.

It wasn't long before the Crown-o-Matic, a jaunty machine that keeps the drill block from hitting the crown block, cut off the fingers of his right hand.

The Crown-o-Matic needed to go higher, to give the drill block greater momentum when pounding the drill into the earth, and the man was the one with the right wrenches. He was hanging onto the drill line—a metal cable that guides the drill into the well—and was working the wrench with his other hand. Two bolts had to be loosened up to slide the block where you wanted it to go. But some guy threw the clutch while the man was holding onto the cable, and he couldn't let go. He would have fallen to the bottom, to the black and viscous underneath of the water. As he blacked out from loss of blood and shock and the ghost fire frying his lost fingers, the man was glad in that moment that he hadn't lost sight of land. The rig was within swimming distance of the Louisiana coast, and men covered in oil and gray silt and industrial lubricant ferried him into a small skiff. He regained consciousness in the back of a pickup truck before losing consciousness again; the next time he woke, it was to the blinding pain of a scour and water, knocking loose the dirt and sludge from his hand of stumps. He was in Lafayette, in a hospital, and it looked like he was going to survive—minus a few digits.

He lived the rest of his working life in shifts: seven on, seven off, fourteen on, seven off, and so on. He eventually switched over to a production platform, where injuries are often less grievous. Not content with the known oil field, his brother got hired on with Diamond M and pulled hitches in Cameroon for three months on, one month off. He saw the world, telling stories of the small oilfield villages he lived in outside of Douala, where everyone spoke French and he could collect buckets of oil cash. He had a boat, the *Blond and Clyde*, commissioned while he was in Africa and spent the shrimp seasons in Lake Tambour and Lake Barré, catching shrimp with his wife and oldest son. Sometimes the man would go with his brother, having learned how to shift his dexterity into his left hand, into his knuckles and wrist. He'd never lost the muscle memory, and he went to his bunk nursing the sore muscles of his ghost fingers. He didn't go back out west to Cypremort Point on these trawling trips. Once, as the *Blond and Clyde* turned east before Point à Mast, the man had an uncanny feeling. Ahead there was a *cyprière*, a cypress grove, on a nearly submerged island. All the cypress trees were black and dead.

As every conversation I had with commercial fishers turned to erosion and the necrotic turn in the ecosystem, I heard them blame one entity more than any other: oil. The older the fisher, the more venomous his accusation. After all, they had seen firsthand the death of the lands and waters on which they plied their living, on which they raised their families. Mr. George Sevin said, "The grass don't wanna grow. The dirt is so salty. It's been there just like if you had it in some big pits: in other words, it's brown water, salt. All over, you can pass over the bayou—that's what killed them trees. An oak tree is hard to kill, and they're all along the bayou. You can see them, they're all dead now. That's saltwater intrusion. It started around Betsy. That was '57–1957. The oil companies started before that."

The great canalization of the Louisiana coast sought to facilitate the transportation of goods and machines to a fledgling and highly profitable oil industry in the early twentieth century. But before that, fishers dug *trainasses* to get to more productive water. Before that, the planters and business owners affiliated with the production of sugar harvested by enslaved people dug canals to get the cane to the refineries. Before that, the Chitimachas and Houmas and the pre-Columbian inhabitants of the Louisiana coast shaped the land and water to make it easier for them to live. The difference with the oil industry is that the Louisiana coast had finally entered an age of mechanization and large-scale public works and federal subsidies for big businesses. The Houma Navigational Canal, begun in 1958 and opened in 1962, connected the Intracoastal Waterway, another federally maintained canal, to Cat Island Pass, the open waters between what is left of the Isles Dernières and the Timbalier Islands.[2] Shipping canals, however, are only part of the story. Mincing the coast are also twenty-five thousand miles of pipelines that transport oil and natural gas from reservoirs and wells to onshore processing facilities.[3] These pipes, embedded in swamp and marsh and seabed, required ditches to nestle in. Larger pipelines require full canals. Nearly fifty years of dredging and wash from barges has dissolved the fragile marshes. The canals to the Gulf welcome the Gulf inland. The Gulf becomes a maw, and its sharpest tooth, the hurricane, gnaws at the canals and widens them.

On April 20, 2010, the Deepwater Horizon oil rig exploded and coated Louisiana's coastal wetlands in oil, spoiling oysters, killing shrimp, smothering pelicans, and doing unknowable damage to the Gulf of Mexico. You would think that armed with the knowledge that the oil industry has mangled the coast with little regard for the collateral damage to canals and having lost legal and lobbying battles to require the companies that tore up the marsh to repair the land, the fishers would turn against the oil industry.[4] This is not the case. The fishers I spoke to, while unflinching in accusing big oil of gross, homicidal negligence, recognize the industry as an essential part of their livelihood. ChaCha Sevin, whose business was decimated during the oil spill, told me that President Barack Obama's six-month suspension of new oil drilling in the Gulf of Mexico following the oil spill was a mistake:

> As far as for the moratorium that the president put on offshore drilling, I mean that crippled us bad. You know it's coming back slowly, but you know and I was the first one that said they gotta cut that out, we don't need that. I mean, we could lose our livelihood completely, and then what would we do. But then once I realized what was taking place, well, if there's no drilling offshore with all these companies, then my business ain't gonna survive anyway. So yeah. If the oil spill would have never hit, I wouldn't have felt that or experienced that and realized it. That you need that industry. It's got to be there. It gives so many jobs, it's unbelievable. You know a lot of the products I buy to operate my business is made from petroleum, so without those products, I mean, I guess you'd find ways eventually, but without those products, you wouldn't make it.

What ChaCha realized, with the help of the strong oil lobby that helped characterize oil companies as benevolent masters and benefactors of the Louisiana coast, was that his whole life was infrastructurally linked to the oil industry. As Kate Orff argues, "Louisiana's natural geography has been radically repurposed into a vast network for extracting, storing, and transporting oil and natural gas." She argues that today's hunger for petroleum products, from plastics to fuel, have created a Petroleum Age wherein our primary modes of living are expressed through oil products.[5] Furthermore, in Terrebonne Parish, the proximity of the fishery and oil is highly visible: from oil field infrastructure cutting through the marsh to boat builders transitioning to welding for the companies servicing oilfield platforms. While ChaCha might be overestimating the deleterious effects of government regulation of the industry that doused his livelihood with oil, he is correct in observing that oil is an integral part of the economy in coastal Louisiana, where people regularly find refuge on oil platforms when other industries tank.

The damage the oil industry has wrought to the marsh, however, has invited the Gulf inshore, bringing with it the potential to swallow southern Louisiana, pipes and all.

Gulf

And we do know, don't we:
We will be overcome by waters
—Katie Ford, "Seawater, and Ours a Bed above It"

Witness the genius of the sea, raw and incoherent. Witness the theater of dissolution that commenced when machines carved straight lines from river to gulf. Witness the theater of grief: a place made living by story and the hope that memory brings, scoured of its human life. For fishers of the brackish marsh where the Louisiana land becomes water, home is a buoyant, watery thing, capricious and nurturing, precarious, renewable, and dangerous. To fish the waters is not only to be comfortable with uncertainty, it is to thrive on it, to author a place in a slippery world where success and family and the play of naming and forgetting, of mooring and unmooring, and the sweaty work of dragging things out of the depths must, deliciously, be balanced lest they blink out. The sea is simultaneously forgiving and unforgiving: it brings a source of protein that can feed and support, and it swells and brings death. The improvisatory spirit of the fishers I spoke to in lower Terrebonne, even in discussing the hard things, was joyful. I learned about the exuberant tricks fishers played on one another as they pursued what they believe is a nearly limitless resource. They pretended their engines were dead to gain better positions in choice trawling spots. They were taught to love a life that had goals but no clear path to reach them. One shrimper's father suggested that his son could not join him on the boat until he could rig a skiff. At eight years old, the boy figured it out. The shrimpers I know are full of stories like this. Witness the gulf of knowledge that can be overcome by testing it. Witness the theater of artifice where the sea and its joining with the land become a metaphor for identity and imagination.

Imagination plays a key role in holding together the incongruent desires, accidents of history, and potential futures in a fast-eroding place like the Louisiana coast.[1] Land, the blood of kin and story, and the structured histories handed down formally and informally are agents of the actual: anchors to a shared reality. The sea is a plane of the virtual, the possible, the vague threat, the hope of freedom. Imagination, in its capacity as alchemist of the actual and virtual, produces possibilities, possible stories, possible reorderings. What it does not produce are fixed artifacts or authority. As felt thought, imagination is both embodied and disembodied. It is playful. It moves. Like the estuary, the plane of imagination can flood, threatening to wipe out actuality. But the floodwaters can recede, leaving the landscape revised, transformed, capable of being rebuilt or reflooded. Thinking of imagination this way enables us to foreground the experience of life on the water as procedural, continually negotiating bodies and geographies and structures and institutions and stories both monumental and ephemeral. The shrimper, in contact with both land and water, in a place where the land turns to sand, turns to water beneath his feet, is constantly becoming. The encroachment of water, of the chaos of the virtual, that destabilizes the land can be a hard trial of disidentification, of being unmoored from the self.

Sociologist David M. Burley, who conducted a large-scale ethnographic study of those affected by coastal land loss in southern Louisiana, writes that "when people identify with and define natural places as being regenerative, the decimation of those places simultaneously erodes part of their own self-definitions."[2] In my interviews with shrimpers, I also found that people considered their environment regenerative. They were optimistic about the prospects of shrimp returning year after year. They were skeptical that their actions upset the ecology of the bayou. They considered the hazards of weather and flood to be nadirs on a cycle of death and rebirth. Their lives were pinnacles of the more pagan shades of Catholicism: a life of figurative death and resurrection, mirrored in nature, something both to surrender to and to alter with acts of creativity and will. South Louisianans, according to both Louisiana scholarship and themselves, are survivors.[3] How can they not imagine themselves as survivors? They have found a way not to tame the sea but to live with it. It would stand to reason that Burley's assessment is correct, that the deterioration of shrimpers' land is tantamount to the deterioration of their self-definitions. Though Burley's contribution to documenting the human toll of erosion and subsidence in coastal Louisiana is invaluable and I agree that this changing land changes identity, I disagree slightly with his interpretation of the relationship between coastal people and stable identities. Burley leans too hard on the fixity of identity and place, whereas these shrimpers have created and are actively creating their identities in relation to a place that they are continuously reworking. In other words, the relationship of place and identity is an unstable process of becoming.

In "Idea of Order at Key West," the singer on the coast does not reflect the senseless chaos of spray and wave, she creates it through her singing: "there never was a world for her / Except the one she sang and, singing, made."[4] Though the shrimpers I spoke to certainly imagine their environment as regenerative, it is their stories of survival that have made it so. One man with feet in both oil and seafood told me, "For the real shrimper, like Kim Guy and the ones who do it all their lives, the economy is gonna go up and down for them, but they never gonna give up. It's just something that's in their blood." The theme of blood destiny, discussed earlier, explores some of blood's valences as a governing metaphor. But blood is not the only polyvalent thematic at play: the water itself becomes place and ideal and an endlessly evocative image for the polyvocal imaginary of southern Louisiana. The economy becomes tidal: up and down. The "real" shrimper becomes *oceanic*: never yielding, vast in capacity, something that tides roll through but ultimately do not affect. Here we see the most potent external liquid transformed into the most potent internal one. Shrimpers spend their lives at sea, lost to the landed, who must submit to the tyranny of solid ground, and thus know something about staying the course, about adapting to changing currents and winds and ecosystems. Unlike the landed, the moored, shrimpers never ever get sick at sea.

What is terrifying to the shrimper is not a loss of identity but a loss of place. The processes of becoming are tied up in being able to change the place they are in. The shrimpers' amphibious place is unlike the place of people who live inland. Shrimpers have access to alternate forms of navigation, to a littoral ecosystem consisting of other life-forms that survive on the fringe, and if their characteristic is survivability, it is because they live in a place that is otherwise hostile to human civilization according to rational people.[5] The effects of a hundred years of unchecked land loss, saltwater encroachment, canalization, subsidence, and sea-level rise as a consequence of global warming are stripping coastal people of their liminal place and forcing them into fixity. Several fishers explained to me that a certain amount of saltwater encroachment—which kills salt-intolerant marsh grass, cypress trees, and oaks, whose roots hold the incontinent land together—actually benefited the fisheries by expanding the estuary. The resulting brackish water is necessary for shrimp, who take refuge in the estuaries to spawn. As the sea claims more and more land, amplifying the destructive potential of hurricanes, the landed fought back with stricter levees. As shrimper Steve Billiot told me,

> Now that they building the levee system—which is good because of the hurricane protection—they're stopping a lot of the water from shrimp migrating, so we're

catching less. And especially back in this area where I'm working at. They working right now, the trucks passing, they're building a dam, and they're building a levee system from Bayou Lafourche to Morgan City all the way towards the West. And that stops a lot of the water, which in turn is going to help the hurricane floodwaters so we don't get flooded out, which is good. But on the other hand you got to go where the shrimp are at, where normally we're catching them in my backyard. And that's a matter of speaking. I can leave my dock and go twenty minutes away and start making money. And now that the dam is there, the levee system, I have to go further out.

Once the levees are complete, it will become increasingly difficult to find the brackish water necessary for a shrimp population. The seawall imposes a fascist order: where once the sea transitioned to land, there is only sea, a demarcation, and land. Land, where people yet persist, is now governmentally the sea.

Nowhere is this principle more elegantly expressed than Benh Zeitlin's 2012 film *Beasts of the Southern Wild*. It was filmed in Isle de Jean Charles, a hyperprecarious stretch of road with houses on stilts and a startling lack of land, a few miles from Chauvin. In May 2016, the *New York Times* declared the inhabitants of the island America's first "climate refugees," as the US Department of Housing and Urban Development apportioned $48 million to resettle the community of Houma and Biloxi-Chitimacha-Choctaw Indians elsewhere.[6] The residents of the Bathtub, a fictional coastal village modeled on places like Isle de Jean Charles, have no such support. Instead, a hurricane comes and floods the Bathtub. This time, however, the floodwaters do not recede because the village lies outside an effective seawall levee, which echoes the real-life Morganza-to-the-Gulf project that similarly excludes Isle de Jean Charles from its perimeter of flood protection. The people of the Bathtub, floating on boats made from the beds of pickup trucks, punching catfish, and crushing crabs in their hands, exhaust their capacity to live at sea, having become accustomed to straddling water and earth. So they blow up the levee. Where once they were claimed by water, now they are claimed by the Federal Emergency Management Agency on behalf of the bureaucracy of humans. This, too, is untenable, and they escape their shelters to live and die in the muck.

This parable is made all the more poignant by the mythological point of view of its six-year-old protagonist and narrator, Hushpuppy, played by Terrebonne Parish native Quvenzhané Wallis. Hushpuppy, like the trope of the improvisational and scrappy fisher, can cope when the world is drowning. She knows how to eat the living meat of the waters. She knows how to make her way back home. But she is a six-year-old who has to face down death on multiple fronts: her erratic and dying father who tries to raise her to be muscular in a treacherous world, the daily chore of snuffing out the life of animals so that she might live, the sudden and severe flood that persists until her whole world is drowned. These confrontations with death are made manifest in the figure of the aurochs, a prehistoric bull that Hushpuppy imagines as a giant tusked pig, suddenly free from its glacier, stomping across the globe to wreak havoc on her. In the most iconic scene from the movie, Hushpuppy, a tiny child, looks into the eyes of the aurochs *and does not blink*. The aurochs turns away because this is a movie about hope, but the optics of beast versus girl makes stark the stakes of environmental cataclysm: the people outside the levees are precious and fragile, and they are fighting a chaotic and violent force that might as well be a god from an ancient story, a determined and unrelenting genius loci. The courage to face a destructive spirit and stake a claim on land soon to be called water is prideful and stupid. But it is also romantic, creative, thrilling, and generative. As Stevens writes, "It was her voice that made / The sky acutest at its vanishing."[7]

The plight of shrimpers and others who live on the edges of land, who have been facing routinized environmental disaster for a century or more, is perhaps a last stand against the oblivion of water. The eschatological truth is that coastal Louisiana will be overcome by water. Sooner or later, whether by erosion or subsidence or the rise of the sea, whether or not we mitigate the loss and restore the coast. It is tempting to see flaunting this inevitable fact by living persistently in quickly dissolving mud as a type of nihilism: a romantic and communal suicide, a captain and crew sinking with their ship. And to deny the pervasive melancholy that accompanies what I've been characterizing as joyful improvisation would be to deny the rich and contradictory feelings experienced by those who make their homes in disappearing places. Geographical philosopher Henri Lefebvre writes, "No space ever vanishes utterly, leaving no trace."[8] If the spirit of the coast is to live on, it will be through holding in suspension the devastation and possibilities of the Gulf as well as the structuration and networks of the land. The embrace of suspension and liminality in the littoral zone, the estuarial openness to contradiction and experience and self-mythologizing and self-effacement—these are strategies to cope with a globalizing world. These strategies recognize the doom and ecocide caused by a corporate and governmental rage to order and in seeing that failure trace the outlines of a ghostlier world, one still perilous but flexible enough to be livable.

NETS

In April in the bayou hamlets of lower Terrebonne Parish, thick, muscular fingers pinch ropes into knots, knots into nets. Hands scaly with callouses grip brush and roller, whitewashing the stained hulls of trawl boats. White paint speckles navy blue work coveralls, the one-piece long-sleeve uniform of mechanics and men older than thirty-five in Chauvin. Grease smears on everything: clothes, faces, roping, gears, pulleys, wrenches and plyers, the busted seats of old Dodge trucks, the Formica kitchen counters. It is a dirty time, and one that is urgent. The boats have been moored for a good four months of bad weather, and we know, thanks to William Butler Yeats, that things fall apart. Like the price of shrimp, which tumbled from $3.75 a pound to $2.85 in May 2015 and to $1.66 a year later.[1] Mechanical failure plus cheap shrimp might mean having to lean on a social safety net like food stamps or welfare. It might mean having to find something else to do entirely to make it through the year.

    Shrimpers, especially the ones on small vessels who trawl by season in inshore waters, have a narrow window of time in which they must harvest enough shrimp for a year's income. The waters beyond three nautical miles until the international limit at two hundred nautical miles, known as federal waters, can be trawled year-round but require a big boat, a crew, and an upfront investment in ice, fuel, and food that would set a captain back upward of $30,000. The state of Louisiana divides its waters into two regions: outside waters extend from the three-mile limit to the coastline, and inside waters are the waters inshore of the coastline. Generally, fishers can harvest shrimp from the outside waters from May until December, while the inside waters can only be fished during a brown shrimp season in May and a white shrimp season in autumn. Each year, the Louisiana Department of Wildlife and Fisheries sends out a cadre of scientists who cast nets into the fishing grounds and measure the shrimp they catch. These scientists and other government employees determine when and where to open the waters to trawlers. For many shrimpers, these bureaucrats, scientists, and policy professionals are the villains of the story.

Imagine you learned to drag nets from your daddy. He taught you about proper mesh size and throttle control. He taught you how to determine when to shrimp by feeling the *vents de Carême*, the winds of Lent. He taught you to divine where to drag by looking for muddy water, where frenetic shrimp activity sweeps the seafloor, creating pillars of underwater mud clouds. Your daddy himself learned these things at the knee of his daddy, who can remember standing chest-deep in a lake holding the end of a seine net and who could pick leeches off his ankles as casually as he might pick an orange, heavy and fragrant, off a tree. Imagine you remember going to your daddy's daddy's camp out on Lake Tambour. It was just a little cabin on pilings, and you could see marsh grass and waves if you pressed your eye to the cracks between wall planks. Your daddy was teaching you to fish for speckled trout, how to squeeze worms onto hooks, how to cast a line, how to jerk the pole to give a little extra life to the quartered worm. But what you remember most is your daddy's daddy, your pawpaw, in a ribbed white sleeveless undershirt tucked into pleated khakis, arms red until midway up his biceps, thick-framed glasses that magnified his green eyes, and a busted panama hat shading his face. After putting the fish in the ice chest just as the sun dipped below horizon, he would go out on the pier and light a kerosene lantern and hook it to a piling and light himself an unfiltered Parliament cigarette. You remember that once lit, the cigarette smoldered in the corner of his mouth, pluming smoke glancing off the side of his spectacled left eye. Shrimp would flick against the border between water and air, and your pawpaw dipped into them a long pole with a net at one end. That night, you, your daddy, and your pawpaw would eat shrimp heavily brined in salt and spice and boiled over a butane burner, then dipped into a mix of ketchup and mayonnaise brought with you in an ice chest. It was the beginning of April, still tolerable to sleep in a cabin in the marsh. You loved the way the world looked lit by kerosene and filtered through the mosquito netting hung over your bunk. And you loved listening to your daddy and pawpaw speaking to each other in hushed French, fragments of which you'd whisper to yourself later. *Là, la merde a pris. C'est pas de quoi.* You couldn't quite understand what they were saying, but you imagined it to be some kind of secret method to catching shrimp, some kind of sacred knowledge that you were confident, if you could get better at worming hooks, they would pass on to you one day.

Now imagine that after a lifetime on a boat, the wealth of intergenerational fishing knowledge quickening your muscles and tendons to efficiently pull thousands of shrimp from the water, you get an envelope full of new rules about shrimping. Imagine that officers from a government agency interrupt your rough ballet of raising nets and releasing a catch and culling and icing and steering and navigating. They want to make sure you are not keeping the speckled trout caught by your trawl. Imagine them inspecting your nets to determine the appropriateness of your mesh size—a mesh you learned by manipulating the cords with your fingers, a mesh you would never have considered measuring. Why would you? Your daddy made nets this way and still does, even though he is no longer as seaworthy as he used to be. Each year, you catch a lot of shrimp. Each year, you feed your family with the proceeds from all that shrimp. Imagine another document sent to you requiring you to cut open your nets and install a turtle excluder device (TED). Sure, you've caught a turtle or two in the last twenty years of trawling. One was so big you kept it and got your brothers and in-laws to come out on the boat to pose with it while your wife took a few Polaroids of you men and your big reptile. You cannot imagine that catching a turtle every now and then is really that big a deal. If you catch one, nine times out of ten you are going to eat it anyway if it's dead. If not, it goes back in the drink. But you can imagine the problem of creating an escape hatch in a net. Each trawl will now yield less shrimp, so you will have to work harder and longer to maintain your income. You wonder when having to wait for and receive mail became a crucial part of a career you chose precisely because it licensed you to work with your hands, to be your own boss. You suppose it happened gradually as a governmental body claimed more and more parts of your business.

The worst of it, growing angrier every time you remember it, is that your knowledge of time and ecosystem, the secret, sacred knowledge your dad did eventually pass on to you—in English—a few years after your pawpaw died, this knowledge is now worthless. Instead, you are instructed when to shrimp and when not to. At first it was April 15 through June. Then the opening of the spring shrimp season crept toward May. You hear about the scientists this and the scientists that, but you know in your heart that these people cannot know what you know because you know the things you know because you have a hundred years of practice: you, your daddy, your pawpaw, his daddy. It's in your blood to know. You do not need a measurement because you were taught to be responsible and not to catch tiny shrimp. Who would you sell them to anyway? You feel caught in a net thrown by strangers. Any way you try to move just makes that net tighter. And you know who cast that net. The Bureau of Wildlife and Fisheries. The State of Louisiana. The United States of America. Politicians. Global fishmongers who have lately brought in foreign shrimp that sell for less than the ones caught in American waters. The wound of taking your inherited knowledge away from you and replacing it with regulation mailed to you, regulation you basically paid for when you bought your commercial fishing license, is raw and achy, and it makes you want to wrangle your kids and wife and parents onto the boat and drift away from land for good.

But that network, the one comprised of your family and your obligations to them and the love for them that threatens to spill over into a protective wrath against the institutions that harm them by restricting you, prevents you from quitting this land. You want them to live and live well. You want your kids to join the social networks you will always be excluded from if they want to and can work hard enough. You want your town to survive and have festivals and fresh seafood and sport fishing. You want grandchildren who can come visit from Houston or Atlanta or, God forbid, New York City, and see the kind of man you are: one who can competently seize a life worth living from a wild environment, who can manage to live despite constant interference, who can demonstrate his love by passing on useful knowledge and good food. And the only way to achieve this, to secure the webwork of your family and their security, is to work and work hard and work happily. On days when you've finished your painting for the day or had to stop rigging the nets because of a flash downpour, you stop by your daddy's, where he sits under the carport in an old white undershirt tucked into khakis, bifocals sliding down his nose as his still-nimble fingers weave the shuttle between cords, knotting together a net. He reminds you of this lesson, his most important: just keep working.

Networks, those assemblages of decentralized nodes that connect people in varying configurations, can also do things that nets do: capture, bind, harvest. Shrimpers, like anyone, belong to a series of overlapping and sometimes contradictory networks that when properly identified can invite a host of constricting actions. Governing bodies regulate the networks, familial bonds discipline them, scholars study them. The first chapter in this section, "Ghost Nets," traces shrimpers' struggles against a constricted life. During my fieldwork and in my conversations with commercial fishers over a life lived among them, fishers consistently complain about governmental interference with their trade. Whether it's TED requirements or the micromanagement of fishing seasons and zoning, shrimpers feel trapped in a net cast from afar. They know their acts of resistance (disregarding seasonal limits, selling dead shrimp off a bait license, using nets without bycatch release devices, protesting certain regulations) amount to little even if they somehow escape the notice of the water police. Although the shrimpers resist, they miss the diffuse controls that continue to ensnare them. The following chapter, "Miraculous Draught of Fish," argues that despite these networks of control, shrimpers model a form of living and working that offers small-scale, local strategies of survival. Shrimpers know that there is only one thing they can do if they want to maintain their livelihood in the shrimp fishery: keep working and bending to the movements of various nets that seek to constrict them. At the same time, these shrimpers are weaving nets of their own, nets of work and family and the shared experience of living in a landscape. Although shrimpers feel moored by obligations and family ties, they rage most against the encroachment of governmentality and capitalism in every facet of their life. In their struggle against a master narrative of the American good life, they collect in their nets the ingredients that make it possible to imagine a life lived otherwise: a life of connection, of networks of support and responsibility, a life worth living even if it is impossible.

Ghost Nets

In the early 1860s, the "President of the Fisherman of the North Coast" of England, Richard Crick, recognized the deep danger of the trawl:

> The ever-gaping jaws of this life-destroyer thus receives everything that is loose in the bottom of the sea. Living and dead fish, pieces of stone, iron and coals, masses of sea weed and spawn, and the bones of many a shipwrecked mariner, who lies "nine fathoms deep" in the dark blue sea, and other relics which the storm has laid beside them, are all jolted along together until the net is filled with this *debris* of the ocean.[1]

To trawl is to strain the sea through mesh, collecting its solids. Crick describes bottom trawling, where the net rigging skims the seafloor, and his concern as a line fisher was the mechanical and industrial processing of sea life, which can be a grisly affair: the delicate bodies of fish crushed against other bodies, some delicate, some with the toothy carapaces of crabs. The expanding weight of the collection churns the first-caught to fishy gristle. Crick uses the imagery of the indiscriminate maw of the trawl to attack a problem that governmental bodies still grapple with today: the possibility that individual fishers will catch too many fish. A net, the primary tool of the fisher, becomes a weapon against a suddenly endangered ecology. To be "caught in a net" is a metaphor we use to mean haplessly trapped, to become entangled in a situation one entered without a larger systematic understanding of what is going on, to be stuck in such a way that becoming unstuck is increasingly improbable the longer one is stuck.

For the shrimpers I spoke to, freedom functions both as a core value and as one of several justifications for working in the fisheries. Kim Guy told me that he loved "to come do this": "I mean, [you're] your own boss. You don't have nobody fussing you in the back and say 'Aw, you gotta go do this. Aw, you gotta go do that.' You go when you want, and you come back when you want. You know what you have to do to make your bills and what you have to do to survive. You want it, you gotta go get it." Kim loves working the nets and traps in the estuary and Gulf because it is a way of living free of surveillance, of nagging, of proscribed rules of labor. Kim's tone is matter-of-fact, but it also contains a whiff of disdain for people who need the comfort of management. For Kim, freedom means relying on his own competence to ensure that he and his family survive. It means not being subject to external discipline, not being enclosed in a physical space. It means choosing to do something instead of consenting to follow the orders of a superior. The mere freedom of democratic society—wherein one can vote for leaders and at least theoretically participate in governance as an equal to others—is insufficient for Kim. His idea of freedom is deeper than legal guarantee. Theodor Adorno and Max Horkheimer critique the notion of freedom in free democratic societies: "Formal freedom is guaranteed for everyone. No one has to answer officially for what he or she thinks. However, all find themselves enclosed from early on within a system of churches, clubs, professional associations, and other relationships which amount to the most sensitive instrument of social control."[2] Instead of a formal freedom, Kim and other shrimpers desire a formless one, a state of being left alone. Specifically, Kim resents what Michel Foucault would call disciplinary power: a technology of control that produces individual subjects of the state by shuffling bodies from one enclosed space to another—the school, the factory, the prison—where people conform to schedules of activity and hierarchies through a process of normalization.

Though Kim, at least as an adult, embraces the enclosed system of the church, he trawls to escape from spaces of normalization. The specter of formal schooling surfaces in conversation with him as simultaneously irrelevant and perhaps a little ludicrous: it is an artificial system that threatens to supplant the improvisatory learning of experience and the sacred exchange of techniques passed through kinship. Like other shrimpers, Kim said that he could not wait to get out of school and go out shrimping, which he did with his family during school breaks. When he speaks of his son, T-Kim, and his embrace of schooling, Kim becomes simultaneously self-deprecating and defensive. T-Kim was studying computer science, and Kim claims to "not know what that is," although he clearly does: "We wasn't raised with that! So we don't really got no use for it, for us!" Kim also recounts a story familiar not only to the other shrimpers I spoke with (who repeated a version of this narrative) but also to anyone who has studied the historically francophone populations in southern Louisiana: his parents, raised in French, had to learn English once entering the school system. While Kim did not explicitly describe that process, I know from both my family's stories and from the scholarly record that French was basically beaten, physically and emotionally, out of francophone children in early twentieth-century Louisiana.[3] Figured as a site of humiliation, schooling takes the unruly tongue and kneads it into something "normal," takes the body and breaks its rough edges against a clock, locks children made docile into a place away from their families, depicted as a receding yet primary form of natural support and knowledge. While the machine of mandatory schooling in the early twentieth century may have processed most children into modern American subjects—prepared to function in other enclosed and disciplined spaces like offices and factories—for men like Kim, disciplinary institutions such as education and wage labor are intolerable. For Kim, these places might as well be their logical extension: the prison.[4]

When I arranged meetings with Kim, I never talked to him directly. Even being accessible by phone was too limiting. His wife, Melissa, brokered the interview. My brother and I arrived right after dawn at Kim's house. Two little boys hid behind pilings and each other, watching us. They had spent the night at Pawpaw Kim's house but decided not to make a run when they heard there would be some strangers aboard. When I interviewed Kim in 2015, it was just before the opening of the inshore shrimp season, and so we went crabbing with him. Though crabbing does not take Kim into the open waters of the Gulf, he enjoys the flexible mobility the fishing life affords him. He is not bound by geography. Whereas fishers might sell closer to their home, Kim sells to a dock in the neighboring village, Dulac, a straight shot across Lake Boudreaux by boat. Instead of a proscribed procedure for his trade, he decides who gets his business. When I asked if Dulac's market was especially good, Kim did not respond directly but merely said that he had been selling there for almost twenty years. Even the invisible hand of the market seems unable to pin him down.

Kim briefly held a "regular" job on one occasion, but he lasted no more than a month. He explained, "Life on [my] boat is so much easier. I stayed on a tugboat for about a month, just staying—you don't enjoy yourself." Though it is initially difficult to see how life on his boat could be so different from life as a paid tugboat captain, to him, the aesthetic of life on the water is defined by freedom and flexibility, while the aesthetic of the land is enclosure and obstacle and discipline. Kim says, "If you on a job, you gotta stay on the job, wherever they tell you, you gotta be at." In his eyes, working on a tugboat is no different than working at a factory or sitting in a classroom. Regardless of the scenery, there is still no freedom to move.

Almost all the shrimpers I spoke to had a similar story. Steve Billiot, who moonlights as an Elvis impersonator (figure 25), makes the same gestures

Figure 25. Steve Billiot as Cajun Elvis, 2015. Photograph by Emma Christopher Lirette.

against both schooling and wage labor. He told me outright that he did not like school and that from an early age, he wanted to shrimp for a living. His wife, Connie, however, is from the Westbank of New Orleans, and she at first refused to move with Steve "down the bayou," so he tried to make a life onshore. He worked in a shipyard for six months, then worked on tugboats on the Mississippi River, and then tried truck driving—a progression from enclosure to mobility. The shipyard kept him stationary, working factory-style labor, punching a time clock. To escape, he thought that captaining a tugboat would afford more mobility and autonomy as well as keep him close to the water. When that, too, proved too constricting, he piloted a big rig, traversing a greater geography. But even with the full network of the United States interstate highway system his domain, he could not escape the directives of a boss and the responsibilities to a company not his own. Eventually, he convinced Connie to move with him to Montegut, where Steve could shrimp the inshore waters in a sixteen-foot skiff (figure 26). He traveled greater physical distances on the tugboat and in the eighteen-wheeler, and he almost certainly made more money in any of those jobs than he did when I talked to him in the lean spring shrimp season of 2015. What he did not have, however, was a sense of absolute freedom, of self-direction, of being able to check out and be obliged to no one but himself and Connie and their children. His wife does not work outside the home. During the off-season, Steve refurbishes busted and abandoned skiffs to sell to other fishermen.

Figure 26. Steve Billiot aboard his boat, the *Lady L*, 2015. Photograph by Emma Christopher Lirette.

Talking to Steve does not reveal the amount of scrambling it must require for him to make enough money to support himself and his wife. (Their children are now adults.) I met Steve after he performed as "Cajun Elvis" with a band at Chauvin Fest, a festival I cofounded. He was lobbying to be booked for the following year's festival. Within five minutes, he was showing off a picture of himself lying on a big haul of shrimp in his little boat. An active member of a Native American tribe, the United Houma Nation, he plays family reunions and clubs and other events that require an ethnically specific Elvis. He and his wife restore antiques. They also collect and curate the faux Nudie suits and sunglasses and wigs and sequined shrimp boots that comprise his Elvis costume. While Steve does not exactly enjoy a life of leisure, his easy, garrulous, and friendly attitude makes it seem as though he does. And he indeed sees it that way. He describes rebuffing telemarketers selling cruises by telling them that he already goes on cruises six months out of the year. This is not to say that Steve is naive about the shrimp fishery's decline or the political and infrastructural challenges to his way of life. He told me, "the shrimping industry here where I work in the back of the Terrebonne area is—it's coming to an end."

When I asked shrimpers about the problems facing the shrimp fishery, they responded with the claustrophobic sense of a person hopelessly entangled in a net. A net is a liquid cage: adapting and flowing around the borders of a body. The shrimpers' most acute frustration was not a consequence of the eroding land transforming their fishing grounds, of the toxins and oils spilled into the water by careless corporations, or even really of the foreign farmers whose chloramphenicol-marinated shrimp led to the decline in shrimp prices. According to former shrimper Glynn Trahan, "The biggest problem is the government taking over and telling you what you can and cannot do." Over the course of several meetings, Glynn grew most angry when telling me the myriad ways the government mismanaged the fishery: it enforces turtle excluder devices (TEDs) for trawlers,[5] it stipulates the opening and closing of seasons, and it enforces catch-size limits: "There's a lot to be said about the government. They control our livelihood. They say when we can go shrimping and when we got to stop." One of the great appeals of the shrimping life, the freedom to be one's own boss, is thwarted by regulation. These regulations appear as a perpetual course correction. The shrimpers outfit their boats and gear a certain way and form habits of movement, but then they need to conform to a new protocol incrementally different from the previous one. Once shrimpers adapt to the second protocol, governing bodies that have been monitoring the effects of the change in terms of safety, environmental impact, and economics refigure the protocol yet again and disseminate the new correct way to shrimp. The shrimpers are free in a sense: they can still shrimp, but they must do so within parameters that are constantly assessed and adjusted.

One clear example of this kind of control mechanism involves the requirement that commercial fishing vessels install automatic identification systems. Since February 26, 2016, boats have been required to have devices that provide a variety of information, including name of boat, type of vessel, position, course, and speed.[6] Also, captains of vessels that trawl in federal waters may be selected to participate in the National Marine Fisheries Service's electronic logbook program, which transmits location data to be used to determine fishing effort, estimate landings and incidental sea turtle and red snapper mortality due to bycatch, and generally monitor boats' locations.[7] Despite my alarm at this rule (*surveillance state! panopticon!* I whisper-shouted to myself), shrimpers were nonplussed when I asked about it. They did not feel this geocoordinate system of surveillance infringed on their freedom in the way that TED regulations did. This kind of control masquerades as technology and safety and is ultimately an invisible part of a paradigmatic shift in how social controls manifest. Global positioning—specifically its use in tracking—is precisely the technology Gilles Deleuze writes about in his short essay "Postscript on the Societies of Control." Citing Félix Guattari, Deleuze describes a city where access is controlled by an electronic card: "What counts is not the barrier but the computer that tracks each person's position—licit or illicit—and effects a universal modulation."[8] This technology is not being used to limit a boat's mobility—yet. Deleuze's point is not only that this tracking technology could be used to control the movement of individuals but that the technology of control itself changes the possible ways people might be manipulated, often invisibly, by corporate entities. Such techniques of control, Deleuze argues, *divide* the individual into different data points (such as location, productive potential, buying habits, participation in politics) that can be continually adjusted. Automated and distributed surveillance replaces the institutional gaze that controls human activity in discrete space and time. A society of control is a network comprised of intersecting nets, capturing and culling, cast by coalitions formed by the merging of government and corporation and family and religion—institutions broken apart by changing paradigms in technology, economics, and politics.

Deleuze expands on Foucault's conception of the shifting character of power from sovereign power to disciplinary and biopolitical power with a brief description of a society of control. In a sovereign society, the state in the figure of the monarch exercises power to end life. In a disciplinary society, the state in the figure of institutions makes individuals adapt to constraints in a series of enclosed spaces (the school, the factory, the hospital). In a society of control, institutions are in crisis, and people are divided into subindividual qualities that become data. In this type of society, control is diffuse (coming not necessarily from the state but also from corporations and complex industrial-governmental networks) but targeted (able to pinpoint granular, subindividual qualities to transform or keep static). Deleuze writes, "Enclosures are *molds*, distinct castings, but controls are a *modulation*, like a self-deforming cast that will continuously change from one moment to the other, or like a sieve whose mesh will transmute from point to point."[9] Controls are technologies that shape our free movement, that conform to our unique bodies, that subdivide us into modular keywords that can be manipulated piecemeal. Controls are like a sieve that behaves like a net, a matrix that culls certain data into a dataset and releases the irrelevant rest. Kim and Steve and the rest of the shrimpers who romanticize their free lives feel the tug of this net from time to time without feeling disciplined by a society that would normalize them into the productive citizens of an industrialized state.

Although the shrimpers I spoke to mostly identified governmental intrusion as the foil to their freedom, industry regulations are not controls in the Deleuzian sense. They are still exercises of power characteristic of disciplinary societies: they define the limits of the normal with sanctions. Shrimpers bristle at the rules set forth by Louisiana Wildlife and Fisheries or the US Department of the Interior, rules which, in the most generous reading, intend to promote life—the lives of shrimpers and the lives of the animal populations that sustain them. These efforts to shape lives are visible, enforced with citations and policing. The real danger is in invisible control: ghost nets. A ghost net is a net that has been severed from its fishing vessel, floating unclaimed in the open waters. You feel a ghost net when you are cruising along in a Lafitte skiff, throttle open wide, and your motor lurches and whines, tossing you against the steering wheel, as you drift to a stop. Your propeller catches the invisible net underwater, but you do not need to see it to resign yourself to a ruined motor as you are stranded somewhere off the coast with a hold full of fast-decomposing sea life. We might think of the controls that mold the actions of shrimpers as a ghost net: free-floating, distributed technologies that form as other institutional forms of power break apart, creating an illusion of self-directed freedom while snaring us just underneath our vision.

Two ghost nets tangle up the livelihoods of shrimpers in coastal Louisiana: limited access to knowledge and indebtedness. Both of these nets are remarkably flexible, able to shape the behavior of shrimpers in invisible ways. They haunt the workspace like a whisper that is just too low to hear beneath the roar of the diesel engine. They lie in wait, ready to loose havoc in some cases and in others to confine a person until the water slowly, imperceptibly rises overhead.

Ghost Net One: Limiting Knowledge

Shrimpers feel rejected and confused by the way the state chooses scientific knowledge over the experiential knowledge of the workers in the fishery. They have no input over the body of knowledge that will govern them. Deleuze agrees: "The numerical language of control is made of codes that mark access to information, or reject it."[10] On Good Friday 2015, I sat with Glynn Trahan under his carport and talked about this very subject. We started the morning in a pond about an eighth of a mile behind his house, where he pulled from the shallow brown water traps clicking with crawfish. His son had a sack and carried the shelly life away to boil for a midafternoon meal. In Chauvin—and I suspect elsewhere in Catholic Louisiana—Good Friday is observed by eating crawfish boiled in spice and salt and then dipped in a mix of mayonnaise and ketchup and drinking Miller Hi-Life beer—enough of each to put you in a food coma until the Easter Vigil Mass. The Catholic Church says that Good Friday is an obligatory day of fasting and abstinence, meaning a day with only one meal and no meat.[11] Crawfish does not count as meat. Glynn has a foot in several nonmeat recreational fisheries—crawfish, shrimp, crab, finfish—but now derives his income from alligator hunting and hosting alligator-hunting events for vacationers. Since alligator season is only the month of October, he seems to be semiretired, spending his days how he sees fit, which generally consists of pursuing wild animal protein.

Under the carport, surrounded by manicured lilies and saw palmetto, Glynn rocked on his swing, telling me of the olden days, when ducks were so thick on the ground you could meet your limit with only a tennis racket. He was fifty-four at the time of the interview, but his flat Cajun accent was about as thick as the accent of my francophone grandparents. Unlike ChaCha Sevin, a bait shrimper who trawls daily to supply recreational fishers with shrimp and who had a sinewy and mournful muscularity, Glynn was gregarious. He was not a hungry man. His life was one of recreation and projects. He had four children, only one of whom worked in the fisheries. His rambling conversation style was accommodating, aided no doubt by the fact that he went to high school with my uncle and knew my family well. He was so disarming in person that I did not realize until going back through my recordings that his distrust of institutional knowledge was so great that he insisted on fantastic counternarratives that seem to have only a tenuous mooring in reality. He was the only shrimper I spoke to who repeated the conspiracy theory that the federal government had jammed through TED legislation in the 1980s and 1990s by planting sea turtles so that they would end up in shrimpers' nets.[12] He also told me that one of the reasons he refrains from eating foreign shrimp is that he believes that "foreigners"—here he invokes by name the Islamic State of Iraq and Syria (ISIS)—are trying to kill us, and imported shrimp would be a suitable vector for poison.

Although he exists on the periphery of the commercial fisheries, Glynn was by far the most suspicious of the fishers I interviewed of the government and its various technologies of disciplining the populace. In between dreamy descriptions of the disappearing wetlands, he complained about a set of laws and regulations at the state and federal level known as compensatory mitigation.[13] These rules intend to offset potential coastal loss with a series of consequences—including fines, infrastructural development, and injunctions—for land-damaging projects. As a man with an interest in turning his land into a Louisiana paradise replete with crawfish ponds, deer pens, and boat launches, Glynn regularly runs afoul of mitigation laws. He recognizes the dangers of erosion, a process he keenly and personally feels—a nagging emptiness that colonizes his memories of a good life on the bayou with his family. But he does not think the government is the best steward of a life and landscape he can feel sifting through his fingers. He told me,

> The government has got involved so much in this, you know, trying to regulate, trying to do what they think is best. And sometime it's hard to see that they're doing the right thing. If you get older people here, get the older people who've been doing this and seen everything from year to year, that's the people who ought to be making decisions on the fisheries and whatever, because I think that's the smartest people, you know: they've seen over the years what's going on, how it can be fixed or whatever needs to be not done so we don't continue having the problem we're having.

The "problem we're having" is not only the specific hardship of the 2015 shrimp season but also the general decline of the fisheries and the loss of coastal land. He rejects the expertise of government scientists. He knows how to manage his land. His grandfather knew how to manage his land. They know because they live a life intimately, ecologically enmeshed with that land. ChaCha, who has a larger stake in the shrimp fishery than Glynn, echoes this sentiment after telling me his solutions for ensuring a thriving fishery: "You know this is just my opinion. I'm not a biologist. I'm not one to make the decision on what needs to be done, but with my years of doing only commercial fishing, for forty years, as a kid growing up, you'd think that someone who has that experience—you should take their opinion seriously." Shrimpers know what is in the water because they have dipped their nets in it and pulled out what was there to see. They know what happens when too many shrimpers lower their nets in a small area. They know the salinity encroaching landward is killing the plants that hold the earth together, letting clumps of mud release into the sea. They cannot abide people who have spent their lives indoors except when they are gathering data and do not believe that they can truly understand the magic of being connected to a place or the threats that menace that magic.

Anthropologist Tim Ingold, in an homage to Martin Heidegger, might say that Glynn operates from a "dwelling perspective." Ingold defines this perspective as one in which "the forms people build, whether in the imagination or on the ground, arise within the current of their involved activity, in the specific relational contexts of their practical engagement with their surroundings."[14] In other words, people can properly build something, manage space, only if they are embedded in the complex network of people, landforms, animals, plants, and things in a given locality. The intrusion of regulatory apparatuses from outside, engineered by scientists who may be abstracting conclusions from faraway experiments, is an act of condescension and colonization. In his lecture "Dwelling Building Thinking," Heidegger weaves a network of etymological claims that links *Bauen* (German: building) to *buan* (Old English: to dwell) and *bin* and *bist* (German first- and second-person singular forms of *sein*: to be). In doing so, he argues that to dwell is to abide, to cultivate (to build), and to *be*: "What then does *ich bin* mean? The old word *bauen*, to which the *bin* belongs, answers: *ich bin, du bist* mean: I dwell, you dwell. The way in which you are and I am, the manner in which we humans are on the earth, is *Buan*, dwelling. To be a human being means to be on the earth as a mortal. It means to dwell. The old word *bauen*, which says that man *is* insofar as he *dwells*, this word *bauen* however *also* means at the same time to cherish and protect, to preserve and care for, specifically to till the soil, to cultivate the vine."[15] Dwelling, for Glynn, is distinctly Heideggerian: to be in place is to live, to live is to cultivate his life through an encounter with the land, to dwell is to be. A deep nostalgia and yearning for an authentic life wounds Glynn, propels him to build camps, transform land into crawfish pounds, equip a Lafitte skiff for recreational trawling long after he left the shrimp fishery.

One of the most interesting metaphors Heidegger uses in his discussion of dwelling is that of the bridge. People can build a bridge only if they have a deep, intimate relationship between dwelling and place. The bridge organizes wild nature into places. According to Heidegger, the bridge "does not just connect banks that are already there. The banks emerge as banks only as the bridge crosses the stream. [...] With the banks, the bridge brings to the stream the one and the other expanse of the landscape lying behind them. It brings stream and bank and land into each other's neighborhood. The bridge *gathers* the earth as landscape around the stream."[16] Rather than being a logical connection between two places, the bridge *creates* the places it connects. We could say that the bridge is a type of net: a way of harvesting meaning from an undifferentiated nature. For Glynn, this makes it all the more odious when the Army Corps of Engineers dictates infrastructural projects in a landscape already made meaningful by structures built by people who dwell there. The disconnect between knowledge informed by dwelling and the abstract knowledge of government and university scientists creates the possibility that new structures—such as canals, floodwalls, levees, land augmentation—not only bulldoze local input but threaten the legibility of the land. In this story, you don't leave home; home leaves you. And you watch, small and angry, as the land on which you staked the authenticity of your life erodes underneath your feet.

Heidegger, not writing in English, neglected to trace the strange origin of *dwelling* in English. The word *dwell* comes to us from Old English, in which it means "to lead into error, mislead, delude; to stun, stupefy." It began to mean "to tarry, delay; to desist from action" after borrowing the meaning of the Old Norse word *dvęlja*, "to retard, delay." From here, we arrive at the modern meaning of living in a home.[17] To dwell in the old sense was to err. In 1933 Heidegger erred in joining the Nazi party and subsequently implementing Nazi policies as rector of the University of Freiburg. He spent his summers dwelling in a chalet in the Black Forest, becoming ahistorical and rooted. The romance of origin, homeland, and the "simple" life of self-sufficiency in a secluded patch of earth lends Heidegger's phenomenology of dwelling a fascistic stink. It is not hard to see a similar autochthony in Glynn's testimony. When he describes the intrusion of government regulation, the arm of state bureaucracy is an invading army. He is suspicious of foreign shrimp not only because the aquacultural practices in Southeast Asia might involve dangerous antibiotics and human rights abuses but because he believes that imported shrimp might be a vector for the violence of foreign-born terrorism. I asked him how Chauvin has changed over the years, and in addition to the narratives of changing industries and receding land, he cites the main problem being one of drug addiction: "You know, the people doing all the drugs, the crack and the heroin—that's people not from around here." This dwelling perspective, the valorization of local knowledge over institutional knowledge, this longing for a life free from governance and public responsibility—these qualities can easily tumble into a nativism that is stubborn, reactionary, and incommunicative. This dwelling, if we are to take at face value Heidegger's conflation of dwelling with building and being, can also invite delusion, error. It can stun us, freezing us in an imagined home that has always been out of our grasp. It can stupefy us.

The mistrust of institutions and their disciplinary power fuels the dwelling perspective characteristic of fishers in Chauvin. Driving down the winding two-lane highway along Bayou Petit Caillou, you cannot help but feel the sepia bleeding from old photographs into the atmosphere. If you look closely, you can read the old signs over closed shops even though the letters have long since been swept away in some hurricane, the outlines etched into the paint by generations of sunlight. Everyone seems old. At the end of my first meeting with Glynn, he brought me inside his house to see old photographs of his grandparents that he wanted digitized and enlarged and framed for the wall in a recreation room. My dad collects old photos of people in Chauvin, and so I acted as his proxy once the anthropology part of the meeting was over. But his urge to collect the traces of the olden days was infectious. You can go into Glynn's yard and find decorative bits of old farm machinery. The cement slab under my dad's raised house is an archive, *en plein air*, of jukeboxes, antique boats (some pulled from the bottom of the bayou), the metal Christmas trees that used to top decommissioned oil wells, nineteenth-century Singer sewing machines, MG convertibles, and the cypress he pulled from the houses where his parents' friends lived when they were alive. A rust and rot museum of old Chauvin. In Chauvin, you feel that you are just beyond the reach of an institution like a government. You feel the weight of dwelling and creating your own systems of knowing.

Perhaps the sequestering of administrative knowledge in environmental reports and census statistics invites the fishers of Chauvin to more fiercely entrench in a dwelling perspective. Though both the Louisiana Department of Wildlife and Fisheries and the US Army Corps of Engineers conduct outreach, often through programs like Sea Grant, gates to information still lock out shrimpers. These gates often manifest as lacks: a lack of educational attainment, a lack of scientific or political literacy, a lack of receptiveness to governmental and media communications, a lack of capital, a lack of time. To be in the know, as far as it matters for the regulatory functions of state knowledge, one must not spend one's days on a boat, trawling in a nostalgic haze or in the sharp muscularity of hauling in a net full of shrimp. The dwelling perspective becomes too minute, and the myopia of shrimpers makes them easier to manage. Although they are building structures, both real and imagined, from their engagement with the local environment, they cannot see beyond its horizon to the forces that steer them. They are still resisting in the older way: against enclosure, attempting to escape to a plane of nautical mobility, to rebel against sanctions when they are imposed, to skipping out of schools and quitting waged jobs.

When the National Oceanic and Atmospheric Administration issued a regulation requiring TEDs in 1987, shrimpers—who at the time had considerably more political power in Louisiana—mobilized immediate pushback.[18] US Congressman Billy Tauzin, at the time a Democrat representing Louisiana's Third Congressional District and a member of the Merchant Marine and Fisheries Committee, and his like-minded colleagues delayed for two years the reauthorization of the Endangered Species Act, the passage of which was required to make the regulation enforceable. The Louisiana legislature, in an amazing muster, passed a law that made enforcing TED regulations illegal in state waters.[19] A month after the TED rule went into effect, shrimpers formed an armada of their skiffs, mooring them starboard to port, blocking all naval traffic into Galveston and Port Aransas in Texas. When the Coast Guard fired water cannons into their riggings, angry fishers clung wet and resolute to their nets and shackled boat to boat so that even the tide could not break the blockade. The blockade at Galveston blocked the Houston Ship Channel, which was the entry to Port Houston, the third-largest US port by tonnage handled in 1988.[20] The shrimpers achieved what they wanted: national attention. They imagined themselves civil rights activists, the oppressed standing up for their livelihoods against a cruel and distant government. The public, however, did not see the analogy, and after thirty-six hours or so, the trawl boats left to harvest the last of the spring shrimp.[21] Nothing much changed until 2013, when Monterey Bay Aquarium's Seafood Watch program designated Louisiana-caught shrimp as "seafood to avoid" based on the lack of TED rule enforcement. Seafood Watch partners with a wide range of businesses, including high-end grocery chain Whole Foods. These businesses then will either attach Seafood Watch's designation to their products or avoid red-listed products altogether. The law barring enforcement of TED rules was finally repealed in 2015 (after Governor Bobby Jindal vetoed a repeal in 2010), and as of March 2017, Louisiana shrimp, except for shrimp caught with otter trawls, was reclassified as "a good alternative."[22]

Not only has any resistance to TED regulations failed to change the ultimate force of rules, but commercial shrimp fishers led the charge to overturn the

1987 law that prohibited TED enforcement. The Louisiana Shrimp Task Force, an advisory body to the Louisiana Department of Wildlife and Fisheries, consists mostly of shrimpers and shrimp processors, with nonvoting representation from a biologist, an enforcement agent, an economist, and three political designees. In 2015, the year the price of shrimp bottomed out, this task force voted to support repeal legislation. Shrimpers declared that they had been using TEDs all along and that the law misled the public about the Louisiana shrimp fishery.[23] Kim Guy, ChaCha Sevin, Steve Billiot, and Chad Portier—all active commercial shrimpers—spoke ambivalently about TEDs. They all used them and had for a long time. They never even indicated that there was a conflict between Louisiana state law and the federal regulations. Over the course of thirty years, active resistance to governance gave way to an active compliance with federal law. The shrimpers interviewed in the press around the Seafood Watch designation and the effort to repeal the anti-TED law blamed the government for this dilemma even though the fishery and sympathetic legislators had fought for and gained institutional roadblocks to regulation. In the words of Mark Abraham, the chair of the Shrimp Task Force and the operator of the Gulf Island Shrimp & Seafood processing plant in Dulac, "Having on the books that our own agents can't enforce TEDs sends the wrong message that Louisiana doesn't care about its own marine life."[24] This message was previously the rallying cry of the anti-TED movement. At an anti-TED rally in Thibodaux in 1987, Governor Edwin Edwards reportedly said, "Perhaps some species were just meant to disappear. If it comes to a question of whether it's shrimpers or the turtles—bye-bye turtles."[25] The irony of this callous sloganeering is that shrimpers are the species on the brink of disappearance.

In describing the delicate process of keeping alive bait shrimp, ChaCha describes a scenario that as aptly describes his own situation as a commercial shrimper:

> Shrimp is something that can't take no kind of stress. Anything you do to them, they'll die. Anything you do to stress them out, they'll die. And then you wonder how they can live, going through all kinds of bad weather, hurricanes—but that's in their natural environment. When you take something from its natural environment, and you put it into captivity, you're changing the whole scenario. Whether it's with shrimp, with animals. You know there are some animals you try to capture them—after so many hours or days, they're gonna die. They're not gonna live. They can't take the stress.

ChaCha paints an image of precarious shrimp life, teetering on the edge of annihilation, rocked by water and wind and the relentless violence of the trawl net. This is what ChaCha does: he takes the shrimp from its natural environment, dunks them in a tank of circulating water, and sells them to be skewered on hooks by recreational fishermen and their children. The shrimp are going to die. They are not going to live. They cannot take the stress of grubby hands pulling them from an ice chest where they are nestled between lunch meat sandwiches and cans of sweet tea. They cannot take the stress of the jaws of a redfish swallowing them, hook and all. But a shrimper, like ChaCha, endures considerable stress too: bad weather, hurricanes, but also oil slicks and imported aquacultured shrimp, a home environment that is quickly surpassing the traditional, quiet life of the boat with its networked pleasures. In the last twenty years, the whole scenario has changed: the impossible calculus of increasing fuel prices and decreasing shrimp prices, the increasing ease with which people from Chauvin with limited means can discover a world divorced from the estuaries of their fathers, the shifting political arena that now privileges a parochial and ethnocentric vision of the world while nevertheless refraining from articulating a vision of how a middle-aged man carrying a torch for an industry in rapid deindustrialization might fit in. There is no path by which we might resurrect shrimping whole, the way it lives in memory.

Ghost Net Two: Indebtedness

Deleuze writes that in a society of control, "man is no longer man enclosed, but man in debt."[26] Not only is man in debt, but he also cannot escape the market. This is the ultimate reason that shrimpers accepted the TED regulations as necessary: their anachronistic fight against it resulted in their industry becoming marked as bad, their products avoided. The Louisiana shrimper, portrayed as greedy and reckless, became the bully of the Gulf of Mexico, a cohabitant in a public resource who did not want to play nice with the ecosystem. Unlike the oil industry, the shrimpers could not wage a multipronged and extended public relations campaign to reconfigure the industry's image as a job creator and steward of the lands on which it relies. After the 2010 BP oil spill in the Gulf of Mexico, BP bought Google search terms to keep the company's cleanup efforts at the top of any search for information about the spill, funneling public curiosity to a careful and apologetic explanation of how BP was fixing the problem.[27] It spent millions of dollars on a television advertisement campaign. And they paid people with boats more than twelve hundred dollars per day to aid in cleanup.[28] Kim Guy told me, "The money we made, you wouldn't have made it shrimping. People were like, 'Aw BP this and BP that.' If it wouldn't have been for BP, they had a bunch of people on our bayou that would have lost a bunch of their stuff. Because they were at the end, you know like I was saying? It was hard to make it at the price of the fuel. And then BP came around and—it went to booming again for the whole year. Some people that had one shrimp boat, now had five shrimp boats." Although the oil spill threatened to permanently transform the ecosystem and taint Louisiana seafood by association with toxicity and corporate malfeasance, the cleanup may well have helped shrimpers avoid going out of business. Even though the shrimp fishery was effectively closed in areas impacted by the spill, people made fortunes, expanded operations, bought new trucks and nets, went on vacation—gifts from BP to shrimpers if they merely knelt before it. If they would play nice, BP was happy to be their patron for a year.

Indebtedness is different than enclosure in one key way: although both situations are technologies that limit activity in some way, only indebtedness requires a continuous relationship. In a prison or factory, an overseer does not necessarily need to be there. Prisoners can be thrown into solitary cells. Workers can arrive at the factory and do their jobs and then leave. With enclosures, there is an arbitrary limit to the confinement: either a sentence or a shift. When the limit is reached, the prisoner or worker is free to go. Perhaps they are eager to get out of the classroom and join their daddies on their boats. Fair enough: endure until the end of the day, and a bell will ring and they can go home. With debt, there is no endpoint. Instead, the debt must be repaid. There is a promise and an obligation to perform a certain way. The debtor is free to decide how to fulfill the debt, but it must be fulfilled. If it is not done by an arbitrary time, the debtor becomes further indebted or forfeits possessions. The debtor may be left without anything, tossed around by forces against which they may not be able to defend: the caprice of economics, the sudden and drowning force of disaster. Debtors do not need to be confined because they know that their lives may be seized by creditors if repayment is not finished.

Consider the costs associated with a large boat that seeks to trawl the Gulf of Mexico for a month or so. For an eighty-two-foot shrimp boat with a ten-thousand-gallon fuel capacity, a captain would have spent around $28,000 in diesel in May 2015.[29] One shrimper told me for a boat with a crew of three or four that intends to spend a month at sea, the total up-front cost (covering fuel, ice/refrigeration, and food) would be between $30,000 and $40,000. With the price of shrimp at seventy cents per pound, the boat would have to return with about twenty-eight tons of shrimp to break even. Anything caught beyond the break-even tonnage will be split between the captain and the crew, assuming there are no other expenses such as maintenance, repairs, insurance, licensing, or equipment replacement.[30] Considering that the average boat in the offshore fleet landed about forty-seven tons per year between 2000 and

2013, a single hitch when the shrimp price was at seventy cents would almost certainly mean crippling debt for the boat captain.[31] Consequently, many offshore boats remained moored, waiting for the price to rebound, while their owners depleted their savings from the 2014 boom year. The price of a used steel boat between sixty and eighty feet long runs upward of $250,000. A brine-freezing unit costs between $21,000 and $55,000.[32] When a young man, eager to escape the confinement of the classroom, embarks on a maritime life of freedom and prosperity, he must first go into debt and buy a boat. If he is lucky, his father is a well-established shrimper and can give him a boat. If not, he must work as a deckhand until he accumulates enough capital for a down payment on a twenty- to thirty-year-old boat. He must pay off his debt in good years and bad, for richer or poorer. There is no easy way to divorce debt.

Perhaps this primacy of debt in commercial shrimp fishing contributes to the frequency with which shrimpers talk about greed as a primary motivator for work. An elder fisherman and shrimp-drying mogul who asked not to be named said, "Let me tell you one thing about shrimping: if you're not greedy, you're never gonna make it. You have to be greedy to go out there and hustle for it. The more you hustle, the more you're gonna make it. Nobody's gonna give you nothing. You have to go and earn it." Shrimping promotes a vision of the individual as a competitor, as an entrepreneur, as a person whose primary goal is to extract the absolute maximum limit of possible profit. Shrimpers envision themselves as gold miners: every minute not spent in the vein, panning the river, is a minute wasted. Indeed, some trawl boats run twenty-four hours a day in season: several shrimpers I interviewed described days punctuated by two-hour naps every twelve hours, hauling and culling with frenetic crews of hungry men. If someone could not manage this schedule, the boat captain would radio for another boat to bring that person back to shore. On such a productive vessel, there is no use for deadweight, another mouth to feed, another mouth gnawing away at profits. Unless a boat fishes the federal waters beyond three miles from the coast, all of its yearly income must come in two short seasons. What choice is there? You're gonna have to make it.

The twin ghost nets of access to knowledge and indebtedness wisp in and out of the lives of the shrimpers of the Louisiana Gulf Coast. Unlike the classical trawl net, which piles and crushes together the life of the sea, the ghost net ensnares just a part of *you*: it divides you into your limbs, your propeller, the moorings you cast to not drift at night if you are the kind of shrimper who sleeps. The ghost net does not collect you. It is not a productive tool. It shimmers in its surprise attacks, and you do not fully see it until you are already underwater. In this analogy, shrimpers imagine they are the shrimp and the government is the net, limiting their movement in the predictable ways that a government governs: setting rules, issuing licenses. This, of course, is still true: the US government has not given up its disciplinary exercise of power. It imagines shrimpers as individuals to be fined into submission. It grants freedoms aligned, if we are to be generous, with the promotion of life—life that institutions design and mold through education, spatial design, and the study of human life as possible lives. But there is a spooky power that is perhaps more potent and invisible and distributed. In this analogy, the shrimpers motor along as themselves, individuals capable of being reduced to a foot with the perfect shape to catch old pieces of net, dipped in antirot fluid and still capable of doing what a net does. Who knows who originally cast that net? In this analogy, it could be anyone or any institution.

But the point of this analogy is not to make a facile case for the drowning menace of debt as a type of spectral net. The point is that shrimpers, who have spent their lives cultivating an identity of freedom from the ways that people onshore are disciplined into obedient citizens, have been fighting the wrong battle. The fierce individualism of the yeoman shrimper is anachronistic in two ways: first, it imagines itself as a precapitalistic identity, concerned with self-sustenance and individual liberty and not beholden to the bourgeois class of business owners; second, it rebels against a disciplinary apparatus swiftly being replaced by one that is not even trying to regulate individuals but is instead focused on subindividual qualities that can be measured and regulated en masse. We might call it, as I have been doing, a society of control after Deleuze. But the issue remains that while shrimpers have gained and seek to preserve a certain variety of freedom—wherein they do not have to show up to work on time or report to a boss—at the expense of identifying other methods by which corporate bodies subjugate them to a new logic of the data bank, of password-locked gates to information, of continual, intimate relationships with money and markets and debtors, of a dizzying volume of distributed, multivalent communications. What results is a group of people who rebel in small ways against a controlling government yet entrench themselves in nativist thinking. A group of people who are having an increasingly hard time culling good information from fantasy. A group of people who carry on working to repay debt, a people who are good-natured about it, justifying what they are doing with love, with a desire to carry on traditional occupations into a mysterious future that will almost certainly be presided over by algorithms and automatons. A group of people who yearn for a time (perhaps one that has always been dislodged from history) where a small family might live on a boat, catching shrimp and going to sleep to the cries of seagulls and the buzzing of mosquitos just beyond the net draped over a bunk. In this analogy, we are the shrimpers. In this analogy, our fight to avoid large nets makes us miss the ghost nets pulling at our toes.

Miraculous Draught of Fish

Picture this: the sagging net of the trawl, a fruit ripe and heavy, verging on splitting under its own weight. Within the net are hundreds of brown shrimp. They crash into each other, sometimes loosening heads shackled to the rest of their armored bodies. The net conforms to space: pulled from the water, it is the teardrop shape of harvested life; beneath the water, it flows away from its rigging. A contortionist cage. When you see the net and its contents hanging above the deck before untying the drawstrings holding closed the package of shrimp in what is called the cod end of the net, you also see the pogy fish caught in the mesh, all tails and lethargic, gasping mouths. You see crabs foaming at the mouth. You see slicks of mud and clumps of salty vegetation.

This is the point of nets: to catch that which is big enough to be caught.

Sometimes, there is nothing big enough to catch. Sometimes, as in the story from Luke 5:1–11, you work all night long at the nets, your body stiffening with the repetition of raising and lowering nets full of nothing—at least nothing you can use (figure 27). Then, in the morning, some Christ tells you to get back out on the water. It's your job. And you return with so much consumable life that your nets groan to the point of breaking, and you spill out the catch from the cod end onto your culling table and make your living.

As ChaCha Sevin told me, "It's just about making a living no matter what you do. It's all about work, really, at the bottom line. It's all about work."

What does it mean to make a living? I have been whispering this question to myself as I write this meditation on shrimping and nets and debt and the slow decline of a livelihood that some people doggedly will not give up despite the bust years, despite conspiracy theories about a sinister government out to destroy a small population of old-timey Louisiana shrimpers. This is about work. Work is about making a living, the work of fashioning a

Figure 27. Dawn through skimmer nets, Lake Boudreaux, May 2015. Photograph by Emma Christopher Lirette.

way to be. Work is about making, fabricating, artificing a situation wherein living takes place, wherein something might be alive, wherein someone might make a life worth living and recognizable as alive, worth catching in a net, valuable enough not be thrown overboard. One must make a living regardless of what one does. The living made by the shrimpers I spoke to is made by the seasonal labor of drifting in a body of water, scraping it clean of its marketable shrimp with big nets hauled on deck by winches powered by diesel engines. This is a living that they hope to make—at least as long as it does not bankrupt them first.

Anthropologist Kathleen Stewart's work focuses on these processes of making a living, or the pursuit of living through a life, and how we become attuned to an atmospheric miasma of senses, trajectories, repetitions, and possible futures. She writes, "The labored viscerality of being *in* whatever's happening renders choices and surfaces already weighty with the atmosphere one is literally attuning to. It produces hard-won attachments that can be hard to get out of once you're in."[1] In other words, the atmosphere is a net. These are the things that catch us: the rhythm of life, the work of the body repeating its work routines, the expectation of the smell of the brackish marsh and bushels of shrimp, the whine of the winch pulling up a net, the stillness of the thick, humid air just this side of chilly, blanketing you as you walk from house to dock, from dock to boat, and the spark of your lighter and cigarette against the predawn gloaming. This atmosphere is a dwelling in the Heideggerian sense: a way to carve oneself into a way of being, a way to build a life from the chthonic experience of already living it, a way to preserve something earthy and old into the future by looking directly ahead and persevering. According to ChaCha Sevin and Kim Guy and Glynn Trahan and Chad Portier and Steve Billiot, to survive in this way means to love your work, to throw your weight into the job, to wake up every morning and recommit to a life you believe worth living.

In the preceding chapter, I built a case against the understanding that the shrimping lifestyle affords the type of freedom that shrimpers told me they enjoy. They like shrimping because they are their own bosses. They like the distance of the open water. They hate the enclosed spaces of onshore life—the school, the factory, the machine shop, the office. They hate feeling the touch of government regulation. They want to be unmoored from the ways that people on land are moored. Yet while performing a type of rebellion, these shrimpers are ensnared by a diffuse, nearly invisible but potent style of power that is adaptable, modular, and continuous. This control is not unique to shrimpers. Scholars have been identifying the rise of data collection, market logic, and global communication as a unique threat for much of the late twentieth and twenty-first centuries.[2] The ways in which shrimpers are not free are the ways in which we are all not free. We live in a world governed at all levels by these intersecting nets. We produce that world by living in it. We are attached to it in ways that make it difficult to get out of it. But shrimpers, in an imperfect way, also offer a model of thinking for living differently. I do not mean to recuperate some nostalgic vision or return to an archetypal and rural disconnection from society. Instead, shrimpers offer a novel way of making a living not in the fight against the powers that be but by casting a smaller net, caring for themselves, and conceiving of an alternative ethics and aesthetics of work.

What does it mean to make a living? In the Bible, the tired and fish-less fishermen make a final cast at the behest of Jesus. They come back with a miraculous draught of fish. Jesus tells the fishermen, "Fear not; from henceforth thou shalt catch men."[3] It is unsurprising, then, when Chad, the most devout of the shrimpers I spoke to, says,

> I was gonna quit the other day. You know, like you said: sometimes you get anxiety or something. One day I was wanting to quit. I was like, "I'm just gonna sell all this," and I could live happily ever after and just go fishing. And God says—I feel in my heart, it's like "It's not about you, Chad." You know, "It's not about you, dude." It's about the families that you got right here that you're trying to direct and that you're trying to feed: you're giving them a job. It's about my son's future, where it's gonna go. If I give up and go fishing, I ain't building no boat for him, I ain't got nothing else going on. I'm just sitting there fishing. Yeah, I made it, but what about him?

Chad clearly believes that he has seen a miraculous draught of fish in his lifetime. He inherited a boat-building talent from his father. He and his wife, Angela, run a small fleet of shrimp boats, and he still captains one himself. He knows that he is blessed with a successful business, with a healthy family, with a legacy to maintain, and with the energy and money to do so. But even he is not immune to busts. This admission of wanting to quit was the only time Chad admitted to any negative feelings toward his own position in the industry. I asked about the falling price of shrimp, and he replied, "You gotta take the good with the bad." I asked about other bad years, and he treated the idea that a season could bankrupt him with a blasé faith in his own ability to pull worth from work: "God will provide."[4] But Chad's faith apparently does not encompass the idea that God will provide for the extended network of people who rely on Chad for jobs: God's providence does not exist without Chad's active labor. Chad is a fisher of men in this sense: through his work, he collects people into his realm of responsibility.

The first day I went to interview Chad, he was just this side of hostile to me. He perched on the skeleton of a sixty-foot steel boat in his yard, torch in hand and with no more protection for his face than a pair of Oakley wraparound shades and a camouflage hat with an embroidered yellow cross (figure 28). A small boombox blared the latest in Christian rock music broadcast over FM radio. I wanted to film him working while I interviewed him, but that meant climbing a ladder twelve feet off the ground, then straddling the two-by-fours he had laid across the void where the middle of the boat would eventually be installed. There were rectangles of industrial grating flopped across these slats, and these were what was to pass for solid ground if I wanted to talk to Chad. He grunted an acknowledgment when I introduced myself. The only sentences he muttered at me were patronizing: "It's a long drop down, brah." "You sure you want to bring that camera up here?" "You want me to talk about being a shrimper? It's work." I didn't stick around for long. Chad was standoffish. My camera and audio equipment were imperiled by my own teetering on the grating and my nervousness about breaking them, either in a fall or by catching a spark raining from Chad's welding torch. I didn't particularly want to go back, either, but Angela returned a call later that day, and I met her and Chad on their dock a week later. After my first meeting, I thought it ironic that the shrimper who most strongly identified as a Christian might be the one guy to be a bit of a jerk to me. Perhaps the presence of his wife tempered his distemper. Perhaps it was the golden-hour lighting and the breeze off the bayou.

Since he had been so gruff with me before, I thought he might give me some good material about some shrimping gossip that was making the rounds that spring. The regular openings—questions about the low price of shrimp,

Figure 28. Chad Portier welding the steel frame of a shrimp boat, 2015. Photograph by Emma Christopher Lirette.

the changes in Chauvin over his lifetime—did not yield much. He began the conversation by saying that he would not have much to say but that his wife would not be able to shut up. So I made a joke about the shrimpers who trawl Robinson Canal, the mile-long waterway that connects Bayou Petit Caillou and Lake Boudreaux. The canal is a bottleneck between the lake and Terrebonne Bay, which opens into the Gulf of Mexico. Shrimp grow to maturity in the brackish waters of Lake Boudreaux and then migrate back into the Gulf. In other words, this canal is prime waters for catching shrimp, a fact that draws small thirty- to forty-foot skiffs equipped with skimmer nets to line up and make a quarter-mile circuit to the east of the bridge that crosses the canal. The owner of Robinson Canal, the banks on either side of it, and a convenience store, Terry Lapeyrouse, was the traditional gatekeeper of who could shrimp in the canal. He had recently been denied a writ of mandamus to compel the police to arrest trespassers—in this case, anyone he did not want trawling his canal. The judge dismissed Terry's efforts, and many shrimpers in Chauvin interpreted this as an open invitation to skim the canal. I speculated to Chad that it would be shoulder to shoulder in the canal this year, with shrimpers firing shotgun shells across each other's bows. There was a long tradition of menacing rival shrimpers in the canal for offenses as minor as trawling too slowly. Chad laughed but immediately defended the essential goodness of the people of Chauvin. From this point, Angela could not get a word in edgewise: Chad could not shut up. What caused him to open up was his impassioned defense of the small-scale ethics of work epitomized in shrimping. Over an hour and a half, Chad revealed a much different persona than the gruff one he had on a steel perch wielding a torch. He was demonstrating his complete faith in work and commitment to care for his people.

The foremost group of people on Chad's mind is his family. He does not want to disappoint his son, a thirteen-year-old with a commercial fishing license, by giving in to anxiety (or anything else). His daughter wants to be a nurse, and he wants her to do work that makes her happy. He tells me how he and Angela spent their honeymoon trawling—the best time of his life. One of the few times he and Angela share the narrative, they describe the idyllic paradise of a couple floating on the wild earth, plucking the first fruits from the ocean, in love. Picture this: Angela, eight months pregnant, standing swaybacked on the deck of a steel trawler painted blue. The sun a flame behind the rushes of marsh grass, the water milky and muddy. There are birds and there are bugs, and a sheen of sweat and brackish spray has dampened everything. Chad, pulling up the try-net they use to test for shrimp density. A large female crab, bursting with roe, scuttles across the floor, stopped by Angela's heel. She's near the cabin, where she lights a butane burner and puts on a pot of water and seasonings. If she were inside the cabin, the spices sublimating into the air would make her choke, but out here, it's no big deal. She stands there, live crab underfoot, until the water boils. Then, she dunks the crab into the pot, boils her red. Chad looks up and says, "You serious—you want to boil that one crab?" Angela replies, "I want that crab. I boiled it and I'm gonna eat it." They are wistful as they tell me this story. They tell me that with some crackers and good dip, you can never starve on the boat. Chad and Angela built their life on this boat and cultivated their family on the water. But while the pleasure of their memories of the seafaring life forms the kernel of their family unit, good stewardship sustains Chad's practice of trawling and building boats. He could not quit the shrimp fishery even if he wanted to—which, at times, he does. Sometimes, he just wants to go fishing rather than act pastorally as a fisher of men.

He elaborates that his network of care extends beyond his family:

> You got fifteen families depending off of you, you know. I felt in my spirit, "No, you're not giving up." When the job's finished, that's the day I'm gonna die. When the job's finished, that's when I'm gonna give up. I'm gonna [pantomimes washing his hands] because I believe my eternal reward is in heaven. So I can live this reward: I'm set up. I can sell everything. I can live this reward, but that's not where it's at, brah. It's my good friends' families. I consider these guys like my brothers, brah. I consider these guys, my captains and crews, they're family, and I tell them that. I say, "I love you, brah." You know? I want to see y'all succeed. I don't want to see y'all not succeed. I'm doing all this for y'all could prosper. I'm prospering

along the way with y'all, but I want you to have all that too. So I'm not gonna give up. I don't want to give up for that reason and not just for that, but because my son's coming right behind 'em.

Chad believes in certain mottos: *God will provide. A rising tide raises all ships.* He sees himself as a coach or mentor rather than a boss. He sees himself as a father figure to the people who work for him. He further sees the strengthening of this network as vital to the success of his son, who will need the community of shrimpers to continue if he hopes to make it. And though Chad and his wife do in fact run a profitable wholesale and retail shrimp outfit, Faith Family Shrimp Company, they were among the first in Chauvin to advertise retail shrimp for sale online. The boat Chad was building when I met him had been commissioned for close to a million dollars.[5] Chad was not boasting when he told me that he could probably retire and fish until he gave up the ghost. He was merely stating that his prosperity should not be his alone. While there might be a whiff of emotional martyrdom to his refrain of "I'm doing this for you," it does not come off that way when he gives me this justification on his dock as the sun sets one evening in May 2015. There is a sweetness in how Chad imagines his role as well as an ethics that obliges him to work in an uncertain industry during the worst shrimp season in years.

The care of shrimpers extends to the nonhuman network of landscapes, organisms, tools, plants, and animals. ChaCha offers a proposal for securing the fisheries: "In order to guarantee the fishing industry as a whole for the future—for future generations—is having a little more management. Or having areas that shouldn't be harvested. That would be a definite—an almost definite guarantee that it would always be there for the future. That they should have areas be, I guess, wildlife management areas. Off-limits. And they could—we do have enough in this state that they could close a few areas. And it wouldn't hurt. Everybody could still make their living." ChaCha cannot make a living without having the fisheries continue into the future. Of all of the shrimpers I spoke to, ChaCha was the least nostalgic even as he was the most melancholy. Having lost so much business during the BP oil spill while his brothers, all of whom had left the industry years earlier and were unaffected by the spill, put into relief the economic reality of trawling for a living. By yearning for the olden days, you let the present-day obstacles to thriving blindside you. You dwell errantly. To oppose this, ChaCha advocates for a future-oriented, pragmatic mode of governance. Although he complains about institutional bodies' lack of respect for local knowledge, he nevertheless recognizes the necessity for some kind of institutional management of the fishery. This management manifests in the same mold as Chad's sense of responsibility for his fleet. To continue making a living requires caring for the environment. To hope to continue fishing, to hope that future fishers might fish requires taking care to not overfish. If this means sequestering space as off-limits, so be it. Nature, to men like ChaCha and Chad, is bountiful. God will provide.

We might envision Chad's paternalism and ChaCha's stewardship as a harkening back to what Michel Foucault describes as the dominant principle of Greek antiquity: to take care of oneself (ἐπιμέλεια ἑαυτοῦ). Foucault identified in Greek thought a turning inward, a refocusing of practices toward an elaboration of the self, and a subjugation of knowledge to the cultivation of the self as an ethical actor. This conception of selfhood, for Foucault, is not mere individualism, at least not the way we normally imagine individualism. We might say that the United States has a certain cult of individuality that values libertarian and competitive values, that envisions people as economic agents in a grand, ever-expanding market, that defines the individual by a bill of rights and dares some person or institution to attempt to infringe on those enumerated rights. In many of my interviews with shrimpers, I heard variations on these themes: shrimpers must be greedy to be successful, the government needs to stay out of our business (except to enforce tariffs on foreign shrimp), we must defend our rights—with violence if necessary—against those who would violate our right to property, land, and the ability to shrimp the way we learned how. I asked every person I interviewed why shrimpers did not just unionize and take collective action with processors or protest things besides turtle-exclusion device regulations. One retired processor told me,

> I don't believe they're ever gonna build a union, because everybody's individual. If you got a shrimp boat, and you do your thing with that shrimp boat, where you sell your shrimp is yours: you have the right to sell on the roads or anywheres else. This is never gonna get—we tried years and years ago to try to put all the fishermen together and try to build a union. You know, build one big plant and have all the fishermen bring [their catch] to that plant, and when that plant processes and sells it, well, the profit that they make on it, they still pay the fishermen everyday when they come in, but the profit that they make on it would be split amongst everybody. And you couldn't get them to get together, you know? Half of them agreed to do it, but they didn't show up when it came time to put the package together. [. . .] It's never gonna come to play because every shrimper that has his own boat is gonna control himself. He don't wanna be told when to go out, where to go, and how much to catch and nothing like that. [. . .] People like Kim Guy, you ain't gonna go over there and tell him that that net he's got is not doing him any good, that he needs a bigger mesh net. He's gonna say, "No! Get away from me!" They're a certain kind of people and that's what they are.

This explanation makes sense from a perspective of American individualism: each person—in the capacity of economic agent—in conflict against others, where people just want to be left alone by government, whether that governance comes in the form of governmental regulation or fellow shrimpers trying to build a defined, institutional fishery. The idea that shrimpers might come together and create a self-governing market is as utopian as them becoming liberated from either regulation or controls. But this explanation for the lack of union viability also demonstrates a qualitatively different attitude of individualism: at the end of the day, the shrimper has his own boat, his domain, his household, and he will *control* himself. In describing how the care of the self for the Greeks should not be confused with modern notions of individualism, Foucault differentiates three "realities" we conflate: the amount of independence bestowed on a person by governing institutions, the valorization of a person's private life of the home and interpersonal relationships, and "the intensity of the relations to self, that is, of the forms in which one is called upon to take oneself as an object of knowledge and a field of action, so as to transform, correct, and purify oneself, and find salvation."[6] Foucault identifies this third individualism as the care of the self: the project of transforming the self such that one might *live* well. We might call this making a living.

The Greek care of the self (not to be confused with contemporary notions of self-care, which combine a promotion of healthy lifestyle choices with a simultaneous license to make unhealthy short-term decisions and act hedonistically) involves a rigorous habit of knowing what the self is capable of and identifying spheres of control. The care of the self is also not being self-involved. Foucault clarifies the usage of the noun ἐπιμέλεια (*epimeleia*), care: "The term *epimeleia* designates not just a preoccupation but a whole set of occupations; it is *epimeleia* that is employed in speaking of the activities of the master of a household, the tasks of the ruler who looks after his subjects, the care that must be given to a sick or wounded patient, or the honors that must be paid to the gods or to the dead. With regard to oneself as well, *epimeleia* implies a *labor*."[7] To care is a job. To care is a job directed outward from the process of turning inward. We see this type of care with Chad, who knows what he is capable of, knows how to manage his job. Through a process of looking inward, of knowing himself and his struggle with his occasional desire to quit, he can recognize how his labor, his care, fits into a household, an economy, and a network of persons under his care. We return here to the word οἶκος, the Greek word for "house," "family," and "family property." This tripartite realm is the ancillary target of the care of the self. Foucault explains the care of the self as an ethical exercise of freedom, that elusive and tantalizing goal of shrimpers everywhere. In an interview with Helmut Becker, Raul Fornet-Betancourt, and Alfredo Gomez-

Müller, Foucault responded to a question about how the care of the self might become an easy path to tyranny:

> If you take proper care of yourself, that is, if you know ontologically what you are, if you know what you are capable of, if you know what it means for you to be a citizen of a city, to be the master of a household in an *oikos*, if you know what things you should and should not fear, if you know what you can reasonably hope for and, on the other hand, what things should not matter to you, if you know, finally, that you should not be afraid of death—if you know all this, you cannot abuse your power over others.[8]

Foucault is still talking about Greeks in antiquity here, but the ethical imperative of a shrimper like Chad or ChaCha is likewise predicated on the ability to understand how one fits into a sphere of influence, how one's own life is contingent on working at making that life a life worth living. The shrimpers I spoke to described to me an *ethos* of living, an aesthetic mode by which they understood what they do. They imagine the character of their life to be familial, moored to both their ancestors and to their contemporary blood relations. They imagine their activity to be fundamentally productive: generating wealth, culture, and possible ways of working in the future. They imagine themselves to be free-floating, individualistic agents surviving an assault of institutionalism that threatens to codify them into nonexistence. They imagine their household to extend from their immediate family to their community, to their cultural identity, to the landscape in which they cast nets and yank out shrimp. They imagine themselves to be attuned to an environment of water and rain, of crustacean migration patterns, of fast-eroding land and fast-salinizing water. Most of all, they imagine themselves.

This self-imagining is perhaps the key means by which shrimpers attempt to survive a global world they believe has left them in the wastelands of history. I earlier alluded to Stewart's concept of the atmosphere, an embodied network of material and immaterial intensities. Like Tim Ingold, Stewart uses Heidegger's language to elaborate what she calls atmospheric attunements: "atmospheric attunements are a process of what Heidegger [...] called worlding—an intimate, compositional process of dwelling in spaces that bears, gestures, gestates, worlds."[9] What shrimpers are doing in their mode of caring for themselves is a practice of not only making a living but making a world. They are worlding. For Stewart, what is important about dwelling is not so much that a person might construct a system of knowledge that errs but that the act of dwelling is the technology that fills space with rich worlds always on the edge of transforming. To form these worlds, one must be receptive to the environment, to recognizing one's own practices, and to accounting for one's movement in that world. The strength of the world relies on the strength of attunement (which is not always a conscious activity). The lives of shrimpers are marked not only by the labor of captaining boats, hauling nets, culling the catch, repairing their equipment but also by the experience of working outdoors, the sensitivity to the changes in humidity, wind, and air pressure that might signal a storm or school of fat shrimp. Even as their own bosses, shrimpers generate a rhythm of work, of cycling through hitches of trawling and selling and working on their boats. They create a world where all it takes to be successful is loving the work of fishing and not giving up, even when the price of shrimp bottoms out and they have to go into debt just to get paid. These worlds come into being through practice and belief. We call the creation of worlds a miracle. Making a world, making a living—these are miracles, especially when there are controls out there gerrymandering the field of possible lives, of possible worlds.

These possible worlds, tenuous and whispery, form through the process that Foucault and Deleuze call subjectivation (*assujettissement*): the formation of the self as a subject. This process is not utopian: subjectivation allows individuals both to become identifiable selves and to become objects of study. Subjectivation, therefore, has the sharp bevel of danger. It is a net, gathering a world, a self, into being as well as catching the self, to be crushed in a net dragged through a water thick with other selves. But this process is where we find hope: it is the locus of the care of the self that Foucault identifies as the ethical imperative of Greek antiquity, the interplay with an atmosphere that brings worlds into being. What is most important in attending to the subjectivation of shrimpers in their work, their persistence, and their justifications and self-mythologizing that keeps them on boats is that these shrimpers—although caught in a net of late capital flows, institutional administration, and corporate control—make do, creating lives worth living. Their faith in themselves, which takes no small amount of creativity and confabulation, is perhaps their greatest, albeit unconscious, act of resistance to the colonization of their world by market forces and governmental mismanagement.

Rather than focusing on individuation and personal gratification, the shrimpers I spoke to fabricated lives that sought to form little networks of survival: the family, the fleet, the bayou village. In an interview with Antonio Negri, Deleuze argues that these nonce worlds, created as individuals and groups constitute themselves as selves, offer glimmers of possible rebellions, of possible new modes of ethical practice: "What we most lack is a belief in the world, we've quite lost the world, it's been taken from us. If you believe in the world you precipitate events, however inconspicuous, that elude control, you engender new space-times, however small their surface or volume. It's what you call *pietas*.

Our ability to resist control, or our submission to it, has to be assessed at the level of our every move. We need both creativity *and* a people."[10] Deleuze makes a case for an engaged politics of worlding (even though he would be unlikely to use this term). He describes the ability to maneuver around controls and the self-elaboration of individuals and groups through experimentation at the frontiers of societal knowledge. Like Stewart, Deleuze is trying to name the brief moments when a set of material and imaginative practices click together to bring a precarious world into being. In the question Deleuze responds to, Negri counterposes Spinoza's concept of *pietas*, which Spinoza defines as "the desire to do good generated in us by our living according to the guidance of reason" and a "radical construct."[11] This piety—this morality, this desire to do good, to live ethically—is at the center of how the shrimpers I spoke imagine themselves.

Every shrimper I spoke to insisted on the cooperation that happens on the water. Even as they defined their fellow fishers as competitive, greedy, granular, and individualistic, they talked about how anyone with a radio and a boat would offer help to someone who ran into trouble. These worlds erected on trawl boats are not closed worlds but ones that constantly reconfigure through interactions with others. This is not to reiterate Chad's argument that shrimpers are essentially good. They are not. Nearly every shrimper I talked to espoused nativist beliefs, xenophobia, and a politics dismissive of social justice. They are comfortable with autocratic leaders from the late Governor Huey P. Long to former President Donald Trump. One shrimper told me that he wished he could just shoot another shrimper right in the face. Shrimpers dwell in contradictions: parochial but invested in mobility, libertarian but moored to a mythic past, ethically oriented toward the others in their network but economically invested in the worst forms of American capitalism's will to competition.

In their self-fashioning through storytelling, through engaging with an environment, through holding in suspension memory and futurity, filiation and cultural identity, the corporeal intensity of laboring beneath the nets and the doom of that labor's potential to continue generating income, in these strategies for coping in a world run amok with controls that seek to subdivide the shrimpers into market segments, these men form little worlds of possibility. The possibility of surviving. The possibility of imagining survival. The possibility of gathering a family, an estuary, a set of bodily movements into a net. This net, woven by fingers that rehearse the movements of fingers from a different era, allows shrimpers to unmoor themselves from the death march into industrial oblivion. And that net moors shrimpers to an uncanny memory that, as Michel de Certeau defines it, is crucial to the practice of interventional storytelling. For Certeau, memory, as a spectral technology, is already unmoored:

"Far from being the reliquary or trash can of the past, [memory] sustains itself by *believing* in the existence of possibilities and by vigilantly awaiting them, constantly on the watch for their appearance."[12] Shrimpers teach that to survive our current era, to survive work, to make a living, we need to be vigilant for opportunities of collective world building that are invested in building networks in the places we dwell, of unmooring ourselves from the stultifying destiny of economic determinism and the logic of corporations and global capital. New worlds built through faith in the possibility of making a life worth living may not always yield a better, more compassionate model than the systems of social controls and biopower and disciplinary control and global capital that now, especially now, seem inescapable and inexhaustible in their capacity to crush out forms of life. But in the aesthetics of work fashioned by shrimpers, we might yet imagine an other-directed, ecological ethics of labor. This labor is less concerned with utopian revolution than with getting through the week, with imagining the work as a practice of weaving a net.

Successful shrimpers must be constantly attentive to the environment, to the weather, to the flows of sea life, and to their equipment. In the offseason, some shrimpers spend weeks weaving and reweaving nets. Sometimes the mesh is too small. Sometimes it is too loose. Sometimes the material of the net rakes across some sharp trap in the water, and the net gives up its ghost. The job of the shrimper is to be attentive to these nets, to weave together new nets when the old can no longer compel the catch to stay caught. Likewise, in coping with the end of their industry (and the continuing, accelerating change in global labor practices), shrimpers in coastal villages in southern Louisiana have modeled strategies of persistence. Their self-elaboration—through bodily and imaginative practice, individual and collective world-building—relies on a type of unmooring that orients them toward a different logic of living. Shrimpers are not free. By persisting in a doomed industry, by championing an anachronistic model of work rooted in locality, small networks of care and belonging, and narratives of continuity and freedom, shrimpers offer an alternative possibility of freedom. They have released all anchors but one: an anchor that allows them to reorient themselves toward a future they can imagine inhabiting, where they can do some good for the people in their sphere of influence. Shrimpers are casting a net that gathers together components of a world in which they might experience freedom, a world that might treat them better than the world where their work is no longer wanted. They are weaving a world they can survive.

FISH STORIES
A Methodological Appendix

> I fish for words
> to say what I fish for,
> half-catch sometimes.
> —James Emanuel, "Poet as Fisherman"

In biblical times, a carpenter god put fishers out of business by asking them to become fishers of men.[1] In that moment, the godhead made incorporeal the nets the fishermen apostles had held. In that moment, the fishermen apostles might entrap people with words and story. They themselves become figurative, the structure of their previous vocation as fishers transposed onto the spiritual realm. This, as we know, was the specialty of the Christ: a god who spoke in stories, who is the apotheosis of story.[2] Fishers, a species of liars, likewise speak through story and exaggeration. At least, that's how the story goes.[3] Folklore indexer Stith Thompson included a subsection in his index devoted to the lies fishers tell, †X1150, specifying eight variations: the great catch of fish, the large number of fishers in one spot, fish caught by remarkable tricks, unusual catches by fishers, fishers catch fish with amazing contents, fisher catches fish with larger fish inside, other unusual methods of catching fish, and fish caught with another's cries.[4] The first variation, the great catch of fish (†X1150.1), appears twice in the Christian Gospels: first in the retelling of recruitment of the fisher apostles in Luke; second, postresurrection in John.[5] In both fish stories, Jesus instructs tired fishers to go out again, and they fill their empty nets. The second variation, a large number of fishers in one spot (†X1151), might describe the governing lie of Chauvin, where, over the course of a few summers, I tried to become a fisher of men to gather the stories of people who might persist in a troubled fishery.

I talked to shrimpers and people connected to the shrimp fishery in southern Terrebonne Parish. They were people I knew from growing up in Chauvin, from running a nonprofit and festival there, from my family members and their vast knowledge of the coast and the people living on it. I had access to these people because they knew who I was—if not directly, then through my father, whose popularity along Bayou Petit Caillou has earned him the nickname Mayor of Chauvin.[6] My first instinct was to capture my informants in story, which I could then explain. This is called thick description: to read a culture like a text. This definition leads to a corollary premise: that culture, like a work of literature, is a symbolic structure whose individual parts have meaning both separately and in concert. According to Clifford Geertz, famous for theorizing ethnography as thick description and for inciting an interpretive turn in anthropology, "As interworked systems of construable signs [...] culture is not a power, something to which social events, behaviors, institutions, or processes can be causally attributed; it is a context, something within which they can be intelligibly—that is, thickly—described."[7] For Geertz, culture comprises a network of meanings, an overdetermined web that governs the field of possibility for individual and collective behavior. Understanding culture, then, is a practice of deciphering the hidden meanings, prescriptions, and imaginaries that are the motors of life. It is a process akin to close reading, in the sense of the New Critics: not only should critics attend to the minute particularities of language or symbol, but they should devise how each linguistic fragment functions to create the whole. Reading culture in this way is a type of structuralism: Geertz writes that we should see culture "as a set of control mechanisms—plans, recipes, rules, instructions (what computer engineers call 'programs')—for the governing of behavior."[8] Ethnographers, whom Geertz imagines conducting research through interviews and observation, are writing "fictions, in the sense that [interpretations] are 'something made' [...] not that they are false, unfactual, or merely 'as if' thought experiments."[9] Like a text, we can exhaust a culture through our interpretations; in our precision, we can translate culture to those outside the field we study in a language comprehensible to them.

There is a lot to admire in this formulation of ethnographic scholarship. It relieves some of the tension about cultural anthropology's scientific pretensions by proposing a definite object of study (culture and the web of significations that order human behavior) and clarifying a methodology (fieldwork followed by the analysis of encounter and observation). As Geertz writes, this work is "not an experimental science in search of law but an interpretive one in search of meaning."[10] Geertz's model also satisfies an aesthetic sensibility in writing ethnographies while grounding them in concrete, observable phenomena. Most important, it encourages precision in parsing subtle distinctions of behavior that carry ambiguous meaning. While this vision still holds value in its attention to the minute texture of lived experience and the aesthetics of documenting it, thick description as an ethnographic methodology reinforces problematic tendencies in anthropological inquiry. It upholds the authority of anthropologists as having mastered their subjects through language and privileges a totalizing vision of culture that is deterministic. Geertz's definition of culture, drawn from the language of computer engineering, suggests that semiotic contexts function like scripts, that like the biblical legion of demons possessing the demoniac, they animate the meat of a people who exist in a pre-programmed world. His ethnographer plays the part of an engineering consultant who works culture like an exorcist: tinkering with a system, grasping it, explaining it, so that in his explanation, he might banish any strangeness.

The emphasis on cultural explanation—a theory that enacts subjectivation, the production of legible subjects that can be subject to power—is haunted by the colonial history of anthropology as a discipline, wherein empires mastered subaltern peoples in acts of representation. This critique of ethnography comes to us both from within anthropology—most famously in *Writing Culture*, a collection of essays edited by James Clifford and George Marcus—and from without—in work of postcolonial theorists such as Edward Said in *Orientalism* and Gayatri Spivak in "Can the Subaltern Speak?" Writing an ethnography is a fraught endeavor. Without care, it can turn into the third variation of a fishing lie: a fish caught by a remarkable trick (†X1153). In seeking to understand people met in the field, anthropologists might fix them in representation, the remarkable and virtuosic ability to interpret, to demarcate, to capture in language the precarious and intensive moment of an encounter with others. This remarkable trick is an ethical quandary that the shrimpers I spoke to from 2013 through 2016 would recognize immediately. In fact, they are the ones who described this kind of relationship as tricky. After BP descended on Chauvin to repair the cataclysm it brought in the form of the 2010 Deepwater Horizon explosion, which bled 4.9 million barrels of oil into the Gulf of Mexico, several shrimpers described to me how the company manipulated interview footage to reshape the post-spill narrative.[11] They were wary, even though they knew me, of the remarkable trick of representation. They worried that I would trick them with misrepresentation. I hoped to avoid this lie.

I did go into the field. I did interview shrimpers. I watched them work. I joined them on their boats. I ate crustaceans they pulled from the water that same day. I identified myself as a researcher, an anthropologist. I identified myself as my father and mother's child, a child of Chauvin. I brought with me a camera, a field recorder, a shotgun and lavalier mic, a heavy tripod capable of withstanding the bob of the surf under a boat, and a big lens. Sometimes my brother, Brett, joined me, holding a bounce or leveling audio (figure 29). Although this book does not include any video, I filmed everything. I was (and still am) interested in producing a documentary that conveys the worlds created by shrimpers. Beyond an audiovisual product that can foreground the sensual, embodied experience of the field and produce knowledge and incite experiences that the textual cannot, the work of recording also heightens attention (for everyone involved) to the relationship between producer/researcher and performer/informant and to the shared work of creating knowledge. Armed with camera and mic, the issue of representation remained conspicuous. I tried to follow in the path of Jean Rouch, a filmmaker and anthropologist whose work offers a counter to Geertz a quarter century before his theory of thick description and that the colloquium of ethnographers of *Writing Culture* seems to have forgotten when trying to assess anthropology's literary turn.[12] Extending the concept of *kinopravda* first theorized by Dziga Vertov, Rouch developed a cinema verité, which "designates not 'pure truth' but the particular truth of the recorded images and sounds—a filmic truth."[13] Rouch recognizes the artificiality of both his filmmaking and ethnographic practices: he does not record naive reality, and he certainly is no detached observer or documentarian. In an interview with filmmaker Enrico Fulchignoni, Rouch says, "I have a tendency, when I'm filming, to consider the landscape [...] as precisely the work of God, and the presence of my camera as an intolerable disorder. It's this intolerable disorder that becomes a creative object."[14] This quotation throws into sharp relief the difference between Rouch's practice of ethnography and Geertz's: whereas thick description seeks to prove an ordered reality explaining social situations, Rouch seeks to incite a type of minor chaos in which people re-create a reality in collaboration with a researcher. This rift in the inertia of everyday life finds its origin in the unnatural presence of the filmmaker and his machinery. Considering ethnographic inquiry as playful, exuberant, but nevertheless incisive and communicative, Rouch envisions his work as "shared anthropology," in which "knowledge is no longer a stolen secret, devoured in the Western temples of knowledge; it is the result of an endless quest where ethnographers and those whom they study meet on a path."[15] Rouch's films enact this chaotic polyvocality: in *Moi, un Noir* and *Chronique d'un* été, he actually gives his camera to his subjects, who become collaborators in his project. Furthermore, with his film *Jaguar* and continuing with *Moi, un noir* and *La pyramide humaine*, he begins labeling his work "ethnofiction," wherein "true" ethnographic knowledges combines with staged performances—emphasizing the "filmic truth" of shared aesthetic creation.

This theorizing of the work of anthropology as a type of fiction distinguishes itself from Geertz's formulation (and predates it). For Rouch, what matters is the collision of worlds that creates the fiction. For Geertz, what matters is that culture is a process of constructing a web of symbolic significance, and the

Figure 29. Brett Lirette, 2015. Video still from fieldwork by Emma Christopher Lirette.

anthropologist has a responsibility of remaining faithful to a preconstructed fiction created by ethnographic study. I put these two figures in dialogue to determine what kind of fiction I might be able to tell from my fieldwork, what kind of lie that resists the totalizing narratives that box in human lives, what kind of lie that can open a space of maneuverability. Though my work takes shape as a text, Rouch was my model for fieldwork: inserting myself into an encounter with fishers so that through conversation in the spectacularly artificial space of the camera, we might be able to do something other than capture the cultural practice, hopes, fears, and self-fashioning of "subjects" to be autopsied in the halls of academia. The presence of the camera, the physicality of attaching a microphone to the people I wanted to tell me stories, the ritual of pulling focus and leveling a tripod—these created a space wherein I could emphasize my position as a researcher: a *producer*. No longer just a native daughter, I was something stranger. Also, the people I talked to performed, knowing the stakes, with the wound of misrepresentation still smarting. This relationship made clear the gift of story the shrimpers gave me. Following Rouch (contra Geertz) gave me the chance to embody the next variation (and its subvariations) of a fishing lie: unusual catches by fishers (†X1154), fisher catches fish with amazing contents (†X1154.1), and fisher catches fish with larger fish inside (†X1154.1.1).

Like all fishers, I wanted to have an unusual catch: the surprise of new information, of rifts within systems of knowledge I previously held to be impenetrable. Even though the product of my fieldwork is literary, conducting research in the spirit of Rouch created a specific, contrived, intrusive, and performative relationship between my informants and me. For the most part, the people I interviewed knew me at least through my family. They had children my age or went to high school with me. Instead of trying to use these people as "informants," entry points toward an articulation of cultural life, I engaged with them in conversation that was made formal by ritual tools: camera and lens, microphone and headphone, pen and paper. These people became partners, at least in conversation. In every interview, I brought to bear my own scholarly/theoretical agenda, to the point of reciting the final passage of Foucault's radio address about civilizations without boats. Glynn Trahan said, "Well, you just said a mouthful." After a brief pause, he riffed for two minutes about boats, regulations, governmentality, and the sublime feeling of life on the water. Glynn has no college education, and like other fishers from Chauvin, he spent his educational career waiting for the final bell of the school day, the border wall between him and his family's watercraft. Another shrimper, Chad Portier, snubbed me until I had my camera set up and a microphone aimed at him. Once I said, "Sound speeds," Chad talked in effusive monologues for over an hour. During my first interview of the 2015 season, shrimper Steve Billiot went into his house to don a homemade Elvis Presley costume and pompadour wig and performed a five-song set from the King's oeuvre.

Perhaps these people would have done these things in my absence or in my presence sans equipment, but like Rouch, I wanted to be an interruption in everyday life, to be a creative encounter, to elicit a performance. As a Chauvin native, I could too easily be swayed by my prior impressions of shrimpers I knew. Likewise, my informants, knowing me, might skip over stories they assumed I knew. I brought my gear and the pageantry of filmmaking to encourage shrimpers to tell me stories they wanted to tell. By doing so, I had several unusual catches, some filled with amazing contents. Some, improbably, contained larger fish. The shrimper most connected to the fishery through his family rejected the idea that shrimping could be in someone's blood. Another delivered a moving ode to the swamp's majesty in one breath while suggesting that the government had engaged in a turtle-depositing conspiracy in another. One gruff shrimper told me how he often thinks of quitting but keeps going to support a fleet of families who work his boats. On the weekends, one shrimper dons shrimp boots painted glittery blue to do Elvis impersonations for weddings and family reunions. I was fortunate to share a version of reality larger than I thought it might be, an expanded field that included wide-ranging connections, potentialities, and the inkling of new worlds coming into being. Borrowing a term from William James, I consider my work to be radically empirical, following James's methodology: "To be radical, an empiricism must neither admit into its constructions any element that is not directly experienced, nor exclude from them any element that is directly experienced. For such a philosophy, *the relations that connect experiences must themselves be experienced relations, and any kind of relation experienced must be accounted as 'real' as anything else in the system.*[16]

James sets up this philosophical framework as a type of bridge between rationalism (abstraction and an emphasis on universal truths) and empiricism (the study of concrete and material particularities of experiential facts). The linkages James sees between experiences include causality, meanings, and systems that join particulars together. It is a practice of attending to the *feeling* of experience, the associated possibilities and memories, and the networks of symbols tied to experience. Poet-anthropologist Michael Jackson adapts radical empiricism for ethnography: "Unlike traditional empiricism, which draws a definite boundary between observer and observed, between method and object, radical empiricism denies the validity of such cuts and makes the *interplay* between these domains the focus of its interest."[17] For Jackson, anthropologists in the field are constantly negotiating and renegotiating the viewpoints of their informants as well as experiencing a full complement of sensory information. The experience of encountering others—sharing experience with them at work, on boats, or in carports—is temporal, constantly mutable. To be radically empirical is to widen the field of possible realities to include what Kathleen Stewart would describe as the atmospheric, heterogeneous, affective, relational worlds that constantly become and unbecome.[18] This enterprise neither privileges a rational stance of detached observation nor excludes the body of the ethnographer as potential site for sensory "data"; rather, it seeks to form an account of a lived experience shaped and complicated by lines of force, affective relations, and the commingling of lifeworlds.[19] Jackson's radically empiricist project envisions culture as not as a "finality" but as a coextensive, co-constitutive "instrumentality" for the people who use it: "Persons actively body forth the world; their bodies are not passively shaped by or made to fit the world's purposes."[20] Here, Jackson critiques a version of anthropology that would abstract culture from lived experience and action, giving it a life of its own to order, proscribe, and generally serve as a codex for human behavior. Following Jackson, I see one of my primary interventions into the understanding of "culture" in coastal Louisiana to be dispensing with culture as a pervasive, symbolic matrix that might explain the people who live there. Instead, I perform an embodied, sensuous, and radically empirical act of communication that attends to a world, a big world constantly mutating inside and outside of the people I talked to.

The work of unmooring means studying the imaginative worlds that people carve into an overdense web of meanings inscribed by such discourses as folklore, politics, tourism, history, and sociology—in addition to ones inscribed by family, neighborhood, region, and nation. But unmooring cannot overlook the material world of people and crustaceans and blood and water. Instead, it must trace paths through the dense atmosphere of place. In my fieldwork and the process of writing it into an ethnography, I have entered a sensory field and felt my way through it while allowing myself to be possessed by the imaginations of the people who gifted me their stories and performances. I meant to believe their stories, to live in the places they describe, and to conspire to re-create them with as much texture as possible. This radically empirical ethnography seeks to touch the work of creating worlds that cut across the worlds known through official channels of knowledge and accepted modalities of living. Unmooring, the process by which I identify how shrimpers in southern Louisiana cope with the various forces and accidents that conspire to wipe them out or trap them in statistical knowledge, calls for both a grounding in the worlds that exist and an openness to worlds yet to come. In other words, unmooring calls for being open to the possibility that within the fish you catch, you might be astonished to find even bigger fish. The poetics of my anthropological practice—to again borrow Jackson's language—is to linger in the tenuous worlds and practices and trace the delicate and vulnerable lines of relation that connect them to each other.

Anthropologist Tim Ingold suggests a methodology based on a "*relational* approach," using Gilles Deleuze and Félix Guattari's image of the rhizome as its governing model: the "rhizome is a progeneration, a continually raveling and unraveling relational manifold."[21] Deleuze and Guattari describe their project as a "pragmatics," "composing multiplicities or aggregates of intensity."[22] Ingold's application of rhizomatic analysis forms a methodology that exceeds and undermines the interpretive paradigm in ethnographic study, providing a methodology that traces the lines of relation that comprise the simultaneously hyperlocal and expansive and imaginative space where people live.[23] Connecting social formations and environment through the figure of the rhizome allows for an ecological approach to ethnography that acknowledges the singularity of experience while connecting each singularity to a continually unfolding practice of living that creates, dismantles, and re-creates overlapping worlds. Ingold writes that "such a synthesis would start from a conception of the human being not as a composite entity made up of separable but complementary parts, such as body, mind and culture, but rather as a singular locus of creative growth within a continually unfolding field of relationships."[24] Using an ecological approach for my fieldwork in Louisiana forced me to attend to how my shrimpers navigate a world of discursive, historical, economic, and environmental instability.

Put at risk by ecological and industrial disaster and overdetermined by symbolic frameworks erected by cultural industries and thick descriptions

Fish Stories: A Methodological Appendix   173

written in the name of folklore, these shrimpers nevertheless *make do* with their lives, dwell within them, forge unforeseen relationships to locations, activities, artifacts, and representations of cultural heritage in popular media. They make a living.

The living these shrimpers make is accomplished through bodily practice, hopes, and self-elaboration. In intersecting my life with theirs, with the shifting roles we play, I attuned myself to sensation—my own, primarily—but also the evocation of what the sensory experience of shrimpers might be like. Although I do not presume to tell shrimpers what they feel, my writing posits, suggests, and evokes something of the possibilities of experience that could build literary worlds shared between readers and myself as author, which is itself a narrative space enacted from my shared experiences with commercial fishers in my hometown. In Rouch's concept of the *ciné-transe*, the body of the filmmaker and ethnographer undergoes a transformation: not quite participant, not quite observer, the anthropologist becomes a machine. During a presentation of his film *Tourou et Bitti*, which documents a possession dance among the Songhay-Zarma in Niger, Rouch says, "My 'self' is altered in front of their eyes in the same way as is the 'self' of the possession dancers; it is the 'film-trance' (*ciné-transe*) of the one filming the 'real trance' of the other."[25] Ethnographers in *ciné-transe* dissolve their status as outsiders, translators, interpreters, and scholars in a fit of improvisatory relationality, interacting with subjects, drawing performances from them, and inserting an exuberant provocation that is less about understanding how a cultural group functions than about making a new filmic world with others—in other words, building relations, attuning to an atmosphere of affective connections. Rouch says he equates the potential for a film's success on "whether I have been able to free myself from the weight of filmic and ethnographic theories necessary to rediscover the *barbarie de l'invention*."[26] Rouch ultimately advocates an ethnographic surrender: a surrender to the spark of recognition in the field, to the chance worlds that are on the precipice of emerging, to an improvisatory friendship with the people being studied. This surrender is one of bodily transformation, one that *opens* the body to sensuous experience.

Anthropologist Paul Stoller defines "sensuous scholarship" as that "in which writers tack between the analytical and the sensible, in which embodied form as well as disembodied logic constitute scholarly argument." Stoller identifies in academic ethnography a privilege accorded to semiotics, textuality, and structuralist accounts for human behavior at the expense of the lived experience shared by fieldworkers and the people they encounter. Sensuous scholarship "demands the full presence of the ethnographer's body in the field" and requires "that ethnographers open themselves to others and absorb their worlds."[27] This practice, like Rouch's *ciné-transe*, is a provocation—not just for the subjects faced with the "intolerable disorder" of anthropologists but for the anthropologists themselves. Ethnographers, seen now as porous entities, incorporate the world of the other through sensual perception, makes contact with this world. This contact is less concerned with "knowing" in the sense of documenting and confining within the limits of acceptable discourse than with knowing as a form of connection. Michael Taussig, whose ethnographic practice can also be considered sensuous, might call this form of connection *magic*. Rehabilitating the concept of *mimesis* through the work of Walter Benjamin, Taussig writes, "To ponder mimesis is to become sooner or later caught [...] in sticky webs of copy *and* contact, image *and* bodily involvement of the perceiver in the image, a complexity we too easily elide as nonmysterious, with our facile use of terms such as identification, representation, expression, and so forth—terms which simultaneously depend upon and erase all that is powerful and obscure in the network of associations conjured by the notion of the mimetic."[28] In this passage, Taussig foregrounds the precise moment of seeing in ethnographic work as already a moment of embodiment. The things we see, the people we meet, talk to, hear, touch, the foods we eat—everything we experience in the field involves the body, its way of etching images (which are copies) into our own bodies. The filmmaker becomes a recording apparatus in *ciné-transe*. Taussig argues that in writing ethnographies, we produce reproductions of what we have experienced, and in attending to the strange alchemy of mimesis wherein we join with what we copy, our ethnographies might shift the focus from interpreting the formal unity of a culture to elaborating the lines of sensual and imaginative relationships we co-create with our subjects: "What happens is that the very concept of 'knowing' something becomes displaced by a 'relating to.'"[29] Relating to someone, unlike knowing something, attempts to dismantle the type of penetrative gaze of the interpreting ethnographer, who renders the other knowable.

The displacement in thinking mimetically relies on the simultaneity of mimesis's opposite: alterity. This same/other binary is not a re-creation of the structuralist paradigms that dominated mid-twentieth century anthropology and linguistics. Rather, it is a quality of Benjamin's "dialectical image," which Taussig defines as "dislocating chains of concordance with one hand, reconstellating in accord with a mimetic snap, with the other."[30] Finding these images, the ones that decenter potential readers while shocking them with the suddenness of recognition—this methodology destabilizes the authority of scientific styles of anthropology (including Geertz's thick description) while inviting a plurality of relational configurations: ethnographer–subject, subject–reader, reader–regimes of power. These new possibilities broaden both the generosity and the political relevancy of ethnographic work. Like Rouch, Taussig's methodology forwards a creative anthropological practice that favors connection over distance, uncertainty over structuralism, provocation over taxonomizing, and imagination over knowledge. To be unmoored: to find dialectical images that disturb common understandings while flickering with recognition, to absorb worlds both stable and nonce while sharing the ones I drag with me—in this case, back to the small world into which I was born. Against totalizing descriptions, judgments, and generalization, I let myself be surprised.

This is one way to unmoor: to tell a good lie. To practice an embodied, ecological anthropology that enacts a "barbarism of invention." A central insight from Rouch is that fieldwork is a disruptive force that can generate creativity. That can forge (or whisper) counterstories. When we enter a field to study people, we become part of the ecology of that field, and our presence is not always welcome. In my fieldwork, I followed Rouch's lead: sharing my world, inviting people to co-create stories with me, treating them as interlocutors rather than subjects. I stayed attentive to my own body, the humidity of the estuary, the slick fish blood beneath my feet, the strain of the body to right itself on water, the rumble of the diesel engines punctuated by the cries of seagulls. The sight of bodies at work. The sight of boats. Moreover, I listened to the stories that shrimpers told me and imagined them as the real but invisible linkages between particular facts, whether expressed in scraps of evidence in the archives at Louisiana State University and Tulane or in the physicality of hauling shrimp ashore or in the dwindling accounts that represent the decline of the shrimping economy. I imagined these stories as a reconstruction of facts in the forms of stories. I imagined these stories as types of lies, but really good ones, ones that were so compelling, so weblike in the way they gathered together the material world that the people who told them forgot that they were telling fictions. Fish stories that are handed down from generation to generation, changing only in the number of fish caught in the miraculous catch, only in the surprising objects found in the bellies of unusual fish. To unmoor, as an ethnographic methodology, is not to reconstruct a culture through testimony and observation but to create a new world that mimics the process of contact, of exchange, of absorption and bewilderment. This is a poetics of ethnography: both ποίησις (to produce) and in the sense of poetry. To subvert Geertz's analogy of interpretation as a fiction, I take ethnographic practice as a type of poetry that produces something by relational and metaphoric creativity, by a frictional encounter of the body in the field with other bodies, by an imperfect, mysterious way of writing that something, that world, such that it draws out of readers new worlds.[31] Jackson writes that a certain impulse toward metaphor and poetry is therapeutic: "In forging links between personal, social, and natural worlds and in reforging these links when we break them, poetry fosters wholeness of Being."[32] This wholeness, like the dialectical image, contains both the rupture of meaning and a surprising recognition.[33] This wholeness is metaphor and parataxis, encounter and following the lines of imagination in conversation, of experiment and disruption, and of making, as best you can, a lie worth telling.

This project began as a way to try to write differently: to take the tricks of poetry and fiction and the rigor of scholarly citation and create something compelling, something entertaining and poignant, something that can help people see the rich world in which I grew up and that is now in decline.

When Jackson describes what a poetic practice of anthropology might be, it hinges on knotting ropes between person and environment, society and image, words and worlds, such that we might yoke a wholeness together from the multiplicity. How Deleuzian![34] This understanding of poetry, a birthing forth of worlds through linkages, is compelling and is what I am doing with writing in this work: layering the tropes and tricks of poetry on top of traditional scholarship with its form of argumentation and proof or interpretive description based on empirical fieldwork or an analysis of history and symbols relevant to the plight of shrimpers in the twenty-first century, what might be known as the post-Deleuzian century, a century that might determine that, after all, the shrimping life is a life no longer worth living.

I have not tried to exactly reproduce the world of the shrimpers but rather have sought to co-create a world by putting these shrimpers in conversation with other voices. Literary theorist Jonathan Culler takes issue with a certain paradigm in literary circles that weighs down the lyric as a vehicle for mimesis. Mimesis: the reproduction of reality. A secondhand copy. Not the mysterious transmutation that Taussig writes about, but the base understanding of poetry as something that stands in for a reality "out there." In much the same way that I criticize interpretive schools of ethnography by associating the practice with New Criticism, Culler associates this emphasis on mimesis with New Criticism: "This is the conception of lyric promoted by the New Criticism: with the insistence that interpretation focus on the words on the page rather than the intentions of the author, it became a point of doctrine that the speaker of a lyric is to be treated as a *persona*, not as the poet him- or herself, and the focus becomes the drama of attitudes expressed by this speaker-character."[35] Culler identifies the treatment of the speaker of the poem as a persona-to-be, the kernel that creates the fiction of the poetic world. Culler argues against understanding a poem as a web of symbolic linkages that constitutes a closed, fictional world wrought by placing words on a page. Instead, a poem is a type of "*epideictic* discourse: public poetic discourse about values in this world rather than a fictional world."[36] Beyond this, there are things in poems that either make no sense or lose their value if we interpret the poem as a story: changes in address, lyric techniques such as parataxis, chiasmus, and stranger ways of understanding what metaphor does. At worst, this fictionalization of the lyric defangs it, makes it self-contained and irrelevant to a world beyond its borders, and rips the communicative power of lyric utterance from the actual poet who authored it. Mimesis, as facile representation, is a treachery particular to the so-called human sciences. If we take poetry—its images and similes, its metaphors, repetitions, and utterances—as just a representation of some reality, then employing it in some kind of research context is not only a colonizing impulse but one that obscures and prettifies that process.

In the game of mooring and unmooring, representation, at least in its totalizing aspect, its way of fixing something, killing it, is another anchor to be loosed. We are talking, as we have been, as we will be, about freedom. Culler writes that we imagine a fictional poetic speaker whose utterances we overhear because "we want to believe that our subjectivity is free and independent of contexts to which we might belong, and imagining the language of a poem as coming from a fictive, nearly contextless speaker, reflects back to us an image of the subject we imagine ourselves to be."[37] This desire to be above the mud, above the institutions and ideas and systems and people that compete to fashion subjectivity, is a desire shrimpers expressed to me both explicitly and otherwise. They want to be free. They want their desires not to be manufactured by a national culture. They want their livelihood not to be contingent on a host of fragmentary and diffuse forces that entrap them. Like them, readers of poetry posit a specific yet ahistorical speaker: a role on which they can co-create a fictional world that can explain away the strange, incantatory, sometimes atavistic voice of the poet. To consider the worlds authored into being by poetry as mere fictions would be to sterilize them, make them graspable and interpretable as closed systems of meaning, render their experiments and caesurae and fragmentations curious artifacts: a terrarium in a velvet study—ornamental, fascinating, and impotent.

When Stewart talks of the spaces on the side of the road that form fecund openings in the master narrative we call America, she is talking not about glass worlds in studies but about spaces that are performative, improvisational, and real: "At once concrete and ephemeral, tactile and uncanny, restive and caught in a deadly calm, [the space on the side of the road] exceeds the space allotted to it by its own history. It replaces bourgeois notions of order with its own more lyrical order, interrupting the hierarchy of system over accident or reality over fiction long enough to imagine something more or 'Other.'"[38]

The key word here is *excess*. Like the space on the side of the road, the worlds I encountered with shrimpers in Louisiana exceed the meanings ascribed to them by scholarly, institutional, and folkloric bodies of knowledge. The space of the boat, the imagination born of water and blood, the laboring body in motion are identifiable signs whose capacity for connection, fabulation, experimental living, and culture are infinite negotiations with materiality, happenstance, hope, and the ways shrimpers make sense of their lives through work and story. Fiction is not the enemy of the lyric but rather a tool to complicate the pretense that language might encapsulate something as big as reality, a person, a subjectivity, a world brought into being. It is a tool for imagining something other than the fatal product of history. The lyric form, which poet Marianne Moore described as "imaginary gardens with real toads in them," offers a methodology that mixes the real with the unreal, that can communicate fiercely in unreal ways, that creates a truth through the performance of the kinds of real but imaginative connections that James (or Jackson) places within the radical expansion of the real.[39] By employing lyric techniques (metaphor, direct and indirect address, allusion, repetition, rhythm, rhyme, fiction), I have written a book that is both genuine and hopefully useful, that seeks not to define but to prod and play, that covers a diverse corpus of material and immaterial works, of people, and of voices that can suggest (but not fix) the possibilities of living and thinking differently.

My writing in this book has been an experiment of multiple genres, of using the long-form monograph as a space in which I can enact and perform my theoretical and aesthetic concerns—mainly the ways in which work and culture are procedural, creative, heterogeneous modes that contain the possibility of workshopping and revising the systems of knowledge that seem to be all-encompassing. I write elliptically, riffing on themes that my main interlocutors, Louisiana shrimpers in and around my hometown, introduced to me during my fieldwork. I re-create and fictionalize my own experiences both conducting this research and growing up in Chauvin. I do not abandon the genre of scholarly writing, but I try to subvert it by making academic authority no greater than the authority of the blue-collar fisher or the authority of lyric utterance. I also draw from a capacious archive of texts, putting the scholarly and ethnographic voices in conversation—sometimes explicitly, sometimes silently—with poets, Scripture writers, fishing experts from the nineteenth century, mapmakers, government bureaucrats, and others. In doing so, I hope that this kind of lyrical scholarship exceeds the arguments it makes. I want to be a splinter that nags, a rope burn, a threat. The theme of this book, unmooring, is fundamentally a story of how far a person has to go to be able to justify a constricted life, how much freedom one can carve into the walls, how much a person can use the given world, the master stories, and environment and social connections as a springboard for an exploration. The danger is that the anchor I cast, the final mooring, does not catch and that this writing is disoriented, unable to latch onto the real world into which a poet makes a lyric utterance, a desperate sort of communication. The hope is to be troubling and defiant, to return again and again to the site of the estuary, the space of the boat, the littoral plain, the body of person and literature, so that this time, during this workshop, during this improvisation, this experiment, we might be able to see a day beyond the day that has become. A day, I hope, that we can survive.

Notes

Unmooring for Beginners

1. From a mid-nineteenth-century nautical manual, to unmoor is "to reduce a Ship to a single Anchor, after riding by two" (Brady, *Naval Apprentice's Kedge Anchor*, 244). Today, this usage is archaic.
2. Stewart, *Space on the Side of the Road*, 3.
3. Berlant, *Cruel Optimism*, 3.

Lesson One: Making Space

1. Mine, *Louisiana Shrimp Value Chain*.
2. Karl Marx and Friedrich Engels specifically use *utopian* as a slur to mean unrealistic political projects based in fantasy rather than reality. They used this term against other systems of early nineteenth-century socialist thought advocated by Henri de Saint-Simon, Robert Owen, and Charles Fourier. While Marx and Engels acknowledge the revolutionary potential of imagining a utopia that is critical of contemporary society, they conclude that followers of "Critical-Utopian Socialism and Communism" ultimately "endeavor [. . .] to deaden the class struggle" and become conservative and reactionary (*Manifesto of the Communist Party*, 516). In addition, Marx and Engels critiqued economists such as Jean Charles Léonard de Sismondi, who critiqued capitalism from a nonsocialist perspective, as simultaneously "reactionary and Utopian" because this type of thought valorizes precapitalist economic systems, specifically the petite bourgeoisie (509).
3. Bloch, *Principle of Hope*, 1:145.
4. Bloch, *Principle of Hope*, 1:623. In describing youth and newness that accompany changes in society, Bloch uses another gestational image: "a society pregnant with a new one" (118). This metaphor has a decidedly different tone than the violent image from Marx and Engels's *Manifesto of the Communist Party*: "The weapons with which the bourgeoisie felled feudalism to the ground are now turned against the bourgeoisie itself" (490).

5. Muñoz, *Cruising Utopia*, 37.
6. Marcuse, Eros and Civilization, 27.
7. Marcuse writes, "The relegation of real possibilities to the no-man's land of utopia is itself an essential element of the ideology of the performance principle" (*Eros and Civilization*, 150).
8. Much to the chagrin of the shrimpers of Chauvin, Muñoz might describe this utopian dream as queer futurity. He resurrects the concept of utopia in the spirit of Bloch, proposing that queerness is futurity: "We have never been queer, yet queerness exists for us as an ideality that can be distilled from the past and used to imagine a future" (*Cruising Utopia*, 1). He calls for a haunting, an imagination of a fragmented past that inspires utopian visions. Queerness, like utopia, is that which is out of sync, an anticipatory mode that finds no home in the present. Like Bloch, Muñoz argues for a concrete utopia rooted in materialist history, one that longs for something other than the catastrophe of history. The remains of the past, the no-longer-conscious, living undead lives through memory and material traces, allow us to imagine the not-yet-here, the anticipation of a world to come.
9. Foucault, *Order of Things*, xix.
10. Foucault, *Order of Things*, xix.
11. Foucault, "Of Other Spaces," 24.
12. My translation. The French reads: "C'est—le jeudi après-midi—le grand lit des parents. C'est sur ce grand lit qu'on découvre l'océan, puisqu'on peut y nager entre les couvertures; et puis ce grand lit, c'est aussi le ciel, puisqu'on peut bondir sur les ressorts; c'est la forêt, puisqu'on s'y cache ; c'est la nuit, puisqu'on y devient fantôme entre les draps; c'est le plaisir, enfin, puisque, à la rentrée des parents, on va être puni."

The audio is available on Foucault, "Les hétérotopies" (compact disc). For the French text, see Foucault, "Les hétérotopies," in *Le corps utopique*, 24.

13. In French: "Le navire, c'est l'hétérotopie par excellence. Les civilisations sans bateaux sont comme les enfants dont les parents n'auraient pas un grand lit sur lequel on puisse jouer; leurs rêves alors se tarissent, l'espionnage y remplace l'aventure, et la hideur des polices la beauté ensoleillée des corsaires" (Foucault, "Les hétérotopies" [compact disc]; Foucault, "Les hétérotopies," 36).

Lesson Two: Stories and Scholarship

1. Again, this isn't meant to be accurate—it's a fairy tale about Cajun/Louisiana history. For Acadian history, see Griffiths, *Contexts of Acadian History*; Faragher, *Great and Noble Scheme*. For a comparative historical analysis of Acadian life that refutes many of the romantic notions of pastoral Acadie, see Kennedy, *Something of a Peasant Paradise?* For early Cajun history, see Carl A. Brasseaux, *Acadian to Cajun*; Carl A. Brasseaux, *Founding of New Acadia*; Carl A. Brasseaux, "Acadian Education."
2. For studies of Louisiana politics, see Parent, Inside the Carnival; Zebrowski, Hydrocarbon Hucksters; Wetta, Louisiana Scalawags; Barnes, Louisiana Populist Movement.
3. Certeau, Practice of Everyday Life, 43.
4. Most scholarly work that specifically addresses Chauvin, Louisiana, appears in unpublished dissertations and theses from sociology and linguistic anthropology: Parr, "Glossary"; Pierron, "Sociological Study"; LeCompte, "Word Atlas"; Gordon, "Rhetoric of Community

Ritual"; Walton, "Flat Speech"; Rottet, "Language Shift and Language Death"; Dajko, "Ethnic and Geographic Variation"; Hubbard, "Blessing of the Fleet."

5. For a well-cited history written in a "local color" style (replete with a bewildering section of portraits of Cajun "celebrities" and concepts as well as a discussion of "Cajunism" as a "neo-pagan" practice), see Rushton, *Cajuns*. For the first serious treatment of Cajuns from a sociocultural perspective, see Dormon, *People Called Cajuns*.

6. On cultural identity, see Bernard, *Cajuns*; Esman, "Festivals, Change, and Unity"; Green, "Louisiana Cajuns"; Henry, "From 'Acadien' to 'Cajun' to 'Cadien'"; Rees, "From 'Grand Dérangement' to Acadiana"; Stivale, *Disenchanting les Bons Temps*; Webre, "Among the Cybercajuns." On representation, see Ancelet, "Negotiating the Mainstream"; Carl A. Brasseaux, *French, Cajun, Creole, Houma*; Camoin, *Louisiane*; Dubois and Horvath, "Sounding Cajun"; Hebert-Leiter, *Becoming Cajun*; Sexton, "Cajun or Coonass?"; Sexton, "Cajun Mardi Gras"; Wiley, "Wilderness Theatre." On "traditional" life, see Ancelet, *Cajun Country*; Ancelet, *"Capitaine, Voyage Ton Flag"*; Ancelet, "Theory and Practice"; Comeaux, "Cajun Barn"; Del Sesto and Gibson, *Culture of Acadiana*; Estaville, "Changeless Cajuns"; Gould, *Cadiens d'Asteur*; Hallowell, *People of the Bayou*; Lindahl, "Presence of the Past"; Sexton, "Cajun and Creole Treaters"; Sexton, "Ritualized Inebriation"; Tidwell, *Bayou Farewell*; Ware, *Cajun Women and Mardi Gras*. On folklore and music, see Ancelet, *Cajun Music*; Ancelet and Gould, *One Generation at a Time*; Ancelet, *Cajun and Creole Folktales*; Caffery, *Traditional Music in Coastal Louisiana*; Bernard, *Swamp Pop*; Blank and Strachwitz, *J'ai Été au Bal*; Borders, "Researching Creole and Cajun Musics"; Ryan Brasseaux, *Cajun Breakdown*; Ryan Brasseaux and Fontenot,, *Accordions, Fiddles, Two-Step, and Swing*; LeMenestrel, "French Music"; Reese and Allen, *Mamou*; Smith, "Cajun Music." On Cajun boundaries, see David, "(Re)Turn of the Native"; DeWitt, *Cajun and Zydeco Dance Music*; Dubois and Horvath, "Creoles and Cajuns"; Henry, "What Has Become of the Cajuns?"; Henry and Bankston, *Blue Collar Bayou*; Heylen, "Kill the Devil"; Natsis, "Legislation and Language"; Rottet, *Language Shift*; Sexton, "Cajun-French Language Maintenance and Shift"; Tentchoff, "Ethnic Survival"; Trépanier, "Cajunization of French Louisiana."

Lesson Three: A Brief History of the Pre-Bust Louisiana Shrimp Fishery

1. Goode, Fisheries and Fishery Industries of the United States, Section II, 535.
2. 1 Corinthians 15:20 (King James Bible).
3. Goode, Fisheries and Fishery Industries of the United States, Section II, 578.
4. Goode, *Fisheries and Fishery Industries of the United States, Section II*, 576. Two hundred thousand dollars is roughly equivalent to $4.4 million today (Sahr, "Inflation Conversion Factors").
5. Davis, *Washed Away?* 339.
6. Seferovich, "Survey," 20–21.
7. Johnson and Lindner, *Shrimp Industry*, 9–19; Becnel, "History of the Louisiana Shrimp Industry," 6.
8. Johnson and Lindner, *Shrimp Industry*, 40–43.
9. Davis, *Washed Away?* 306–7; Hebert, "Shrimp Boats Is Anettin' Millions"; Lorillard D. Sampsell, "The Recent Storm on the Gulf Coast," *Frank Leslie's Weekly*, October 26, 1893, 270; "Mrs. Quong Is up to Date," *Detroit Free Press*, February 2, 1896; "Louisiana's Queerest

Colony," *Boston Daily Globe*, December 7, 1898; "Trade in Dried Fish," *Washington Post*, February 1, 1903. Quong Sun was not officially established until the early 1920s, but evidence indicates that the company operated at least as early as 1913 (Kaplan-Levenson, "Little Company That Could"; *Soards' New Orleans City Directory for 1912*, 1282). It is unclear to what extent the Chinese population overlapped with the Philippine population, and though contemporary accounts seem to conflate the two groups, scholars seem to agree that the shrimp-drying process comes from Chinese immigrants, though Filipino (as well as Italian, Croatian, German, and Cajun) groups participated in this industry (Davis, *Washed Away?* 305–10; Higgins, "Story of the Shrimp Industry," 440).

10. Johnson and Lindner, *Shrimp Industry*, 25, 37.

11. George W. Dunbar, George H. Dunbar, and Francis B. Dunbar, "Improvement in Methods of Preserving Shrimps and Other Shell-Fish," US Patent 178916A, filed February 1, 1876; issued June 20, 1876, https://patents.google.com/patent/US178916A/en.

12. Goode, Fisheries and Fishery Industries of the United States, Section V, 810.

13. Becnel, "History of the Louisiana Shrimp Industry," 14.

14. Johnson and Lindner, *Shrimp Industry*, 30.

15. Percy, "Louisiana Shrimp Story," 102.

16. Johnson and Lindner, *Shrimp Industry*, 23–40.

17. Johnson and Lindner, *Shrimp Industry*, 6; Percy, "Louisiana Shrimp Story," 102.

18. It is unclear why this gear is named for the otter. Perhaps it has to do with otter fishing, wherein trained otters chased fish into nets. Perhaps it has to do with the bobbing of the boards in the water if they are insufficiently weighted, as a Baton Rouge newspaper article from 1999 claims (Bruce Schultz, "Tests under Way on New Version of Trawl Doors," *New Orleans Advocate*, August 23, 1999). Perhaps it is based on the boards used to stretch the hides of otters.

19. Typically, there are two open shrimping seasons for state waters up to three miles from the coast: a brown shrimp season from May to mid-June, and a white shrimp season from August through December. For discussion of shrimping regulation as it affects the shrimpers I spoke to in 2015, see "Nets," in this volume. Louisiana has had regulated open and closed shrimp seasons since 1910 after a law introduced by Representative Robert B. Butler of Terrebonne Parish (An Act for the Protection of Salt Water Shrimp, to Provide the Manner in Which Said Crustaceans May Be Caught, to Fix the Season in Which They May Be Caught, to Authorize the Issuance of Licenses to Seine, and to Provide Penalties for the Violations of This Act, act 245, sess. 2 [July 7, 1910]). Not until the late 1930s did marine biologists begin to understand shrimp populations in the waters of Louisiana enough to thoughtfully designate open shrimping seasons (Colten, "Environmental Management in Coastal Louisiana," 703).

20. Skladany and Harris, "On Global Pond," 178; Goss, Burch, and Rickson, "Agri-Food Restructuring," 516–17.

21. Goss, Burch, and Rickson, "Agri-Food Restructuring," 518–21.

22. Tran, "Food Safety," 708; Harrison, *Buoyancy on the Bayou*.

23. Import Alert, 8; Harrison, Buoyancy on the Bayou, 22–25.

24. De Schryver, Defoirdt, and Sorgeloos, "Early Mortality Syndrome Outbreaks," 1; "Thailand: Thai Shrimp Association Explains Impact of EMS Epidemic," *Asia News Monitor*, December 20, 2013.

25. US Food and Drug Administration, *Import Alert 16-127*.

26. Marschke and Vandergeest, "Slavery Scandals," 40–41.

Syllabus

1. Postelection analysis has revealed that at least in the case of the 2016 US election, the concept that white, working-class voters comprised the majority of Trump supporters is false. Based on an analysis of American National Election Study data, political scientists Nicholas Carnes and Noam Lupu demonstrate that "white non-Hispanic voters without college degrees making below the median household income made up only 25 percent of Trump voters," which they characterize as "a far cry from the working-class-fueled victory many journalists have imagined" ("It's Time to Bust the Myth: Most Trump Voters Were Not Working Class," *Washington Post*, June 5, 2017, https://www.washingtonpost.com/news/monkey-cage/wp/2017/06/05/its-time-to-bust-the-myth-most-trump-voters-were-not-working-class/).

Blood

1. Foucault, *History of Sexuality*, 1:147–48.

Bloodlines

1. Carsten, "Introduction," S2.
2. Harrison, Buoyancy on the Bayou, 76.
3. The "T" is short for *petit*, the French word for small, but in this case, it's the Louisiana French way of saying "Jr."
4. Connerton, How Modernity Forgets, 68.
5. Even the language of shrimping is tinged with lunar lore: when the moon's crescent is angled, shrimpers commonly say that "the moon is dumping shrimp into the bayous." This phrase promises a good catch.
6. Carsten, "Introduction," S11.
7. I explore the call of water and this elegant phrase in the following chapter.
8. Ingold, *Lines*, 117.
9. Schneider, *American Kinship*, 25.
10. See Douglas, Natural Symbols; Douglas, Purity and Danger.
11. Foucault, *History of Sexuality*, 1:143.
12. Foucault, *History of Sexuality*, 1:148.
13. Foucault, *History of Sexuality*, 1:149.
14. Carsten, "Introduction," S12, S13.
15. Marx, *Capital*, 342.
16. Associated Press, "Louisiana Shrimping: Lower Prices This Year and Rise in Imported Shrimp," *Gulf Live*, March 29, 2015, http://www.gulflive.com/news/index.ssf/2015/03/louisiana_shrimping_lower_pric.html; Associated Press, "Louisiana Shrimpers Decry Low Prices, Damage Caused by Imports," NOLA.com, August 12, 2015, https://www.wdsu.com/article/shrimpers-decry-low-prices-damage-caused-by-imports/8517170#; Associated Press, "Shrimp Prices Plummet in 2015," *Washington Times*, May 26, 2015, http://www.washingtontimes.com/news/2015/may/26/shrimp-prices-plummet-in-2015/.

Blood Magic and Cruelty

1. In Louisiana, people with last names end that would end in *eau* in Acadie have added an *x* to the end: Boudreaux, Thibodeaux (more commonly spelled Thibodaux in Louisiana), Gautreaux.

2. Chuck and his first wife made up the last name *Emmrys*, and he used it while they were married. Though raised bilingual, he lived most his life in English.

3. Especially among the Acadians I met during my year in Canada and in a subsequent visit during the Congrès Mondial des Acadiens, it seems to be common knowledge that Acadians and Mi'kmaq intermarried. Several branches of my family lineage trace back to "unknown Mi'kmaq woman" in the seventeenth and eighteenth centuries or have surnames historically associated with Mi'kmaq bands. For more on the Acadians, the Mi'kmaq, and le Grand Dérangement, see Carl A. Brasseaux, *French, Cajun, Creole, Houma*; Carl A. Brasseaux, *Quest for the Promised Land*; Carl A. Brasseaux, *Scattered to the Wind*; Dickason, "La 'guerre navale' des Micmacs"; Dickason, "Louisbourg and the Indians"; Mathis-Moser and Bischof, *Acadians and Cajuns*; Rushton, *Cajuns*; Scott, "Mi'kmaw Armed Resistance."

4. Strong and van Winkle, "'Indian Blood,'" 551. The phenomenon of claiming native ancestry without actual ties to indigenous society allows white people to reap cultural benefits without suffering racism. This practice recently came under increased public scrutiny when Senator Elizabeth Warren's claim of Native American ancestry caused a scandal during the 2020 presidential election primaries.

5. Strong and van Winkle, "'Indian Blood,'" 551.

6. See Bernard, *Cajuns*, 85–111.

7. Although Black francophones in Louisiana often share surnames, French dialect, and ways of living, few identify as Cajun, and they are usually considered Creole, a highly contested term in Louisiana that can at turns mean people born in the New World of European descent or Black francophones. See Binder, *Creoles and Cajuns*, 57–61; Spitzer, "Monde Créole."

8. *Coonass* is the "official" slur for a Cajun. No one is really sure where it comes from, but coonasses will often give an explanation a go if you ask nicely. Or you could read a scholarly exploration of the term: Sexton, "Cajun or Coonass?" 273–74.

9. Momaday, *Way to Rainy Mountain*, 7.

10. Woodard, *Ancestral Voice*, 22.

11. Krupat, *Voice in the Margin*, 14; Strong and van Winkle, "'Indian Blood,'" 562.

12. Berlant, *Cruel Optimism*, 2–3.

13. For more of the story of that summer, see Feldman and Lirette, "New Adventures."

14. Stivale, *Disenchanting les Bons Temps*, 121.

15. Berlant, *Cruel Optimism*, 23.

16. Berlant, *Cruel Optimism*, 1.

17. Kassie Bracken, "Oil and Water," *New York Times*, July 19, 2010, http://www.nytimes.com/video/us/1247468464693/oil-and-water.html.

18. Susan Saulny, "Cajuns on Gulf Worry They May Need to Move on Once Again," *New York Times*, July 19, 2010.

Ecology and the Body

1. This view of culture has been a prevalent way of understanding culture in anthropology and elsewhere in the twentieth and twenty-first centuries. According to Bronisław Malinowski, "This social heritage is the key concept of social anthropology. It is usually called culture. [. . .] Culture comprises inherited artifacts, goods, technical processes, ideas, habits, and values" (cited in Kroeber and Kluckhohn, *Culture*, 47). In Clifford Geertz's definition, "Culture is best seen not as complexes of concrete behavior patterns—customs, usages, traditions, habit clusters—as has, by and large, been the case up to now, but as a set of control mechanisms—plans, recipes, rules, instructions (what computer engineers call 'programs')—for the governing of behavior" (*Interpretation of Cultures*, 44). For more on Geertz's view of culture, see "Miraculous Draught of Fish," in this volume. Both of these definitions emphasize the status of culture as a system of knowledge and the passed-along nature of cultural knowledge.

2. Ingold, *Perception of the Environment*, 25.

3. Ingold argues that our emphasis on genealogy has even penetrated and become naturalized by our scientific models. Instead of blood, we get genes: "Nowadays, one is as likely to hear it said of some feature of a person that it is 'in the genes' as to be told that it is 'in the blood.' But the sense of such pronouncements has hardly been altered by the substitution of genetic for sanguinary metaphors. If anything, the science of genetics has not so much challenged as taken on board—and in turn lent authority to—the founding principles of the genealogical model, namely that persons embody certain attributes of appearance, temperament and mentality by virtue of their ancestry, and that these are passed on in a form that is unaffected by the circumstances or achievements of their life in the world" (*Perception of the Environment*, 137)

4. Ingold, *Perception of the Environment*, 144.

5. Ingold, *Perception of the Environment*, 148.

6. Ingold, *Perception of the Environment*, 147–48.

7. See Carrigan, *Saffron Scourge*.

8. Jeff Adelson, "National Recession May Be Catching up with Louisiana, Census Figures Indicate," NOLA.com, September 20, 2012, https://www.nola.com/news/business/article_050b50a8-909b-5a95-8635-5bc07fe2a690.html.

9. After the development of such technologies as the otter net, butterfly nets, ice boats, and refrigeration, shrimpers stopped working for processing plants and started working for themselves. See Harrison, *Buoyancy on the Bayou*, 17–19; Landry, "Shrimping in Louisiana."

10. One possible channel for shrimpers is in the direct retail market. SeaGrant, a university-affiliated research, advocacy, and support organization targeting coastal communities and fisheries, has developed the Louisiana Direct Seafood marketing initiative. LA Direct Seafood, based on a 2010 program in Delcambre, Louisiana, gives shrimpers and other fishers a platform to sell and market their seafood online.

11. Carsten, "Introduction," S7.

12. See Gutierrez, *Cajun Foodways*; Richardson, "Local Diet."

13. For a popular litany of shrimp dishes, see Zemeckis, *Forrest Gump*.

14. Ingold, *Perception of the Environment*, 143.

15. Berlant, *Cruel Optimism*, 122.

16. Berlant, *Cruel Optimism*, 122.

Water

1. Couvillion et al., *Land Area Change in Coastal Louisiana*; Marshall et al., "Losing Ground."
2. Saikku, *This Delta, This Land*, 141.
3. Powell, *Accidental City*, 8–10.
4. Powell, *Accidental City*, 43–51.
5. Saikku, *This Delta, This Land*, 156–59.
6. Mizelle, *Backwater Blues*, 44–47.
7. Flood Control Act, ch. 596, sess. 1 (May 15, 1928).
8. Seed et al., *Investigation of Performance*, 4–8.
9. Kesel, "Decline in the Suspended Load."
10. Turner, "Discussion Of: Olea, R. A. and Coleman, J. L., Jr., 2014," 1332–33.
11. Knabb, Rhome, and Brown, *Tropical Cyclone Report*, 11.
12. As of 2022, this flood control system, the Morganza to the Gulf of Mexico Project, is under the auspices of the Army Corps of Engineers until its completion.
13. See Misrach and Orff, *Petrochemical America*, 119, 131–35, 169–77.
14. Stevens, "Idea of Order at Key West," lines 38–40.
15. Stevens, "Idea of Order at Key West," lines 3–4.
16. Deleuze and Guattari, *Thousand Plateaus*, 4.
17. Stevens, "Idea of Order at Key West," lines 53–56.
18. Stevens, "Idea of Order at Key West," lines 45–46, 49.
19. Stevens, "Idea of Order at Key West," lines 42–43.

Bodies of Water

1. Guyton, *Textbook of Medical Physiology*, 274.

Names of Water, or the Idea of Order at Mare à Clay

1. Fortier, *Louisiana*, 201.
2. US Department of the Interior, *Decisions of the United States Board on Geographical Names*, 8.
3. Bill Ellzey, "Flooding Sparks a Lawsuit for Crop Damage," *Houma Courier*, January 18, 2012; Bill Ellzey, "Lake's Name Change Is a Mystery," *Houma Courier*, January 21, 2012; Bill Ellzey, "Time for the Lights to Be Turned On," *Houma Courier*, January 25, 2012.
4. Ryan, Weinstein, and Pearson, *Houma Navigation Canal Deepening Project*, 59–60.
5. May, "John A. Quitman and His Slaves," 556.
6. William McCulloh, *Township 19S, Range 18E, Southeastern District West of the Mississippi River*, official plat map (Donaldsonville, LA: Surveyor General Office, 1856), https://wwwslodms.doa.la.gov/WebForms/DocumentViewer.aspx?docId=522.00853&category=H#1.
7. Ingold, *Perception of the Environment*, 219.
8. Massey, *Space, Place, and Gender*, 3.

Bodies on the Water

1. Deleuze and Guattari, *Thousand Plateaus*, 151.
2. Deleuze and Guattari write, "You have to keep enough of the organism for it to reform each dawn; and you have to keep small supplies of signifiance and subjectification, if only to turn them against their own systems when the circumstances demand it" (*Thousand Plateaus*, 160).
3. Deleuze and Guattari, *Thousand Plateaus*, 151.
4. Carla Ghere and Carolyn Tillman, two women in the fisheries whose stories are out of the scope of this project on shrimpers, were notable exceptions to this ideal during my fieldwork. They ran crab boats, alone or together, that acted as the only female-bodied space available to them in the fisheries. This world, too, was permeable and highly visible. Others on the water noticed and hailed them. Adopting a persona that was brash, profane, and skillful, Carla was well respected by nearly every fisherman I talked to: they admired her drive and success in furthering her family's fishery legacy. Her younger sister, Carolyn, who also maintained a job at a grocery store that she went to after crabbing in the morning, was less rough but did not need to secure herself as a fleet leader. When I asked Carolyn what the most challenging thing was about being a woman in the masculine world of the fisheries, she replied, "Peeing."
5. Even more grimly, Kim rode out 2021's Hurricane Ida on his boat. This deadly category 4 storm hovered over the Chauvin area, causing cataclysmic destruction. Against all odds, Kim survived, and he was interviewed first by Megan Wyatt, journalist for the *Acadiana Advocate*. Megan Wyatt, "Commercial Fisher Recalls Riding Out Hurricane Ida in His Boat before 140 mph Winds Flipped It," *Acadiana Advocate*, September 7, 2021, https://www.theadvocate.com/acadiana/news/weather_traffic/article_8bd91596-1023-11ec-94c7-337d9 0de622d.html.
6. For more on what it is like to drown and save the drowning, see Pia, "Observations."

Land's End

1. *Bayou Lafourche* means "Bayou the Fork," and if very old maps are to be trusted, it was previously considered "La Fourche des Chetimacha" and the "Chetimacha River"; it later appears as "Bayou la Fourche des Chetimachas" in church records. See Decercelier, *Carte du Missicipy ou Louissiane depuis la Baye de lascension jusqua la pointe de la Mobille*, 1718–29), Archives nationales d'outre-mer, Aix-en-Provence, France; John Ross, *Course of the River Mississippi, from the Balise to Fort Chartres; Taken on an Expedition to the Illinois, in the Latter End of the Year 1765* (London: Sayer, 1765), Louisiana Research Collection, Tulane University, New Orleans; Woods and Nolan, *Sacramental Records*, 28, 198).
2. D. C. Houston, *Military Approaches to New Orleans*, Department of the Gulf Map 10, prepared by order of Major General Nathaniel P. Banks (New Orleans: US Department of the Gulf, 1863), figure 18, RG 77, M 106-1, National Archives, Washington, DC; Becnel, *Barrow Family*, 46–57.
3. "Caillou Island House," *Thibodaux Minerva*, May 6, 1854, 20; Jonathan C. White and Louis F. Anderson, "The Gulf House," *Thibodaux Minerva*, July 14, 1855, 30.
4. Dixon, *Last Days of Last Island*, 22.

5. Jonathan C. White and Louis F. Anderson, "Notices," *Thibodaux Minerva*, September 22, 1855, 40.

6. Finn-Fon-Boo [pseud.], "Sea Shore Correspondence," *Thibodaux Minerva*, September 23, 1854, 40.

7. On rheumatism, see Jonathan C. White and Louis F. Anderson, "Notices," *Thibodaux Minerva*, October 7, 1854, 42.

8. Klepp, *Revolutionary Conceptions*, 98–106.

9. Studyx [pseud.], "Last Island," *Houma Ceres*, August 30, 1855, 1, 7.

10. Emerson, *Essays*, 212–13.

11. Emerson, *Essays*, 205–6, 193.

12. Quoted in Dixon, *Last Days of Last Island*, 72. The following summary of the storm relies on Dixon's scholarship and narrative.

13. DeSantis, "Labors of Love.",

14. Paul Virilio, "Primary Accident," 211–12.

15. Corbin, *Lure of the Sea*, 249.

Oil and Water

1. Harrison, *Buoyancy on the Bayou*, esp. 32.

2. Ryan, Weinstein, and Pearson, *Houma Navigation Canal Deepening Project*, 1.

3. Misrach and Orff, *Petrochemical America*, 143.

4. For instance, in *Terrebonne Parish School Board v. Castex Energy, Inc.*, the Louisiana State Supreme Court ruled that because the original lease allowed an oil lessee to alter the land, the company was not required to remedy the damage caused by digging pipeline canals even though the damage was unequivocally acknowledged and was not limited to the leased plot of land (Theriot, *American Energy, Imperiled Coast*, 212; *Terrebonne Parish School Board v. Castex Energy, et al.*, No. 04-C-0968, Supreme Court of Louisiana [2005]).

5. Misrach and Orff, *Petrochemical America*, 131, 127.

Gulf

1. This discussion of imagination borrows from philosopher Brian Massumi, who defines imagination as "the involuntary and elicited no-difference between perception, cognition, and hallucination" (*Parables for the Virtual*, 207). In theorizing how a person might navigate a reality that includes the virtual and the actual, Massumi characterizes imagination as a methodology:

> Imagination is the mode of thought most precisely suited to the differentiating vagueness of the virtual. It alone manages to diagram without stilling. Imagination can also be called intuition: a thinking feeling. Not feeling something. Feeling thought—as such, in its movement, as process, on arrival, as yet unthought-out and unenacted, postinstrumental and preoperative. Suspended. Looped out. Imagination is felt thought, thought only-felt, felt as only thought can be: insensibly unstill. Outside any given thing,

outside any given sense, outside actuality. Outside coming in. The mutual envelopment of thought and sensation, as they arrive together, pre–what they will have become, just beginning to unfold from the unfelt and unthinkable outside: of process, transformation in itself. (34)

2. Burley, *Losing Ground*, 54. Burley was a research assistant with the Center for Hazards Assessment, Response and Technology (CHART) and the University of New Orleans, which employed a team of ethnographers to interview people in coastal parishes. CHART is an applied sociology think tank that develops disaster-response strategies for Louisiana communities.

3. Carl A. Brasseaux, Cajun historian par excellence, writes, "It is clear that the story of the Acadians is one of survival against all odds" (*French, Cajun, Creole, Houma*, 6).

4. Stevens, "Idea of Order at Key West," lines 42–43.

5. Austin, "Coastal Exploitation," 687–88; Dokka, "Modern-Day Tectonic Subsidence"; Dokka, "Louisiana's Coast Is on Life-Support." Dokka further argues that current efforts at coastal restoration are misguided at best because although human activity certainly has damaged the wetlands, tectonic forces are also sinking the landmass.

6. Coral Davenport and Campbell Robertson, "Resettling the First American 'Climate Refugees,'" *New York Times*, May 3, 2016, http://www.nytimes.com/2016/05/03/us/resettling-the-first-american-climate-refugees.html.

7. Stevens, "Idea of Order at Key West," lines 34–35.

8. Lefebvre, *Production of Space*, 164.

Nets

1. *Fishery Market News*, https://www.fisheries.noaa.gov/national/sustainable-fisheries/fishery-market-news.

Ghost Nets

1. This quotation is part of a reproduction of a "large sheet" written by Crick in a pamphlet intended to refute this anti-trawling jeremiad: Hull Defence Committee, *Trawl Fishing*, 6.

2. Adorno and Horkheimer, *Dialectic of Enlightenment*, 120.

3. Teachers would rap knuckles with rulers, hit students with rubber hoses, and force them to write lines or wear nooses, among other things. See Bernard, *Cajuns*, 18–19, 33–34; Phillips, "Spoken French of Louisiana," 173.

4. See Foucault, *Discipline and Punish*, 135–305.

5. I distinguish here between trawlers (shrimpers who employ "otter trawl" fishing gear, which consists of great nets attached to an outrigger boom that stay entirely submerged during the drag) and shrimpers who use skimmers or butterfly net gear, neither of which currently require TEDs.

6. AIS Requirements, Code of Federal Regulations, Title 33 (2015): 164, § 164.146 ¶ (b) ibid.: 164.146 ¶ (j).

7. Recordkeeping and Reporting, Code of Federal Regulations, Title 50 (2015): 622, § 622.651.

8. Deleuze, "Postscript," 7.
9. Deleuze, "Postscript," 4.
10. Deleuze, "Postscript," 5.
11. Days of Penance, canon 1251, in *Code of Canon Law*.
12. I cannot understand what possible motivation a federal organization like National Marine Fisheries would have to plant turtles or what possible benefit anyone could receive by sabotaging a relatively small industry in a relatively negligible way. Harrison documents this conspiracy theory in *Buoyancy on the Bayou*, 51–53.
13. For US federal regulations, see Compensatory Mitigation for Losses of Aquatic Resources, Code of Federal Regulations, 33 (2015): 325, 332; Compensatory Mitigation for Losses of Aquatic Resources, Code of Federal Regulations, 40 (2015): 230 §§ 230.91–230.98. For Louisiana law, see Mitigation of Coastal Wetlands Losses, Louisiana Revised Statutes, 49 (2011): § 49:214.41.
14. Ingold, *Perception of the Environment*, 186.
15. Heidegger, "Building Dwelling Thinking," 145.
16. Heidegger, "Building Dwelling Thinking," 150.
17. "dwell, v.," Oxford English Dictionary.
18. Sea Turtle Conservation; Shrimp Trawl Requirements, Federal Register, 52 (Washington, DC, 1987) 217, 22, 227, § 24244.
19. Turtle Excluder Devices; Findings; Enforcement of Federal Requirements; Rules and Regulations, Louisiana Revised Statutes, 56 (2011): § 56:57.2.
20. US Department of Transportation, Maritime Administration, *Report to the Congress*, 6.
21. Margavio and Forsyth, *Caught in the Net*, 31–42.
22. Provides Relative to Fisheries Management by the Department of Wildlife and Fisheries, 2010 Regular Session, HB 1334; Repeals the Prohibition on Enforcement of the Federal TEDs in Shrimp Nets Requirement, 2015 Regular Session, HB 668; Ostdahl, *Warmwater Shrimp*, 2–3.
23. Benjamin Alexander-Bloch, "Louisiana Shrimp Task Force Votes to Repeal Turtle-Excluder Device Enforcement Prohibition," NOLA.com, April 1, 2015.
24. Alexander-Bloch, "Louisiana Shrimp Task Force Votes."
25. Rudloe and Rudloe, "Shrimpers and Lawmakers Collide," 50.
26. Deleuze, "Postscript," 6.
27. Friedman, "BP Buys 'Oil' Search Terms."
28. Outzen, "Gulf Oil Spill."
29. *U.S. No 2 Diesel Ultra Low Sulfur (0–15 Ppm) Retail Prices*, US Energy Information Administration (2017) https://www.eia.gov/dnav/pet/PET_PRI_GND_A_EPD2DXL0_PTE_DPGAL_M.htm.
30. Exact figures on expenses for an average trawler are difficult to determine. Insurance may be as high as $15,000 per month for the largest vessels or $1,200 for mid-sized vessels to $83 for the smallest, inshore boats in Louisiana. For a good breakdown of shrimper expenses in 2005, see LaFleur, Yeates, and Aysen, "Estimating the Economic Impact."
31. Mine et al., *Louisiana Shrimp Value Chain*, 20.
32. Mine et al., *Louisiana Shrimp Value Chain*, 19.

Miraculous Draught of Fish

1. Stewart, "Atmospheric Attunements," 451.
2. See especially Castells, *Rise of the Network Society*; Foucault, *Birth of Biopolitics*; Galloway, *Protocol*; Harvey, *Spaces of Global Capitalism*; Massey, *World City*; Negri and Hardt, *Empire*; Povinelli, *Geontologies*.
3. Luke 5:10 (King James Bible).
4. The theme of God providing, of course, appears throughout Christian and Jewish Scripture, and Chad was not the only shrimper to tell me that God would provide.
5. This boat, even for its large size, was considered expensive by others in Chauvin, but it involved a significant amount of customization and luxury styling. When I talked to them in 2016, when the boat was still incomplete, many shrimpers were skeptical that the purchaser would be able to recoup the cost.
6. Foucault, *History of Sexuality*, 3:42.
7. Foucault, *History of Sexuality*, 3:50; emphasis added.
8. Foucault et al., "Ethics of the Concern of the Self."
9. Stewart, "Atmospheric Attunements," 445.
10. Deleuze, "Control and Becoming," 176.
11. Spinoza, *Ethics*, 218. Curley translates *pietas* as "morality." In the Latin: "Cupiditatem autem bene faciendi, quae ex eo ingeneratur, quod ex rationis ductu vivimus, pietatem voco" (Spinoza, *Ethica Ordine Geometrico Demonstrata*, 356).
12. Certeau, *Practice of Everyday Life*, 87.

Fish Stories: A Methodological Appendix

1. Matthew 4:18–20 (King James Bible).
2. "In the beginning was the Word, and the Word was with God, and the Word was God" (John 1:1 [King James Bible]).
3. In fact, the idiom *fish story*, based on fishers' supposed propensity to stretch the truth, means a story too incredible to be true.
4. Thompson, *Motif-Index of Folk-Literature*, 524.
5. Luke 5:1–11; John 21:1–14
6. Chauvin actually has no mayor, as it falls under the jurisdiction of the consolidated Terrebonne Parish government.
7. Geertz, *Interpretation of Cultures*, 14.
8. Geertz, *Interpretation of Cultures*, 44.
9. Geertz, *Interpretation of Cultures*, 15.
10. Geertz, *Interpretation of Cultures*, 5.
11. US Coast Guard, *On Scene Coordinator Report*, 33.
12. While Geertz towered over interpretive cultural anthropology in the United States in the late twentieth century, he was not the first to combine aesthetic and "scientific" concerns in anthropology. For a brief sampling, see Malinowski, *Argonauts of the Western Pacific*; Mead, *Coming of Age in Samoa*; Leiris, *L'Afrique fantôme*; Lévi-Strauss, *Tristes tropiques*; Dumont, *Headman and I*.
13. Rouch, *Ciné-ethnography*, 98.
14. Rouch, *Ciné-ethnography*, 154.

15. Rouch, *Ciné-ethnography*, 100–101.
16. William James, *Essays in Radical Empiricism*, 42.
17. Jackson, *Paths toward a Clearing*, 8.
18. "The ordinary hums with the background noise of ruts and disorientations, intensities and resting points. An atmospheric fill buzzes with the resonance of nascent forms quickening or sloughing off, materialities pressing into the expressivity of something coming into existence" (Stewart, "Atmospheric Attunements," 446).
19. Jackson proposes studying not culture but the lifeworld: "a world whose horizons are open, the quotidian world in which we live, adjusting our needs to the needs of others, testing our ideas against the exigencies of life" (*Paths toward a Clearing*, 1). The term *lifeworld* (*Lebenswelt*) comes from philosopher Edmund Husserl (*Crisis of European Sciences*, 108–9). For the introduction of lifeworld in social theory, see Schütz, *On Phenomenology and Social Relations*, 72–78.
20. Jackson, *Paths toward a Clearing*, 1, 136.
21. Ingold, *Perception of the Environment*, 140.
22. Deleuze and Guattari, *Thousand Plateaus*, 15. According to Massumi's interpretation of Deleuze and Guattari, their philosophy shares with James, associated with the American school of pragmatism, a "radical empiricism," a term that Deleuze and Guattari themselves discuss as "when immanence is no longer immanent to something other than itself" (*What Is Philosophy?* 46). See also Massumi, *Parables for the Virtual*.
23. "To find one's way is to advance along a line of growth, in a world which is never quite the same from one moment to the next, and whose future configuration can never be fully known. Ways of life are not therefore determined in advance, as routes to be followed, but have continually to be worked out anew. And these ways, far from being inscribed upon the surface of an inanimate world, are the very threads from which the living world is woven" (Ingold, *Perception of the Environment*, 242).
24. Ingold, *Perception of the Environment*, 4–5.
25. Rouch, *Ciné-ethnography*, 99. For the film, see Rouch, *Tourou et Bitti*.
26. Rouch, *Ciné-ethnography*, 100.
27. Stoller, *Sensuous Scholarship*, 23.
28. Taussig, *Mimesis and Alterity*, 21.
29. Taussig, *Mimesis and Alterity*, 26.
30. Taussig, *Mimesis and Alterity*, 19.
31. Geertz writes that the texts ethnographers write are "fictions, in the sense that [interpretations] are 'something made' [. . .] not that they are false, unfactual, or merely 'as if' thought experiments" (*Interpretation of Cultures*, 15).
32. Jackson, *Paths toward a Clearing*, 154.
33. Taussig defines the dialectical image as "dislocating chains of concordance with one hand, reconstellating in accord with a mimetic snap, with the other" (*Mimesis and Alterity*, 19).
34. In what might be the most famous French poststructuralist comedy bit, Michel Foucault deadpans, "Perhaps one day, this century will be known as Deleuzian" ("Theatrum Philosophicum," 885.
35. Culler, *Theory of the Lyric*, 109.
36. Culler, *Theory of the Lyric*, 115.
37. Culler, *Theory of the Lyric*, 116.
38. Stewart, *Space on the Side of the Road*, 205.
39. Moore, "Poetry," 24.

Bibliography

Adorno, Theodor W., and Max Horkheimer. *Dialectic of Enlightenment: Philosophical Fragments*. Edited by Gunzelin Schmid Noerr. Translated by Edmund Jephcott. Stanford: Stanford University Press, 2002.
Ancelet, Barry Jean. *Cajun and Creole Folktales: The French Oral Tradition of South Louisiana*. New York: Garland, 1994.
Ancelet, Barry Jean. *Cajun Country*. Jackson: University Press of Mississippi, 1991.
Ancelet, Barry Jean. *Cajun Music: Its Origins and Development*. Lafayette: Center for Louisiana Studies, 1989.
Ancelet, Barry Jean. *"Capitaine, Voyage Ton Flag": The Traditional Cajun Country Mardi Gras*. Lafayette: Center for Louisiana Studies, 1989.
Ancelet, Barry Jean. "Negotiating the Mainstream: The Creoles and Cajuns in Louisiana." *French Review* 80, no. 6 (2007): 1235–55.
Ancelet, Barry Jean. "The Theory and Practice of Activist Folklore: From Fieldwork to Programming." In *Working the Field: Accounts from French Louisiana*, edited by Jacques M. Henry and Sara LeMenestrel, 81–100. Westport, CT: Praeger, 2003.
Ancelet, Barry Jean, and Philip Gould. *One Generation at a Time: Biography of a Cajun and Creole Music Festival*. Lafayette: Center for Louisiana Studies, 2007.
Austin, Diane E. "Coastal Exploitation, Land Loss, and Hurricanes: A Recipe for Disaster." *American Anthropologist* 108, no. 4 (2006): 671–91.
Barnes, Donna A. *The Louisiana Populist Movement, 1881–1900*. Baton Rouge: Louisiana State University Press, 2011.
Becnel, Thomas. *The Barrow Family and the Barataria and Lafourche Canal: The Transportation Revolution in Louisiana, 1829–1925*. Baton Rouge: Louisiana State University Press, 1989.
Becnel, Thomas. "A History of the Louisiana Shrimp Industry, 1867–1961." Master's thesis, Louisiana State University, 1962.
Berlant, Lauren. *Cruel Optimism*. Durham: Duke University Press, 2011.
Bernard, Shane. *The Cajuns: Americanization of a People*. Jackson: University Press of Mississippi, 2003.
Bernard, Shane. *Swamp Pop: Cajun and Creole Rhythm and Blues*. Jackson: University Press of Mississippi, 1996.

Binder, Wolfgang, ed. *Creoles and Cajuns: French Louisiana/La Louisiane Française*. New York: Lang, 1998.
Blank, Les, and Chris Strachwitz, dirs. *J'ai Été au Bal: Roots of Cajun and Zydeco Music*. Brazos Films, 2003.
Bloch, Ernst. *The Principle of Hope*. Translated by Neville Plaice, Stephen Plaice, and Paul Knight. 2 vols. Cambridge: MIT Press, 1986.
Borders, Florence. "Researching Creole and Cajun Musics in New Orleans." *Black Music Research Journal* 8, no. 1 (1988): 15–31.
Brady, William N. *The Naval Apprentice's Kedge Anchor, or Young Sailor's Assistant*. New York: Frye and Shaw, 1841.
Brasseaux, Carl A. "Acadian Education: From Cultural Isolation to Mainstream America." In *The Cajuns: Essays on Their History and Culture*, edited by Glenn Conrad, 212–24. Lafayette: Center for Louisiana Studies, 1978.
Brasseaux, Carl A. *Acadian to Cajun: Transformation of a People, 1803–1877*. Jackson: University Press of Mississippi, 1992.
Brasseaux, Carl A. *The Founding of New Acadia: The Beginnings of Acadian Life in Louisiana, 1765–1803*. Baton Rouge: Louisiana State University Press, 1987.
Brasseaux, Carl A. *French, Cajun, Creole, Houma: A Primer on Francophone Louisiana*. Baton Rouge: Louisiana State University Press, 2005.
Brasseaux, Carl A, ed. *Quest for the Promised Land: Official Correspondence Relating to the First Acadian Migration to Louisiana, 1764–1769*. Lafayette: Center for Louisiana Studies, 1989.
Brasseaux, Carl A. *Scattered to the Wind: Dispersal and Wanderings of the Acadians, 1755–1809*. Lafayette: Center for Louisiana Studies, 1991.
Brasseaux, Ryan. *Cajun Breakdown: The Emergence of an American-Made Music*. Oxford: Oxford University Press, 2009.
Brasseaux, Ryan, and Kevin Fontenot, eds. *Accordions, Fiddles, Two-Step, and Swing: A Cajun Music Reader*. Lafayette: Center for Louisiana Studies, 2006.
Burley, David M. *Losing Ground: Identity and Land Loss in Coastal Louisiana*. Jackson: University Press of Mississippi, 2010.
Caffery, Joshua Clegg. *Traditional Music in Coastal Louisiana: The 1934 Lomax Recordings*. Baton Rouge: Louisiana State University Press, 2013.
Camoin, Cécilia. *Louisiane: La théâtralité comme force de vie*. Paris: PUPS, 2013.
Carrigan, Jo Ann. *The Saffron Scourge: A History of Yellow Fever in Louisiana, 1796–1905*. Lafayette: Center for Louisiana Studies, 1994.
Carsten, Janet. "Introduction: Blood Will Out." *Journal of the Royal Anthropological Institute* 19 (2013): S1–S23.
Castells, Manuel. *The Rise of the Network Society*. Cambridge: Blackwell, 1996.
Certeau, Michel de. *The Practice of Everyday Life*. Edited by Luce Giard. Translated by Stephen F. Rendall. Berkeley: University of California Press, 1984.
Chapman, George. *The Widdowes Teares: A Comedie*. London: Browne, 1612.
Clifford, James, and George E. Marcus, eds. *Writing Culture: The Poetics and Politics of Ethnography*. Berkeley: University of California Press, 1986.
The Code of Canon Law: Latin-English Edition. Washington, DC: Canon Law Society of America, 1983.
Colten, Craig. "Environmental Management in Coastal Louisiana: A Historical Review." *Journal of Coastal Research* 33, no. 3 (2017): 699–711.
Comeaux, Malcolm. "The Cajun Barn." *Geographical Review* 79, no. 1 (1989): 47–62.

Connerton, Paul. *How Modernity Forgets*. Cambridge: Cambridge University Press, 2009.
Conrad, Glenn, ed. *The Cajuns: Essays on Their History and Culture*. Lafayette: Center for Louisiana Studies, 1978.
Corbin, Alain. *The Lure of the Sea: The Discovery of the Seaside in the Western World, 1750–1840*. Berkeley: University of California Press, 1994.
Coughlan, John. "Gulf Coast Unemployment Trends, 2000 to 2010: Hurricanes, Recessions, Oil Spills." *Monthly Labor Review* 135, no. 8 (August 2012): 11–18.
Couvillion, Brady R., John A. Barras, Gregory D. Steyer, William Sleavin, Michelle Fischer, Holly Beck, Nadine Trahan, Brad Griffin, and David Heckman. *Land Area Change in Coastal Louisiana (1932 to 2010)*. Reston, VA: US Geological Survey, 2011. http://purl.fdlp.gov/GPO/gpo8208.
Culler, Jonathan. *Theory of the Lyric*. Cambridge: Harvard University Press, 2015.
Dajko, Nathalie. "Ethnic and Geographic Variation in the French of the Lafourche Basin." PhD diss., Tulane University, 2009.
David, Marc. "(Re)Turn of the Native: Insider Ethnography and the Politics of Fieldwork in South Louisiana." In *Working the Field: Accounts from French Louisiana*, edited by Jacques M. Henry and Sara LeMenestrel, 101–20. Westport, CT: Praeger, 2003.
Davis, Donald W. *Washed Away?: The Invisible Peoples of Louisiana's Wetlands*. Lafayette: University of Louisiana at Lafayette Press, 2010.
Deleuze, Gilles. "Control and Becoming." Translated by Martin Joughin. In *Negotiations, 1972–1990*, 169–76. New York: Columbia University Press, 1995.
Deleuze, Gilles. "Postscript on the Societies of Control." *October* 59 (1992): 3–7.
Deleuze, Gilles, and Félix Guattari. *A Thousand Plateaus: Capitalism and Schizophrenia*. Minneapolis: University of Minnesota Press, 1987.
Deleuze, Gilles, and Félix Guattari. *What Is Philosophy?* New York: Columbia University Press, 1994.
Del Sesto, Steven, and Jon Gibson, eds. *The Culture of Acadiana: Tradition and Change in South Louisiana*. Lafayette: University of Southwestern Louisiana, 1975.
DeSantis, John. "Labors of Love and Many Helping Hands." *Point of Vue*, July 1, 2015. https://dokumen.tips/reader/f/pov-july-2015.
De Schryver, Peter, Tom Defoirdt, and Patrick Sorgeloos. "Early Mortality Syndrome Outbreaks: A Microbial Management Issue in Shrimp Farming?" *PLoS Pathogens* 10, no. 4 (April 24, 2014). https://doi.org/10.1371/journal.ppat.1003919.
DeWitt, Mark. *Cajun and Zydeco Dance Music in Northern California: Modern Pleasures in a Postmodern World*. Jackson: University Press of Mississippi, 2008.
Dickason, Olive P. "La 'guerre navale' des Micmacs contre les Britanniques, 1713–1763." In *Micmacs et la mer*, edited by Charles Martijn, 233–48. Montreal: Récherches amérindiennes au Québec, 1986.
Dickason, Olive P. "Louisbourg and the Indians: A Study in Imperial Race Relations." In *History and Archeology*, 6:3–206. Ottawa: National Historic Parks and Sites Branch, Parks Canada, Deptartment of Indian and Northern Affairs, 1976.
Dickinson, Emily. "Water Makes Many Beds" (poem 1428). In *The Complete Poems of Emily Dickinson*, edited by Thomas Herbert Johnson, 609. Boston: Little, Brown, 1997.
Dixon, Bill. *Last Days of Last Island: The Hurricane of 1856, Louisiana's First Great Storm*. Lafayette: University of Louisiana at Lafayette Press, 2009.
Dokka, Roy K. "Louisiana's Coast Is on Life-Support: Can the Coast Be Saved?" Presentation Louisiana State University Law School, August 26, 2010. http://lecture.lsu.edu/Panopto/Pages/Viewer.aspx?id=28071ff4-f660-4b3d-9ed7-a2af8461d27c.

Dokka, Roy K. "Modern-Day Tectonic Subsidence in Coastal Louisiana." *Geology* 34, no. 4 (2006): 281–84.
Dormon, James. *The People Called Cajuns: An Introduction to an Ethnohistory*. Lafayette: Center for Louisiana Studies, 1983.
Douglas, Mary. *Natural Symbols: Explorations in Cosmology*. London: Routledge, 2003.
Douglas, Mary. *Purity and Danger: An Analysis of Concepts of Pollution and Taboo*. London: Routledge, 2003.
Dubois, Sylvie, and Barbara Horvath. "Creoles and Cajuns: A Portrait in Black and White." *American Speech* 78, no. 2 (2003): 192–207.
Dubois, Sylvie, and Barbara Horvath. "Sounding Cajun: The Rhetorical Use of Dialect in Speech and Writing." *American Speech* 77, no. 3 (2002): 264–87.
Dumont, Jean-Paul. *The Headman and I: Ambiguity and Ambivalence in the Fieldworking Experience*. Austin: University of Texas Press, 1978.
Emanuel, James A. "Poet as Fisherman." In *Deadly James and Other Poems*, 78–79. Detroit: Lotus, 1987.
Emerson, Ralph Waldo. *Essays: Second Series*. Boston: Monroe, 1845.
Esman, Marjorie. "Festivals, Change, and Unity: The Celebration of Ethnic Identity among Louisiana Cajuns." *Anthropological Quarterly* 55, no. 4 (1982): 199–210.
Estaville, Lawrence, Jr. "Changeless Cajuns: Nineteenth-Century Reality or Myth?" *Louisiana History* 28, no. 2 (1987): 117–40.
Faragher, John Mack. *A Great and Noble Scheme: The Tragic Story of the Expulsion of the French Acadians from Their American Homeland*. New York: Norton, 2005.
Feldman, Lindsey, and Emma Christopher Lirette. "New Adventures in Tandem Ethnography." *Southern Spaces*, October 7, 2013. http://southernspaces.org/blog/new-adventures-tandem-ethnography.
Ford, Katie. "Seawater, and Ours a Bed above It." In *Colosseum*, 55–56. St. Paul: Graywolf, 2008.
Ford, Katie. "The Vessel Bends the Water." In *Colosseum*, 28. St. Paul: Graywolf, 2008.
Fortier, Alcée. *Louisiana: Comprising Sketches of Parishes, Towns, Events, Institutions, and Persons, Arranged in Cyclopedic Form*. Madison, WI: Century Historical Association, 1914.
Foucault, Michel. *The Birth of Biopolitics: Lectures at the Collège de France, 1978–79*. Edited by Michel Senellart, François Ewald, Alessandro Fontana, and Arnold Davidson. Translated by Graham Burchell. New York: Palgrave Macmillan, 2008.
Foucault, Michel. *Discipline and Punish: The Birth of the Prison*. New York: Vintage, 1995.
Foucault, Michel. "Les hétérotopies." In *Le corps utopique—Les hétérotopies*, edited by Daniel Defert, 21–36. Paris: Lignes, 2009.
Foucault, Michel. "Les hétérotopies." *Utopies et hététerotopies* (compact disc). L'Institute national de l'audiovisuel, 2004.
Foucault, Michel. *The History of Sexuality*. Volume 1, *An Introduction*. Translated by Robert Hurley. New York: Vintage, 1990.
Foucault, Michel. *The History of Sexuality*. Volume 3, *The Care of the Self*. Translated by Robert Hurley. New York: Pantheon, 1986.
Foucault, Michel. "Of Other Spaces." *Diacritics* 16 (1986): 22–27.
Foucault, Michel. *The Order of Things: An Archaeology of the Human Sciences*. New York: Routledge, 1989.
Foucault, Michel. "Theatrum Philosophicum." *Critique* 282 (1970): 885–908.

Foucault, Michel, Helmut Becker, Raul Fornet-Betancourt, and Alfredo Gomez-Müller. "The Ethics of the Concern of the Self as a Practice of Freedom." In *Ethics: Subjectivity and Truth*, edited by Robert Hurley and Paul Rabinow, 281–301. New York: New Press, 1997.

Friedman, Emily. "BP Buys 'Oil' Search Terms to Redirect Users to Official Company Website." ABC News, June 5, 2010. https://abcnews.go.com/Technology/bp-buys-search-engine-phrases-redirecting-users/story?id=10835618.

Galloway, Alexander R. *Protocol: How Control Exists after Decentralization*. Cambridge: MIT Press, 2004.

Geertz, Clifford. *The Interpretation of Cultures: Selected Essays*. New York: Basic Books, 1973.

Goode, George Brown. *The Fisheries and Fishery Industries of the United States, Section II: A Geographical Review of the Fisheries Industries and Fishing Communities for the Year 1880*. US Commission of Fish and Fisheries. Washington, DC: US Government Printing Office, 1887.

Goode, George Brown. *The Fisheries and Fishery Industries of the United States, Section V: History and Methods of the Fisheries*. US Commission of Fish and Fisheries. Washington, DC: US Government Printing Office, 1887.

Gordon, Barbara Elizabeth. "The Rhetoric of Community Ritual: The Blessing of the Shrimp Fleet at Chauvin, Louisiana." PhD diss., Louisiana State University and Agricultural and Mechanical College, 1991.

Goss, Jasper, David Burch, and Roy E. Rickson. "Agri-Food Restructuring and Third World Transnationals: Thailand, the Cp Group and the Global Shrimp Industry." *World Development* 28, no. 3 (2000): 513–30.

Gould, Philip. *Les Cadiens d'Asteur*. Baton Rouge: Louisiana State University Press, 1991.

Green, Joe. "The Louisiana Cajuns: The Quest for Identity through Education." *Theory into Practice* 20, no. 1 (1981): 63–69.

Griffiths, N. E. S. *The Contexts of Acadian History, 1686–1784*. Montreal: McGill-Queen's University Press, 1992.

Gutierrez, Paige. *Cajun Foodways*. Jackson: University Press of Mississippi, 1992.

Guyton, Arthur C. *Textbook of Medical Physiology*. 8th ed. Philadelphia: Saunders, 1991.

Hallowell, Christopher. *People of the Bayou: Cajun Life in Lost America*. New York: Dutton, 1979.

Harrison, Jill Ann. *Buoyancy on the Bayou: Shrimpers Face the Rising Tide of Globalization*. Ithaca: Cornell University Press, 2012.

Harvey, David. *Spaces of Global Capitalism: Towards a Theory of Uneven Geographical Development*. London: Verso, 2006.

Hebert, George N. "Shrimp Boats Is Anettin' Millions." *Nation's Business*, May 1952, 54.

Hebert-Leiter, Maria. *Becoming Cajun, Becoming American: The Acadian in American Literature from Longfellow to James Lee Burke*. Baton Rouge: Louisiana State University Press, 2009.

Heidegger, Martin. "Building Dwelling Thinking." Translated by Albert Hosftadter. In *Poetry, Language, Thought*, 143–59. New York: Harper Perennial, 2001.

Henry, Jacques. "From 'Acadien' to 'Cajun' to 'Cadien': Ethnic Labelization and Construction of Identity." *Journal of American Ethnic History* 17, no. 4 (1998): 29–62.

Henry, Jacques. "What Has Become of the Cajuns of Yore?" *Louisiana History* 46, no. 4 (2005): 465–81.

Henry, Jacques, and Carl L. Bankston, III. *Blue Collar Bayou: Louisiana Cajuns in the New Economy of Ethnicity*. Westport, CT: Praeger, 2002.

Heylen, Romy. "Kill the Devil or Marry an American: Descent and Consent among the Cajuns." *French Review* 67, no. 3 (1994): 453–65.

Higgins, Elmer. "A Story of the Shrimp Industry." *Scientific Monthly* 38, no. 5 (May 1934): 429–43.

Hubbard, Audriana. "The Blessing of the Fleet: Heritage and Identity in Three Gulf Coast Communities." Master's thesis, Louisiana State University and Agricultural and Mechanical College, 2013.

Hull Defence Committee. *Trawl Fishing: The Arguments against Trawling Considered and Refuted.* Hull, UK: Yorkshire Printing and Publishing, 1863.

Husserl, Edmund. *The Crisis of European Sciences and Transcendental Phenomenology: An Introduction to Phenomenological Philosophy.* Translated by David Carr. Evanston, IL: Northwestern University Press, 1970.

Import Alert: Government Fails Consumers, Falls Short on Seafood Inspections. Food and Water Watch, 2007. https://www.foodandwaterwatch.org/sites/default/files/import_alert_report_may_2007.pdf.

Ingold, Tim. *Lines: A Brief History.* London: Routledge, 2007.

Ingold, Tim. *The Perception of the Environment: Essays on Livelihood, Dwelling and Skill.* New York: Routledge, 2000.

Jackson, Michael. *Paths toward a Clearing: Radical Empiricism and Ethnographic Inquiry.* Bloomington: Indiana University Press, 1989.

James, William. *Essays in Radical Empiricism.* London: Longmans, Green, 1912.

Johnson, Fred Francis, and Milton Jerome Lindner. *Shrimp Industry of the South Atlantic and Gulf States.* US Department of Commerce, Bureau of the Fisheries, Investigational Report 21. Washington, DC: US Government Printing Office, 1934.

Kaplan-Levenson, Laine. "The Little Company That Could: How a New Orleans Immigrant Created a Global Dried Shrimp Business." TriPod: New Orleans at 300, October 8, 2015. http://wwno.org/post/little-company-could-how-new-orleans-immigrant-created-global-dried-shrimp-business.

Kennedy, Gregory M. W. *Something of a Peasant Paradise? Comparing Rural Societies in Acadie and the Loudunais, 1604–1755.* Montreal: McGill-Queen's University Press, 2014.

Kesel, Richard H. "The Decline in the Suspended Load of the Lower Mississippi River and Its Influence on Adjacent Wetlands." *Environmental Geology and Water Sciences* 11, no. 3 (1988): 271–81.

Klepp, Susan E. *Revolutionary Conceptions: Women, Fertility, and Family Limitation in America, 1760–1820.* Chapel Hill: University of North Carolina Press, 2009.

Knabb, Richard D., Jamie R. Rhome, and Daniel P. Brown. *Tropical Cyclone Report: Hurricane Katrina, 23–30 August 2005.* National Hurricane Center, 2005. https://www.nhc.noaa.gov/data/tcr/AL122005_Katrina.pdf.

Kroeber, A. L., and Clyde Kluckhohn. *Culture: A Critical Review of Concepts and Definitions.* Cambridge, MA: Peabody Museum of American Archaeology and Ethnology, Harvard University, 1952.

Krupat, Arnold. *The Voice in the Margin: Native American Literature and the Canon.* Berkeley: University of California Press, 1989.

LaFleur, Elizabeth, Diane Yeates, and Angelina Aysen. "Estimating the Economic Impact of the Wild Shrimp, Penaeus Sp., Fishery: A Study of Terrebonne Parish, Louisiana." *Marine Fisheries Review* 67, no. 1 (2005): 28–42.

Landry, Laura. "Shrimping in Louisiana: Overview of a Tradition." *Folklife in Louisiana: Louisiana's Living Traditions*. [1990] 2003. http://www.louisianafolklife.org/LT/Articles_Essays/creole_art_shrimping_overv.html.
LeCompte, Nolan Philip. "A Word Atlas of Terrebonne Parish." Master's thesis, Louisiana State University and Agricultural and Mechanical College, 1962.
Lefebvre, Henri. *The Production of Space*. Oxford: Wiley-Blackwell, 1992.
Leiris, Michel. *L'Afrique fantôme*. Paris: Gallimard, 1934.
LeMenestrel, Sara. "French Music, Cajun, Creole, Zydeco: Ligne de couleur et hiérarchies sociales dans la musique franco-louisianaise." *Civilisations* 53, nos. 1–2 (2006): 119–47.
Lévi-Strauss, Claude. *Tristes tropiques*. New York: Criterion, 1961.
Lindahl, Carl. "The Presence of the Past in the Cajun Country Mardi Gras." *Journal of Folklore Research* 33, no. 2 (1996): 125–53.
Malinowski, Bronisław. *Argonauts of the Western Pacific: An Account of Native Enterprise and Adventure in the Archipelagoes of Melanesian New Guinea*. London: Routledge, 1922.
Marcuse, Herbert. *Eros and Civilization: A Philosophical Inquiry into Freud*. Boston: Beacon, 1966.
Margavio, Anthony V., and Craig J. Forsyth. *Caught in the Net: The Conflict between Shrimpers and Conservationists*. College Station: Texas A&M University Press, 1996.
Marschke, Melissa, and Peter Vandergeest. "Slavery Scandals: Unpacking Labour Challenges and Policy Responses within the Off-Shore Fisheries Sector." *Marine Policy* 68 (2016): 39–46.
Marshall, Bob, the Lens, Brian Jacobs, and Ali Shaw. "Losing Ground." ProPublica, August 28, 2014. http://projects.propublica.org/louisiana/.
Marx, Karl. *Capital: A Critique of Political Economy*. Translated by Ben Fowkes. Vol. 1. New York: Penguin, 1976.
Marx, Karl, and Friedrich Engels. *Manifesto of the Communist Party*. In *Karl Marx, Frederick Engels: Collected Works*, 6:477–519. New York: International, 1975.
Massey, Doreen B. *Space, Place, and Gender*. Minneapolis: University of Minnesota Press, 1994.
Massey, Doreen B. *World City*. Cambridge: Polity, 2007.
Massumi, Brian. *Parables for the Virtual: Movement, Affect, Sensation*. Durham: Duke University Press, 2002.
Mathis-Moser, Ursula, and Günter Bischof, eds. *Acadians and Cajuns: The Politics and Culture of French Minorities in North America/Acadiens et Cajuns, politique et culture de minorités francophones en Amérique du Nord*. Innsbruck, Austria: Innsbruck University Press, 2009.
May, Robert E. "John A. Quitman and His Slaves: Reconciling Slave Resistance with the Proslavery Defense." *Journal of Southern History* 46, no. 4 (1980): 551–70.
Mead, Margaret. *Coming of Age in Samoa: A Psychological Study of Primitive Youth for Western Civilisation*. New York: Morrow, 1928.
Mine, Sarah, Rui Chen, Shelby Shelton, and Marcy Lowe. *Louisiana Shrimp Value Chain: Price Dynamics, Challenges, and Opportunities*. Datu Research, 2016. http://www.crcl.org/images/Shrimp.pdf.
Misrach, Richard, and Kate Orff. *Petrochemical America*. New York: Aperture Foundation, 2012.
Mizelle, Richard M. *Backwater Blues: The Mississippi Flood of 1927 in the African American Imagination*. Minneapolis: University of Minnesota Press, 2014.

Momaday, N. Scott. *The Way to Rainy Mountain*. Albuquerque: University of New Mexico Press, 1969.
Moore, Marianne. "Poetry." In *The Norton Anthology of Poetry*, edited by Margaret W. Ferguson, Mary Jo Salter, and Jon Stallworthy, 5th ed., 1329–30. New York: Norton, 2005.
Muñoz, José Esteban. *Cruising Utopia: The Then and There of Queer Futurity*. New York: New York University Press, 2009.
Natsis, James. "Legislation and Language: The Politics of Speaking French in Louisiana." *French Review* 73, no. 2 (1999): 325–31.
Negri, Antonio, and Michael Hardt. *Empire*. Cambridge: Harvard University Press, 2000.
Ostdahl, Maggie. *Warmwater Shrimp: Brown Shrimp, Pink Shrimp, Rock Shrimp, Royal Red Shrimp, Seabob Shrimp, White Shrimp*. Monterey, CA: Seafood Watch, 2015. http://www.seafoodwatch.org/-/m/sfw/pdf/reports/s/mba_seafoodwatch_uswarmwater_shrimp_report.pdf.
Outzen, Rick. "Gulf Oil Spill: BP Pleasure Boat Scandal." *Daily Beast*, June 2, 2010. https://www.thedailybeast.com/gulf-oil-spill-bp-pleasure-boat-scandal.
Parent, Wayne. *Inside the Carnival: Unmasking Louisiana Politics*. Baton Rouge: Louisiana State University Press, 2004.
Parr, Una M. "A Glossary of the Variants from Standard French in Terrebonne Parish: With an Appendix of Popular Beliefs, Superstitions, Medicine and Cooking Recipes." Master's thesis, Louisiana State University, 1940.
Percy, Viosca, Jr. "The Louisiana Shrimp Story." In *Seventh Biennial Report: Louisiana Wild Life and Fisheries Commission, 1956–1957*, 102–6. New Orleans: Division of Education and Publicity, 1958.
Phillips, Hosea. "The Spoken French of Louisiana." In *The Cajuns: Essays on Their History and Culture*, edited by Glenn Conrad, 173–84. Lafayette: Center for Louisiana Studies, 1978.
Pia, Frank. "Observations on the Drowning of Nonswimmers." *Journal of Physical Education* 71, no. 6 (1974): 164–67, 181.
Pierron, Walter Joseph. "A Sociological Study of the French-Speaking People in Chauvin, a Line Village in Terrebonne Parish." Master's thesis, Louisiana State University, 1942.
Povinelli, Elizabeth A. *Geontologies: A Requiem to Late Liberalism*. Durham: Duke University Press, 2016.
Powell, Lawrence N. *The Accidental City: Improvising New Orleans*. Cambridge: Harvard University Press, 2012.
Rees, Mark. "From 'Grand Dérangement' to Acadiana: History and Identity in the Landscape of South Louisiana." *International Journal of Historical Archaeology* 12, no. 4 (2008): 338–59.
Reese, William Dean, and Charles McKinley Allen. *Mamou: Acadian Folklore, Natural History, and Botany of the Mamou Plant*. Lafayette: Center for Louisiana Studies, 2004.
Rich, Adrienne. "Twenty-One Love Poems." In *The Dream of a Common Language: Poems, 1974–1977*, 25–36. New York: Norton, 1978.
Richardson, Maggie Heyn. "The Local Diet." In *The Louisiana Field Guide: Understanding Life in the Pelican State*, edited by Ryan Orgera and Wayne Parent, 126–38. Baton Rouge: Louisiana State University Press, 2014.
Rottet, Kevin. "Language Shift and Language Death in the Cajun French-Speaking Communities of Terrebonne and Lafourche Parishes, Louisiana." PhD diss., Indiana University, 1995.
Rottet, Kevin. *Language Shift in the Coastal Marshes of Louisiana*. New York: Lang, 2001.

Rouch, Jean, dir. *Chronique d'un été*. Argos Films, 1961.
Rouch, Jean. *Ciné-ethnography*. Edited and translated by Steven Feld. Minneapolis: University of Minnesota Press, 2003.
Rouch, Jean, dir. *Jaguar*. Les Films de la Pléiade, 1968.
Rouch, Jean, dir. *La pyramide humaine*. Les Films de la Pléiade, 1961.
Rouch, Jean, dir. *Moi, un noir*. Les Films de la Pléiade, 1958.
Rouch, Jean, dir. *Tourou et Bitti*. Comité du Film Ethnographique, 2005.
Rudloe, Jack, and Anne Rudloe. "Shrimpers and Lawmakers Collide over a Move to Save the Sea Turtles." *Smithsonian*, December 1989, 45–54.
Rushton, William Faulkner. *The Cajuns: From Acadia to Louisiana*. New York: Farrar Straus Giroux, 1979.
Ryan, Joanne, Richard A. Weinstein, and Charles E. Pearson. *Houma Navigation Canal Deepening Project, Terrebonne Parish, Louisiana: Cultural Resources Literature Search, Records Review and Research Design*. US Army Corps of Engineers, New Orleans District. Contract DACW29-01-D-0016, delivery order. 0005. Baton Rouge: Coastal Environments, 2005.
Sahr, Robert. "Inflation Conversion Factors." Oregon State University, College of Liberal Arts—School of Public Policy, Political Science, n.d. http://liberalarts.oregonstate.edu/spp/polisci/research/inflation-conversion-factors.
Said, Edward W. *Orientalism*. New York: Pantheon, 1978.
Saikku, Mikko. *This Delta, This Land: An Environmental History of the Yazoo-Mississippi Floodplain*. Athens: University of Georgia Press, 2005.
Schneider, David Murray. *American Kinship: A Cultural Account*. Chicago: University of Chicago Press, 1980.
Schütz, Alfred. *On Phenomenology and Social Relations: Selected Writings*. Edited by Helmut R. Wagner. Chicago: University of Chicago Press, 1970.
Scott, Tod. "Mi'kmaw Armed Resistance to British Expansion in Northern New England (1676–1761)." *Journal of the Royal Nova Scotia Historical Society* 19 (2016): 1–18.
Seed, Raymond B., Remon I. Abdelmalak, Adda G. Athanasopoulos, et al. *Investigation of Performance of the New Orleans Flood Protection Systems in Hurricane Katrina on August 29, 2005*. Independent Levee Investigation Team at University of California at Berkeley, 2006. http://projects.ce.berkeley.edu/neworleans/.
Seferovich, George H. "A Survey of the Louisiana Fresh Oyster Industry." *Louisiana Conservation Review*, Summer 1938, 20–23.
Sexton, Rocky. "Cajun and Creole Treaters: Magico-Religious Folk Healing in French Louisiana." *Western Folklore* 51, nos. 3–4 (1992): 237–48.
Sexton, Rocky. "Cajun-French Language Maintenance and Shift: A Southwest Louisiana Case Study to 1970." *Journal of American Ethnic History* 19, no. 4 (2000): 24–48.
Sexton, Rocky. "Cajun Mardi Gras: Cultural Objectification and Symbolic Appropriation in a French Tradition." *Ethnology* 38, no. 4 (1999): 297–313.
Sexton, Rocky. "Cajun or Coonass? Exploring Ethnic Labels in French Louisiana Regional Discourse." *Ethnology* 48, no. 4 (2009): 269–94.
Sexton, Rocky. "Ritualized Inebriation, Violence, and Social Control in Cajun Mardi Gras." *Anthropological Quarterly* 74, no. 1 (2001): 28–38.
Sidney, Philip. *The Countess of Pembroke's Arcadia*. London: Ponsonby, 1590.
Skladany, Martin, and Craig Harris. "On Global Pond: International Development and Commodity Chains in the Shrimp Industry." In *Food and Agrarian Orders in the World-Economy*, edited by Philip McMichael, 164–94. Westport, CT: Praeger, 1995.

Smith, Lindsay. "Cajun Music: The Oral Poetry of the Cajun People." PhD diss., Emory University, 1995.
Soards' New Orleans City Directory for 1912. New Orleans: Soards Directory Company, 1912.
Spinoza, Benedict de. *Ethica Ordine Geometrico Demonstrata*. In *Opera Quae Supersunt Omnia*, edited by Carolus Hermannus Bruder, 1:149–416. Leipzig: Tauchnitz, 1843.
Spinoza, Benedict de. *Ethics*. Translated by Edwin M. Curley. In *A Spinoza Reader: The Ethics and Other Works*, edited by Edwin M. Curley, 85–265. Princeton: Princeton University Press, 1994.
Spitzer, Nicholas. "Monde Créole: The Cultural World of French Louisiana Creoles and the Creolization of World Cultures." *Journal of American Folklore* 116, no. 459 (2003): 57–72.
Spivak, Gayatri Chakravorty. "Can the Subaltern Speak?" In *Marxism and the Interpretation of Culture*, edited by Cary Nelson and Lawrence Grossberg, 271–313. Urbana: University of Illinois Press, 1988.
Stevens, Wallace. "The Idea of Order at Key West." In *Collected Poetry and Prose*, 105–6. New York: Library of America, 1997.
Stewart, Kathleen. "Atmospheric Attunements." *Environment and Planning D: Society and Space* 29, no. 3 (2011): 445–53.
Stewart, Kathleen. *A Space on the Side of the Road: Cultural Poetics in an "Other" America*. Princeton: Princeton University Press, 1996.
Stivale, Charles. *Disenchanting les Bons Temps: Identity and Authenticity in Cajun Music and Dance*. Durham: Duke University Press, 2003.
Stoller, Paul. *Sensuous Scholarship*. Philadelphia: University of Pennsylvania Press, 1997.
Strong, Pauline Turner, and Barrik van Winkle. "'Indian Blood': Reflections on the Reckoning and Refiguring of Native North American Identity." *Cultural Anthropology* 11, no. 4 (1996): 547–76.
Taussig, Michael. *Mimesis and Alterity: A Particular History of the Senses*. New York: Routledge, 1993.
Tentchoff, Dorice. "Ethnic Survival under Anglo-American Hegemony: The Louisiana Cajuns." *Anthropological Quarterly* 53, no. 4 (1980): 229–41.
Theriot, Jason P. *American Energy, Imperiled Coast: Oil and Gas Development in Louisiana's Wetlands*. Baton Rouge: Louisiana State University Press, 2014.
Thompson, Stith. *Motif-Index of Folk-Literature: A Classification of Narrative Elements in Folktales, Ballads, Myths, Fables, Medieval Romances, Exempla, Fabliaux, Jest-Books, and Local Legends*. Vol. 5. Bloomington: Indiana University Press, 1957.
Tidwell, Mike. *Bayou Farewell: The Rich Life and Tragic Death of Louisiana's Cajun Coast*. New York: Pantheon, 2003.
Tran, Thi Thu Trang. "Food Safety and the Political Economy of Food Governance: The Case of Shrimp Farming in Nam Dinh Province, Vietnam." *Journal of Peasant Studies* 40, no. 4 (2013): 703–19.
Trépanier, Cécyle. "The Cajunization of French Louisiana: Forging a Regional Identity." *Geographical Journal* 157, no. 2 (1991): 161–71.
Turner, R. Eugene. "Discussion Of: Olea, R. A. and Coleman, J. L., Jr., 2014. 'A Synoptic Examination of Causes of Land Loss in Southern Louisiana as Related to the Exploitation of Subsurface Geological Resources.' *Journal of Coastal Research*, 30(5), 1025–1044." *Journal of Coastal Research* 30, no. 6: 1330–34.
US Coast Guard. *On Scene Coordinator Report: Deepwater Horizon Oil Spill*. Washington, DC: US Department of Homeland Security, US Coast Guard, 2011. https://www.loc.gov/item/2012427375.

US Department of the Interior. *Decisions of the United States Board on Geographical Names: Decisions Rendered between July 1, 1938 and June 30, 1939.* Washington, DC: US Government Printing Office, 1939.

US Department of Transportation, Maritime Administration. *A Report to the Congress on the Status of the Public Ports of the United States 1988–1989.* Washington, DC: Office of Port and Intermodal Development, 1990.

US Food and Drug Administration. *Import Alert 16-127.* Silver Spring, MD: US Food and Drug Administration, 2013. https://www.accessdata.fda.gov/cms_ia/importalert_29.html.

US National Oceanic and Atmospheric Administration, National Marine Fisheries Service. *Fisheries of the United States.* 1995–2015. Silver Spring, MD: Fisheries Statistics Division, 2015.

Virilio, Paul. "The Primary Accident." In *The Politics of Everyday Fear,* edited by Brian Massumi, 211–20. Minneapolis: University of Minnesota Press, 1993.

Walton, Shana L. "Flat Speech and Cajun Ethnic Identity in Terrebonne Parish, Louisiana." PhD diss., Tulane University, 1994.

Ware, Carolyn. *Cajun Women and Mardi Gras: Reading the Rules Backward.* Urbana: University of Illinois Press, 2007.

Webre, Stephen. "Among the Cybercajuns: Constructing Identity in the Virtual Diaspora." *Louisiana History* 39, no. 4 (1998): 443–56.

Wetta, Frank Joseph. *The Louisiana Scalawags: Politics, Race, and Terrorism during the Civil War and Reconstruction.* Baton Rouge: Louisiana State University Press, 2012.

Wiley, Eric. "Wilderness Theatre: Environmental Tourism and Cajun Swamp Tours." *Drama Review* 46, no. 3 (2002): 118–31.

Woodard, Charles. *Ancestral Voice: Conversations with N. Scott Momaday.* Lincoln: University of Nebraska Press, 1989.

Woods, Earl C., and Charles E. Nolan, eds. *Sacramental Records of the Roman Catholic Church of the Archdiocese of New Orleans.* Vol. 6, 1796–99. New Orleans: Archdiocese of New Orleans, 1991.

Zebrowski, Ernest. *Hydrocarbon Hucksters: Lessons from Louisiana on Oil, Politics, and Environmental Justice.* Jackson: University Press of Mississippi, 2014.

Zeitlin, Benh, dir. *Beasts of the Southern Wild.* Cinereach: 2012.

Zemeckis, Robert, dir. *Forrest Gump.* Paramount Pictures, 1994.

Index

Page numbers in **bold** refer to illustrations.

Acadie, 8, 19, 22, 51–53, 54, 184n1, 188nn1–3, 193n3
Adorno, Theodor, 134
Ancelet, Barry Jean, 22–23, 52
anchors. *See* moorings
anticipatory affect, 14–15, 36, 57, 62, 184n8. *See also* fear; hope
assujettissement (subjectivation), 54, 161, 167
atmosphere, 75, 152, 172–73; concept of atmospheric attunement, 160–61
attunement, 17, 29, 100, 152, 173; atmospheric, 160–61

barbarie de l'invention, 173, 175
bayous: Go-to-Hell, 21; Grand Caillou, 93; Lafourche, 105, 124, 191n1; Petit Caillou, 11–12, 17, 34, 63–64, 67, 71, **88**, 88–92, 93, **94**, 144, 147, 154–55, 166; Terrebonne, 105; communities on, 8, 52–53, 113, 127, 136, 161; named for Chinese population, 26; naming of, 26, 78, 118, 191n1; waterway, 6, 18, 26, 77–78, 83, 96, 119, 122, 141
Beasts of the Southern Wild, 124–25
Bergson, Henri, 44
Berlant, Lauren, 8, 55, 57–58, 62, 71–72
Benjamin, Walter, 174
Bienville, Jean-Baptiste Le Moyne, Sieur de, 76–77

Billiot, Connie, 136–37
Billiot, Steve, 33, 42, 123–24, 135–37, 139, 146, 153, 170
biopower, 36–37, 45, 71, 139, 163
Blanchard, James, 42
Bloch, Ernst, 3, 14–15, 183n4, 185n8
blood, 33–34, 37, 43–46, 49–50, 65, 68–70, 84, 114, 118, 172, 175; of Christ, 34, 45, 70; as imaginative force, 3, 30, 34, 37, 46, 50, 53–55, 58, 62, 67, 72–73, 99–100, 122, 178; "it's in my blood," 6–7, 9, 29, 30, 33–37, 40–43, 46–50, 53–54, 56–57, 60, 62–63, 66, 68–69, 71–73, 78, 81, 99–100, 123, 129, 170, 189n3; and kinship, 5, 9, 29–30, 34–35, 37, 39–46, 50–54, 57–58, 61–62, 66, 69–72, 81, 122, 134, 160; magic, 30, 37, 50, 56, 58, 61, 68, 71–72; memory, 40, 53–54, 57; metaphorical meanings of, 34, 37, 39–40, 43–47, 50, 68–70, 123; purity of, 44–46, 52–53; reckoning, 51–52, 188n4; society of, 36–37, 45; as truth, 33, 42, 46–47, 50, 71; vocation, 7, 29, 33–37, 40–44, 46, 50, 58, 60, 62, 71–73, 81, 84, 114
Boat Blessing, 11–13, 17, 64–66
boats: as affective charged space, 6–7, 9, 14–18, 42, 55–63, 72–73, 147, 152, 160–62, 170, 177–79; building, 79, 101, 120, 153–57, 195n5; canots, 86; challons, 86; generic watercraft, 81, **94**, 98, 124, 138, 141, 147, 157; ice, 26–27, 189n9; in oil industry, 8,

12, 79, 117–19, 136; passenger ships, 19, 52; pirogues, 78, 86, 94–96, 116; sailboats, 3–4, 25; shipwrecks, 125, 133; skiffs, 6, 27, 33, 98, 105, 117–18, 121, 136–37, 139, 143–45, 155, 191n4; steamboats, 105, 111; trawl, 5–6, 8, 11–18, 26–27, 33–34, 41–42, 49–50, 53, 55–63, 64–70, 81, 99, 101–3, 114, 117–18, 121, 127–30, 135, 137–38, 145, 147–50, 154–62, 167, 170–71, 175, 191n5, 194n30; tugboats, 47, 79, 135–36
body, 17, 30, 36, 39, 42, 45–46, 54, 60–61, 66, 71, 75, 99–100, 104, 105, 111, 115, 135, 137, 179; of Christ, 68, 70; of ethnographer, 171–75; male, 101–3; at work, 7, 29, 37, 40–41, 47–50, 56–57, 62–63, 100, 151–52, 178
Body without Organs (BwO), 80–81, 100
Brasseaux, Carl, 23, 193n3
Broussard, Joseph (Beausoleil), 19–20, 52
Burley, David M., 122, 193n2

Cajun Elvis, **136**. *See also* Billiot, Steve
Cajuns, 8–9, 19–23, 51–53, 56, 141, 184n1
canals: Boudreaux, 64, 78, 94, 117; canalization, 30, 77–79, 123; Cutoff à Tchonque, 87, 93, 117; Houma Navigational, 119; oil industry, 77–79, 112, 114, 119–20, 192n4; Placid, 86–87; Robinson, 86, **88–90**, 93, 155; *trainasse*, 94, 96, 111, 119; waterway, 81, 83, 86, 105, 143
capitalism: alienation under, 15, 48; and competition, 161–63; global, 6–8, 27, 45, 50, 101, 163; laissez-faire, 20; precapitalist imagination, 43, 47, 150; in the twenty-first century, 14, 18, 30, 36–37, 43, 54, 69–73, 81, 131, 163, 183n2
care of the self, 158–61
Carsten, Janet, 39, 43, 46, 69–71
Catholicism, 11–12, 21, 34, 101, 122, 140
Certeau, Michel de, 22, 162–63
ChaCha. *See* Sevin, O'neil "ChaCha"
Chapman, George, 39
Chauvin, David, 102–3
Chauvin, Louisiana, 6, 8, 11–13, 17, 21–22, 26, 29, 34, 40–42, 49, 53, 55, 59–60, 64–66, 76, 79, 87, 93–97, 113, 124, 127, 137, 140,
144, 147, 155, 157, 165–67, 170, 178, 184n8 (Lesson One), 184n4 (Lesson Two), 191n5, 195nn5–6
chloramphenicol, 5, 27, 137, 143
ciné-transe, 173–74
civilisations sans bateaux, 17, 184n13
Connerton, Paul, 43
Conrad, Glenn R., 22–23
Corbin, Alain, 111–12
Crick, Richard, 133, 193n1
cruel optimism, 7, 36, 56–59, 68
Culler, Jonathan, 176–77
culture, 3–9, 13, 16–18, 20–23, 30, 39–40, 50, 51–54, 57, 66–70, 81, 160–62, 166–67, 168, 171, 172, 174, 175, 177, 178, 189n1, 196n19

Deepwater Horizon Oil Spill, 3, 8, 21, 27, 36, 50, 55–56, 58, 60, 62–63, 111, 119–20, 147–48, 157, 167
Deleuze, Gilles, 56, 80, 100, 138–40, 147, 150, 161–62, 172, 176, 191n2, 196n22, 196n34
debt, 7, 58, 117, 140, 147–51, 161
dialectical images, 174–76, 196n33
Dickinson, Emily, 98
disciplinary power, 134–35, 139, 144, 163
Douglas, Mary, 44
dwellings, 18, 142–45, 152, 160

ecology, 14, 18, 37, 44, 50, 53, 61, 66–69, 71, 79, 122, 133, 142, 163, 172, 175
Edwards, Edwin, 20, 146
Emanuel, James, 165
Emerson, Ralph Waldo, 110
environment, 7, 13, 18, 23, 29, 36, 47, 49, 54, 57, 61, 66–68, 71, 76–78, 95–96, 122–25, 130, 138, 144–47, 158–63, 172, 176, 178
Eros, 15
erosion, 21, 30, 50, 79–80, 81, 83, 87, 96, 112, 119, 120, 121, 122, 125, 141
Eschete, Dudley, 11, 93, 141
Eschete, Henry "Tchonque," 78, 87, 93, 96, 117
ethnography, 23, 29, 55, 62–63, 93, 166–79

family: author's, 33–34, 37, 52, 61, 64, 66, 114–18, 166, 188n3; as social formation, 5–7, 13–15, 18, 30, 33–36, 41–47, 49, 53,

55–60, 66, 69–71, 81, 83, 121, 129–31, 134, 139, 141, 150, 154, 156, 159–62. *See also* blood: as kinship
fear, 13, 15, 18, 23, 36, 39, 62–63, 101, 153, 160, 169
Feldman, Lindsey, 55, 59, 61, 188n13
femininity, 43, 55, 191n4
fiction, 22, 29, 166, 168–69, 175–78, 196n31
Finn-Fon-Boo. *See* Thuer, John
first fruits, 25–26, 156
floods, 75–79, 83, 116, 122, 124–25
Ford, Katie, 105, 121
forgetting, 30, 93–94, 100, 121
Fortier, Alcée, 93
Foucault, Michel, 15–17, 36, 45, 134, 139, 158–61, 170, 184nn12–13, 196n34
freedom, 3–7, 10, 12–15, 17, 30–31, 47, 56, 69, 81, 100, 122, 129, 133–40, 144, 148–50, 153, 159, 163, 173, 177–78
future: dark, 6, 12, 30, 42, 60, 150; hope for, 5, 13–18, 57, 71, 157–58, 163, 184n8; possibilities, 23, 53, 96, 122, 152–53, 160, 196n23; queer, 15, 184n8; surprise, 36, 111, 149, 169, 175. *See also* utopia

Geertz, Clifford, 166–69, 174–75, 189n1, 196n31
genius loci, 75, 79, 104, 125
Ghere, Carla, 191n4
ghosts: in haunted spaces, 15, 30, 57, 94, 110, 125; haunted time, 7, 58, 184n8; as hidden form, 45, 48, 52, 80–81, 167; nets, 130–31, 139–40, 149–50; spirits, 15–16, 72–73, 75–76, 94, 96, 157
gods: Christ as a fisher-, 5, 153–54, 157–58, 165, 195n4; Judeo-Christian, 11–12, 19–20, 25, 83–84, 110, 168; murder-drunk, 104. *See also* Catholicism
good life, 8, 55; as aspirational, 9–10, 14, 56–58, 131, 141; and good old days, 12, 140; as worth living, 7, 13, 46–47, 99, 130–31, 152–53, 160, 163, 176. *See also* nostalgia
Great Flood of 1927, 77
grocery stores, 8, 12, 70, 145, 191n4; Boudreaux Canal, 94, 117; Lapeyrouse Seafood, Bar, Grocery, and Campground, 155; Piggly Wiggly, 12, 26; Rouses, 12; Whole Foods, 12, 145
Guattari, Félix, 80, 100, 138, 172, 191n2, 196n22
Gulf of Mexico, 3–5, 16, 49, 75–76, 78, 80, 84, 87, **95**, 105, **106**, 110, 190n12; coastal communities and, 3, 11, 22, 70–72, 79, 98–99, 112, 122–25; ecological disaster, 36, 61–62, 71, 79, 111, 119–20, 147–49, 155, 167; erosion and subsidence, 21, 30, 50, 79–80, 81, 83, 96, 112, 119–20, 121, 141; fishery location, 5, 25–26, 37, 134–35, 147; offshore oilfield, 113–14, 116. *See also* Deepwater Horizon Oil Spill
Guy, Kimothy "Kim," 11, 25, **32**, 33–34, 40–49, 63, 69, 96, 99, 102–4, 123, 133–35, 139, 146–47, 153, 158, 191n5

Harrison, Jill Ann, 40–41, 116–17, 189n9, 194n12
Heidegger, Martin, 142–44, 152–53, 160–61
heterotopia, 16–18
hope: affect, 3, 5–6, 14–16, 21, 56–59, 62–63, 71–72, 75, 81, 121–22, 125, 160–61; specific desires, 5, 37, 48, 59, 152, 157–58, 169, 173, 178–79
Horkheimer, Max, 134
hurricanes: Andrew, 76, 116; effects of, 8, 30, 50, 71, 77, 98, 119, 123–24, 144, 146–47; Grand Isle (1909), 98; Ida, 191n5; Juan, 76; Katrina, 27, 51, 77–78, 81, 111; Last Island (1856), 110–12; Rita, 27, 78, 111; season, 3, 27; tropical cyclone, 8, 75–76; unnamed (Old Man Boudreaux), 94

Iberville, Pierre Le Moyne, Sieur d', 76
imagination, 121–22, 192n1; cultural, 3, 9, 17, 19–23, 122–23, 142, 145, 166; pasts, 14–15, 19–22, 30–31, 36, 53–58, 71–72, 184n8; realms of possibility, 4, 6, 9–10, 12, 14–15, 17–18, 30–31, 36–37, 40, 42–43, 47, 61, 71–72, 81, 96, 107, 131, 150, 162–63, 171–72, 174–78, 183n2, 184n8; self-, 6, 10, 122, 145, 150, 157–58, 162; unimaginable, 110–11
improvisation, 13, 16, 68, 100, 121, 124–25, 134, 173, 177, 179
Ingold, Tim, 44, 66–68, 71, 94–96, 142, 160, 172, 189n3, 196n23

islands, 26, 75, 83; barrier, 49, 81, 116; Caillou, 105, 107, 117; Canary, 52; Isle de Jean Charles, 124; Isle Dernière, 105, 107, 110–12; Timbalier, 105, 119

Jackson, Michael, 171–72, 175–76, 178, 196n19
James, William, 170–71, 178, 196n22
Jindal, Bobby, 145

knowledge: cultural, 7, 9, 40, 63, 66–67, 168–70, 177–78, 189n1; experiential, 8, 31, 40, 59–60, 100, 123, 140–43; institutional, 87, 94–97, 119–20, 127–30, 135, 140–46, 172, 174–75, 178; intergenerational, 14, 41–42, 44–45, 73, 128–30; -power, 45–46, 53–54, 71, 144–45, 149–50, 161–62; local, 94–97, 124, 140–46, 157, 188n3, 196n23; not knowing, 30, 35, 36, 56, 62, 99–100, 121, 134–35, 166; of the self, 48–50, 157–63

La Salle, René-Robert Cavelier, Sieur de, 78
lakes, 25, 78, 105; Barré, 87, **95**, 118; Boudreaux/Quitman, 33, 59, 61, 64–67, 87, **88**, **89–92**, 93–97, **98**, 135, **152**, 155; Caillou, 117; Gero, **91–92**, 97; Pelto, 78, 117; Tambour, 87, 118, 128
Lapeyrouse, Terry, 155
Lefebvre, Henri, 125
levees, 30, 64, 77–79, 81, 83, 103, 112, 116, 123–25, 143
Lewis, Sinclair, 21
life on the water, 5–7, 9–10, 16, 30, 59, 73, 78–79, 81, 98–101, 116, 122, 135, 156, 170
lifeworld, 67, 171, 196n19
Lindahl, Carl, 23
Lirette, Brett, 33, 59, 63, 71, 135, 167, **169**
Lirette, Linda, 55, 66
Lirette, Kurt, 33, 55, 59, 61–62, 76, 93, 112, **115**, 144; fictionalized, 113–16; mayor of Chauvin, 166–67, 195n6
Lirette, Sandra, 34, 70, 73, 167
Long, Huey, 21, 162
Louisiana: culture, 17, 19–23, 54, 70–71, 81, 134–35, 140–41, 171–72; Department of Wildlife and Fisheries, 127–28, 139, 144–46; fishery, 24–28, 36, 40–43; governance, 127–29, 139, 144–46, 186n19; history, 19–21, 51–52, 68–70, 87, 93–94, 96–97, 111–12; imaginary, 3, 8–9, 19–23, 123–25; place, 5–7, 11, 29–30, 37, 51, 76–80, 87–93, **95**, **108–9**, 119–20, 127; Shrimp Task Force, 146; and studies as academic discipline, 22–23, 122, 177–78

magic. *See* blood: magic
Malinowski, Bronisław, 189n1
Marcuse, Herbert, 15, 184n7
Mare à Clay, 86–87, **88**, 96–97
Marx, Karl, 47–48, 69, 183n2, 183n4
masculinity, 12–13, 17, 40–44, 55, 101–3, 107, 191n4
Massey, Doreen, 96
Massumi, Brian, 192n1
May, Robert E., 93
memory: collective, 17, 37, 40, 43, 53–56, 107; forgetting, 30, 93–94, 100, 121; imagined, 14–15, 30, 55–56, 75, 121, 147, 162–63, 184n8; muscle, 119; remembering, 7, 23, 24, 60, 66–68, 70, 86–87, 93, 96, 104, 112, 113–14, 116, 128–29
Mi'kmaq, 19, 21, 51–52, 188n3
mimesis, 174, 176–77, 196n33
minoritization, 8–9, 20
misrecognition, 71–72
Mississippi River, 20, 76–77, 80–81, 105, **106**, **108–9**, 121, 136
Momaday, N. Scott, 53–54
Moore, Marianne, 178
moorings: as literal anchors, 3–5, 76, 98, 101, 145, 149, 183n1; as metaphor, 3–5, 7, 9, 14–15, 34, 37, 75, 81, 101, 122, 141, 163, 177–78. *See also* unmooring
Muñoz, José Esteban, 14–15, 184n8
myth, 7–9, 16–18, 22, 41, 46, 53, 57–58, 68, 71–72, 83, 110, 124–25, 151, 161–62, 165

naming, 16, 21, 30, 44, 51–52, 75–78, 83–84, 86–87, 93–94, 96–97, 118, 186n18, 188nn1–3
Negri, Antonio, 161–62
nets: butterfly, 57, 189n9, 193n5; cast, 25, 86, 160; dip, 25, 156; gill, 27; as metaphor for control, 16, 30–31, 129–31, 137–40; as

metaphor for gathering, 43, 129–31, 143, 151–54, 161–63; seine, 17, 25–26, 78–79, 86, 128; skimmer, 25, 63, 117, 152, 155, 193n5; social safety, 43, 127; trawl, 5, 12, 26–27, 33–36, 41, 49, 56, 59–61, 63, 67, 72, 85, 99–100, 114, 117, 127–31, 133–34, 142, 145–47, 149–50, 151, 158, 165, 186n18, 189n9, 193n5. *See also* Turtle Excluder Devices (TEDs)

networks: affective, 56, 59, 62, 71–72, 142, 147, 157, 160–61, 166; of care, 7, 130–31, 156–59, 162–63; of control, 5, 7, 31, 130, 139; culture as, 166; familial, 5, 43, 46, 114, 130; information, 54; infrastructural, 120, 125, 136; social, 6, 15, 22, 43, 54–55, 100, 114, 154, 156–57, 162; social media, 6, 15, 43–44, 55, 99; of symbols, 166, 174

New Orleans, 11, 20–21, 25–26, 51, 76–77, 81, 105, **108**, 114, 136

normalcy, 7, 8, 15, 30, 36, 54, 55, 71, 72, 134–35, 139

nostalgia, 6, 12, 20, 43, 54, 143

Obama, Barack, 120

oil industry: effects on shrimp fishery, 8, 62–63, 77–79; environmental disaster, 3, 30, 50, 58–59, 62–63, 71, 79, 86, 111–12, 119–20, 137, 148, 167, 171, 192n4; offshore work, 6, 8, 12, 20, 30, 59, 61, 69, 79, 84, 113–14, 116–19; support for, 21, 120. *See also* Deepwater Horizon Oil Spill

Orff, Kate, 120

Our Lady of the Sea, 111

passéisme. See nostalgia

pasts: imagined, 14–15, 19–22, 30–31, 36, 53–58, 71–72, 184n8; relation to present and future, 13–16, 42, 68, 71–72, 162–63, 184n8; uncanny, 5, 13, 54. *See also* memory; nostalgia

Picou Cemetery, 98

pietas, 161–62, 195n11

pirates, 17, 93, 107, 110, 184n13

pirogues, 78, 86, 94–96, 116

Portier, Angela, 101–2, 154–56

Portier, Chad, 101–2, 146, 153–60, 162, 170, 195n4

possibility, 5–7, 18, 30, 62, 72, 82, 100, 162–63, 166, 172, 178. *See also* imagination: realms of possibility

power, 5–7, 36–37, 39, 45, 50, 54, 56, 134, 139–40, 144–45, 150, 153, 160, 166–67, 174

present, 5, 7, 14–18, 29–30, 43, 54–55, 57, 59–62, 71–72, 157, 184n8

Quitman, John A., 93, 96–97

Quong Sun Company, 26, 186n1

radical empiricism, 170–72, 178, 196n22

rationalization, 43, 50, 61, 77, 171; order, 30, 75–82, 86, 87, 94, 96–97, 99, 110, 112, 122–26, 166, 168, 171, 177; quantification, 7, 12, 16, 24–25, 36, 45, 52–54, 150; scientists, 23, 24, 45, 87, 127–29, 140, 142–44, 166–67, 174, 177, 189n3, 195n12

regulations, 5–6, 14, 17, 36, 45, 116, 120, 128–31, 138–39, 141–47, 150, 153–55, 158–59, 170

rhizomes, 66, 172

Robinson, James Baker, 93, 96–97

Said, Edward, 167

Saikku, Mikko, 76

saltwater intrusion, 17, 77–79, 112, 119, 123

Schneider, David, 44

Sea Grant, 144

Seafood Watch (Monterey Bay Aquarium), 145–46

self: dismantling of, 30, 56–57, 81, 83–84, 100, 122–23, 125, 173; elaboration of, 10, 125, 158–63, 169; selfhood, 6–7, 16, 36, 45–47, 79–80; -sovereignty, 6, 8, 14, 42, 58, 136, 140

sexuality, 15, 36, 45, 184n8

Sevin, George, 34, **35**, 86–87, **88**, 112, 119

Sevin, O'neil "ChaCha," 34–36, 42, 49–50, 55–63, 64, 68–69, 71, 73, 86, 120, 141–42, 146–47, 151, 153, 157–58, 160

shrimping: as addiction, 35–36; and Chinese in Louisiana, 25–26, 185n9; dried shrimp, 25–26, 93, 96, 117, 149, 185n9; enslaved laborers in fishery, 28; as family practice, 7, 9, 14, 37, 39–44, 55, 58, 70–71, 121, 128–30, 134–36; and

Filipinos in Louisiana, 26, 185n9; fishery, 3, 6, 8, 12–14, 24–28, 42–43, 48, 58, 60, 62–63, 69, 72–73, 112, 127, 129, 137–38, 147, 160, 176, 189n9; and foreign aquaculture, 5, 27–28, 58, 71, 141, 143–44; intergenerational rejection, 6–7, 13, 29, 33–34, 37, 40–44, 55, 57–59, 63, 68–69, 73, 130, 134, 144; persistence of, 8, 14, 24, 28, 29–31, 33–34, 48, 50, 58, 72–73, 130–31, 138, 147, 160, 173; price of shrimp, 12, 50, 116, 127, 154, 161; seasons, 5, 11, 118, 127–29, 142, 186n19; unionizing, 34–35, 69, 145, 158–59

Sidney, Philip, 51

skiffs, 6, 27, 33, 98, 105, 117–18, 121, 136–37, 139, 143–45, 155, 191n4

slavery: and laborers in fishery, 28; in the United States, 20–21, 24, 93–94, 96, 105, 119

society of control, 139, 147, 150

Spinoza, Baruch, 162, 195n11

Spivak, Gayatri, 167

Stearn, Silas, 25

Stevens, Wallace, 30, 75, 78–82, 84, 125

Stewart, Kathleen, 7–8, 17, 23, 152, 160, 162, 171, 177, 196n18

Stivale, Charles, 23, 56

Stoller, Paul, 173–74

stories: as cultural determination, 7–9, 12–13, 18, 19–22, 46, 51–52, 62, 93–94, 98, 103–4, 113–16, 134–36, 177–78; telling as practice of freedom, 9, 16, 22, 47, 162, 178–79; telling as wayfinding, 94–96, 121–22

Strong, Pauline Turner, 52–54

Studyx, 107, 110

Taussig, Michael, 174–76, 196n33

Thompson, Stith, 165

Thuer, John, 105, 107

Tillman, Carolyn, 191n4

Trahan, Glynn, 40, 47–48, 99–100, 138, 140–44, 153, 170

Trump, Donald, 4, 30, 162, 187n1

Turtle Excluder Devices (TEDs), 129, 138, 141, 145–46, 158, 170, 193n5, 194n12

United Houma Nation, 21, 52, 119, 124, 137

United States Army Corps of Engineers, 77, 84, 112, 143–44

United States Geological Survey, 87, **88–92**, 96

unmooring, 4–5; game of mooring and, 8, 16, 18, 121, 177; nautical, 5, 183n1; practice, 7, 9, 14, 23, 30, 61, 72, 81–82, 100, 122, 153, 162–63, 171–72, 175, 178–79

utopia, 4, 7, 13–18, 159, 161, 163, 183n2, 184n8

vampires, 21–22, 47, 68

van Winkle, Barrik, 52–54

Vertov, Dziga, 168

Virilio, Paul, 111

world-making, 7–9, 13–18, 23, 30–31, 42–43, 48, 57–59, 61–62, 67–68, 71–72, 79–82, 95–96, 110, 121, 123, 153, 168, 170–73, 175–79; worlding, 160–63

Writing Culture, 167–68

Yeats, William Butler, 127

Yim, Lee, 26

About the Author

Emma Christopher Lirette is a writer and independent scholar. After growing up on the Louisiana Gulf Coast, she earned an MFA in creative writing from Cornell University and a PhD in American studies from Emory University. She currently works in the field of User Experience Research.

www.ingramcontent.com/pod-product-compliance
Lightning Source LLC
Chambersburg PA
CBHW021840220426
43663CB00005B/334